Wanderings In Corsica

Its History And Its Heroes
Vol. I

by

Ferdinand Gregorovius

Wanderings In Corsica
Its History And Its Heroes
Vol. I
by Ferdinand Gregorovius

ISBN: 978-93-68095-86-6

Published by

DOUBLE 9 BOOKS

2/13-B, Ansari Road
Daryaganj, New Delhi – 110002
info@double9books.com
www.double9books.com
Tel. 011-40042856

ABOUT THE AUTHOR

Ferdinand Gregorovius was a German historian, born on January 19, 1821, in Nidzica, Poland, and is best known for his work on the medieval history of Rome. Gregorovius developed a deep interest in the city of Rome and its historical significance, dedicating much of his career to exploring its medieval past. His most renowned work, History of the City of Rome in the Middle Ages, is a comprehensive study that spans several volumes and provides a detailed examination of the city's political, cultural, and religious developments during the medieval period. Gregorovius's scholarship is characterized by a thorough analysis of primary sources and a keen understanding of the historical forces that shaped Rome's evolution. His works also include studies on key figures in Roman history, such as Lucrezia Borgia: Daughter of Pope Alexander VI, which highlights his interest in the intricate lives of historical personalities. Throughout his career, Gregorovius was recognized for his intellectual rigor and contributions to historical research. He passed away on May 1, 1891, in Munich, Germany, leaving behind a legacy of important historical writings that continue to influence the study of medieval Rome and its role in European history.

CONTENTS

BOOK II
HISTORY

BOOK III
WANDERINGS IN THE SUMMER OF 1852

PREFACE

It was in the summer of the past year that I went over to the island of Corsica. Its unknown solitudes, and the strange stories I had heard of the country and its inhabitants, tempted me to make the excursion. But I had no intention of entangling myself so deeply in its impracticable labyrinths as I actually did. I fared like the heroes of the fairy-tales, who are allured by a wondrous bird into some mysterious forest, and follow it ever farther and farther into the beautiful wilderness. At last I had wandered over most of the island. The fruit of that summer is the present book, which I now send home to my friends. May it not meet with an unsympathetic reception! It is hoped that at least the history of the Corsicans, and their popular poetry, entitles it to something better.

The history of the Corsicans, all granite like their mountains, and singularly in harmony with their nature, is in itself an independent whole; and is therefore capable of being presented, even briefly, with completeness. It awakens the same interest of which we are sensible in reading the biography of an unusually organized man, and would possess valid claims to our attention even though Corsica could not boast Napoleon as her offspring. But certainly the history of Napoleon's native country ought to contribute its share of data to an accurate estimate of his character; and as the great man is to be viewed as a result of that history, its claims on our careful consideration are the more authentic.

It is not the object of my book to communicate information in the sphere of natural science; this is as much beyond its scope as beyond the abilities of the author. The work has, however, been written with an earnest purpose.

I am under many obligations for literary assistance to the learned Corsican Benedetto Viale, Professor of Chemistry in the University of Rome; and it would be difficult for me to say how helpful various friends were to me in Corsica itself. My especial thanks are, however, due to the exiled Florentine geographer, Francesco Marmocchi, and to Camillo Friess, Archivarius in Ajaccio.

Rome, *April 2, 1853.*

The Translator begs to acknowledge his obligations to L. C. C. (the translator of Grillparzer's *Sappho*), for the translation of the Lullaby in the first volume; the Voceros the second volume, and the poem which concludes the work.

Edinburgh, *February 1855.*

BOOK I
HISTORY

CHAPTER I
EARLIEST ACCOUNTS

The oldest notices of Corsica we have, are to be found in the Greek and Roman historians and geographers. They do not furnish us with any precise information as to what races originally colonized the island, whether Phœnicians, Etruscans, or Ligurians. All these ancient races had been occupants of Corsica before the Carthaginians, the Phocæan Greeks, and the Romans planted their colonies upon it.

The position of the islands of Corsica and Sardinia, in the great western basin of the Mediterranean, made them points of convergence for the commerce and colonization of the surrounding nations of the two continents. To the north, at the distance of a day's journey, lies Gaul; three days' journey westwards, Spain; Etruria is close at hand upon the east; and Africa is but a few days' voyage to the south. The continental nations necessarily, therefore, came into contact in these islands, and one after the other left their stamp upon them. This was particularly the case in Sardinia, a country entitled to be considered one of the most remarkable in Europe, from the variety and complexity of the national characteristics, and from the multifarious traces left upon it by so many different races, in buildings, sculptures, coins, language, and customs, which, deposited, so to speak, in successive strata, have gradually determined the present ethnographic conformation of the island. Both Corsica and Sardinia lie upon the boundary-line which separates the western basin of the Mediterranean into a Spanish and an Italian half; and as soon as the influences of Oriental and Greek colonization had been eradicated politically, if not physically, these two nations began to exercise their determining power upon the islands. In Sardinia, the Spanish element predominated; in Corsica, the Italian. This is very evident at the present day from the languages. In later times, a third determining element, but a purely political one—the French, was added in the case of Corsica. At a period of the remotest antiquity, both Spanish and Gallo-Celtic or Ligurian tribes had passed over to Corsica; but the Spanish characteristics which struck the philosopher Seneca so forcibly in the Corsicans of his time, disappeared, except in so far as they are still visible in the somewhat gloomy and taciturn, and withal choleric disposition of the present islanders.

The most ancient name of the island is Corsica—a later, Cyrnus. The former is said to be derived from Corsus, a son of Hercules, and brother of Sardus, who founded colonies on the islands, to which they gave their names. Others say that Corsus was a Trojan, who carried off Sica, a niece of Dido, and that in honour of her the island received its appellation. Such is the fable of the oldest Corsican chronicler, Johann della Grossa.

Cyrnus was a name in use among the Greeks. Pausanias says, in his geography of Phocis: "The island near Sardinia (Ichnusa) is called by the native Libyans, Corsica; by the Greeks, Cyrnus." The designation Libyans, is very generally applied to the Phœnicians, and it is highly improbable that Pausanias was thinking of an aboriginal race. He viewed them as immigrated colonists, like those in Sardinia. He says, in the same book, that the Libyans were the first who came to Sardinia, which they found already inhabited, and that after them came the Greeks and Hispanians. The word Cyrnos itself has been derived from the Phœnician, *Kir*—horn, promontory. In short, these matters are vague, traditionary, hypothetical.

So much seems to be certain, from the ancient sources which supplied Pausanias with his information, that in very early times the Phœnicians founded colonies on both islands, that they found them already inhabited, and that afterwards an immigration from Spain took place. Seneca, who spent eight years of exile in Corsica, in his book *De Consolatione*, addressed to his mother Helvia, and written from that island, has the following passage (cap. viii.):—"This island has frequently changed its inhabitants. Omitting all that is involved in the darkness of antiquity, I shall only say that the Greeks, who at present inhabit Massilia (Marseilles), after they had left Phocæa, settled at first at Corsica. It is uncertain what drove them away—perhaps the unhealthy climate, the growing power of Italy, or the scarcity of havens; for, that the savage character of the natives was not the reason, we learn from their betaking themselves to the then wild and uncivilized tribes of Gaul. Afterwards, Ligurians crossed over to the island; and also

Hispanians, as may be seen from the similarity of the modes of life; for the same kinds of covering for the head and the feet are found here, as among the Cantabrians—and there are many resemblances in words; but the entire language has lost its original character, through intercourse with the Greeks and Ligurians." It is to be lamented that Seneca did not consider it worth the pains to make more detailed inquiry into the condition of the island. Even for him its earliest history was involved in obscurity; how much more so must it be for us?

Seneca is probably mistaken, however, in not making the Ligurians and Hispanians arrive on the island till after the Phocæans. I have no doubt that the Celtic races were the first and oldest inhabitants of Corsica. The Corsican physiognomy, even of the present time, appears as a Celtic-Ligurian.

CHAPTER II
THE GREEKS, ETRUSCANS, CARTHAGINIANS, AND ROMANS IN CORSICA

The first historically accredited event in relation to Corsica, is that immigration of the fugitive Phocæans definitely mentioned by Herodotus. We know that these Asiatic Greeks had resolved rather to quit their native country, than submit to inevitable slavery under Cyrus, and that, after a solemn oath to the gods, they carried everything they possessed on board ship, and put out to sea. They first negotiated with the Chians for the cession of the Œnusian Islands, but without success; they then set sail for Corsica, not without a definite enough aim, as they had already twenty years previously founded on that island the city of Alalia. They were, accordingly, received by their own colonists here, and remained with them five years, "building temples," as Herodotus says; "but because they made plundering incursions on their neighbours, the Tyrrhenians and Carthaginians brought sixty ships into the seas. The Phocæans, on their side, had equipped a fleet of equal size, and came to an engagement with them off the coast of Sardinia. They gained a victory, but it cost them dear; for they lost forty vessels, and the rest had been rendered useless—their beaks having been bent. They returned to Alalia, and taking their wives and children, and as much of their property as they could, with them, they left the island of Cyrnus, and sailed to Rhegium." It is well known that they afterwards founded Massilia, the present Marseilles.

We have therefore in Alalia, the present Aleria—a colony of an origin indubitably Greek, though it afterwards fell into the hands of the Etruscans. The history of this flourishing commercial people compels us to assume, that, even before the arrival of the Phocæans, they had founded colonies in Corsica. It is impossible that the powerful Populonia, lying so near Corsica on the coast opposite, with Elba already in its possession, should never have made any attempt to establish its influence along the eastern shores of the island. Diodorus says in his fifth book:—"There are two notable cities in Corsica—Calaris and Nicæa; Calaris (a corruption of Alalia or Aleria) was founded by the Phocæans. These were expelled by the Tyrrhenians, after they had been some time in the island. The Tyrrhenians founded

Nicæa, when they became masters of the sea." Nicæa is probably the modern Mariana, which lies on the same level region of the coast. We may assume that this colony existed contemporaneously with Alalia, and that the immigration of the entire community of Phocæans excited jealousy and alarm in the Tyrrhenians, whence the collision between them and the Greeks. It is uncertain whether the Carthaginians had at this period possessions in Corsica; but they had colonies in the neighbouring Sardinia. Pausanias tells us that they subjugated the Libyans and Hispanians on this island, and built the two cities of Caralis (Cagliari) and Sulchos (Palma di Solo). The threatened danger from the Greeks now induced them to make common cause with the Tyrrhenians, who also had settlements in Sardinia, against the Phocæan intruders. Ancient writers further mention an immigration of Corsicans into Sardinia, where they are said to have founded twelve cities.

For a considerable period we now hear nothing more about the fortunes of Corsica, from which the Etruscans continued to draw supplies of honey, wax, timber for ship-building, and slaves. Their power gradually sank, and they gave way to the Carthaginians, who seem to have put themselves in complete possession of both islands—that is, of their emporiums and havens—for the tribes of the interior had yielded to no foe. During the Punic Wars, the conquering Romans deprived the Carthaginians in their turn of both islands. Corsica is at first not named, either in the Punic treaty of the time of Tarquinius, or in the conditions of peace at the close of the first Punic War. Sardinia had been ceded to the Romans; the vicinity of Corsica could not but induce them to make themselves masters of that island also; both, lying in the centre of a sea which washed the shores of Spain, Gaul, Italy, and Africa, afforded the greatest facilities for establishing stations directed towards the coasts of all the countries which Rome at that time was preparing to subdue.

We are informed, that in the year 260 before the birth of Christ, the Consul Lucius Cornelius Scipio crossed over to Corsica, and destroyed the city of Aleria, and that he conquered at once the Corsicans, Sardinians, and the Carthaginian Hanno. The mutilated inscription on the tomb of Scipio has the words—Hec cepit Corsica Aleriaque vrbe. But the subjugation of the wild Corsicans was no easy matter. They made a resistance as heroic as that of the Samnites. We even find that the Romans suffered a number of defeats, and that the Corsicans several times rebelled. In the year 240, M. Claudius led an army against the Corsicans. Defeated, and in a situation of imminent danger, he offered them favourable conditions. They accepted them, but the Senate refused to confirm the treaty. It ordered the Consul, C. Licinius Varus, to chastise the Corsicans, delivering Claudius at the same time into their hands, that they might do with him as they chose. This was frequently the policy of the Romans, when they wished to quiet their religious scruples about an oath. The Corsicans did as the Spaniards and Samnites had done in similar instances. They would not receive the innocent general, and sent him back unharmed. On his return to Rome, he was strangled, and thrown upon the Gemonian stairs.

Though subdued by the Romans, the Corsicans were continually rising anew, already exhibiting that patriotism and love of freedom which in much later times drew the eyes of the world on this little isolated people. They rebelled at the same time with the Sardinians; but when these had been conquered, the Corsicans also were obliged to submit to the Consul Caius Papirus, who defeated them in the bloody battle of the "Myrtle-field." But they regained a footing in the mountain strongholds, and it appears that they forced the Roman commander to an advantageous peace.

They rose again in the year 181. Marcus Pinarius, Prætor of Sardinia, immediately landed in Corsica with an army, and defeated the islanders with dreadful carnage in a battle of which Livy gives an account—they lost two thousand men killed. The Corsicans submitted, gave hostages and a tribute of one hundred thousand pounds of wax. Seven years later, a new insurrection and other bloody battles—seven thousand Corsicans were slain, and two thousand taken prisoners. The tribute was raised to two hundred thousand pounds of wax. Ten years afterwards, this heroic people is again in arms, compelling the Romans to send out a consular army: Juventius Thalea, and after him Scipio Nasica, completed the subjugation of the island in the year 162.

The Romans had thus to fight with these islanders for more than a hundred years, before they reduced them to subjection. Corsica was governed in common with Sardinia by a Prætor, who resided in Cagliari, and sent a *legatus* or lieutenant to Corsica. But it was not till the time of the first civil war, that the Romans began to entertain serious thoughts of colonizing the island. The celebrated Marius founded, on the beautiful level of the east coast, the city of Mariana; and Sulla afterwards built on the same plain the city of Aleria, restoring the old Alalia of the Phocæans. Corsica now began to be Romanized, to modify its Celtic-Spanish language, and to adopt Roman customs. We do not hear that the Corsicans again ventured to rebel against their masters; and the island is only once more mentioned in Roman history, when Sextus Pompey, defying the triumvirs, establishes a maritime power in the Mediterranean, and takes possession of Corsica, Sardinia, and Sicily. His empire was of short duration.

CHAPTER III
STATE OF THE ISLAND DURING THE ROMAN PERIOD

The nature of its interior prevents us from believing that the condition of the island was by any means so flourishing during the long periods of its subjection to the Romans, as some writers are disposed to assume. They contented themselves, as it appears, with the two colonies mentioned, and the establishment of some ports. The beautiful coast opposite Italy was the region mainly cultivated. They had only made a single road in Corsica. According to the Itinerary of Antonine, this Roman road led from Mariana along the coast southwards to Aleria, to Præsidium, Portus Favoni, and Palæ, on the straits, near the modern Bonifazio. This was the usual place for crossing to Sardinia, in which the road was continued from Portus Tibulæ (*cartio Aragonese*)—a place of some importance, to Caralis, the present Cagliari.

Pliny speaks of thirty-three towns in Corsica, but mentions only the two colonies by name. Strabo, again, who wrote not long before him, says of Corsica: "It contains some cities of no great size, as Blesino, Charax, Eniconæ, and Vapanes." These names are to be found in no other writer. Pliny has probably made every fort a town. Ptolemy, however, gives the localities of Corsica in detail, with the appellations of the tribes inhabiting them; many of his names still survive in Corsica unaltered, or easily recognised.

The ancient authors have left us some notices of the character of the country and people during this Roman period. I shall give them here, as it is interesting to compare what they say with the accounts we have of Corsica in the Middle Ages and at the present time.

Strabo says of Corsica: "It is thinly inhabited, for it is a rugged country, and in most places has no practicable roads. Hence those who inhabit the mountains live by plunder, and are more untameable than wild beasts. When the Roman generals have made an expedition against the island,

and taken their strongholds, they bring away with them a great number of slaves, and then people in Rome may see with astonishment, what fierce and utterly savage creatures these are. For they either take away their own lives, or they tire their master by their obstinate disobedience and stupidity, so that he rues his bargain, though he have bought them for the veriest trifle."

Diodorus: "When the Tyrrhenians had the Corsican cities in their possession, they demanded from the natives tribute of resin, wax, and honey, which are here produced in abundance. The Corsican slaves are of great excellence, and seem to be preferable to other slaves for the common purposes of life. The whole broad island is for the most part mountainous, rich in shady woods, watered by little rivers. The inhabitants live on milk, honey, and flesh, all which they have in plenty. The Corsicans are just towards each other, and live in a more civilized manner than all other barbarians. For when honey-combs are found in the woods, they belong without dispute to the first finder. The sheep, being distinguished by certain marks, remain safe, even although their master does not guard them. Also in the regulation of the rest of their life, each one in his place observes the laws of rectitude with wonderful faithfulness. They have a custom at the birth of a child which is most strange and new; for no care is taken of a woman in child-birth; but instead of her, the husband lays himself for some days as if sick and worn out in bed. Much boxwood grows there, and that of no mean sort. From this arises the great bitterness of the honey. The island is inhabited by barbarians, whose speech is strange and hard to be understood. The number of the inhabitants is more than thirty thousand."

Seneca: "For, leaving out of account such places as by the pleasantness of the region, and their advantageous situation, allure great numbers, go to remote spots on rude islands—go to Sciathus, and Seriphus, and Gyarus, and Corsica, and you will find no place of banishment where some one or other does not reside for his own pleasure. Where shall we find anything so naked, so steep and rugged on every side, as this rocky island? Where is there a land in respect of its products scantier, in respect of its people more inhospitable, in respect of its situation more desolate, or in respect of its climate more unhealthy? And yet there live here more foreigners than natives."

According to the accounts of the oldest writers, we must doubtless believe that Corsica was in those times to a very great extent uncultivated, and, except in the matter of wood, poor in natural productions. That Seneca exaggerates is manifest, and is to be explained from the situation in which he wrote. Strabo and Diodorus are of opposite opinions as to the character of the Corsican slaves. The former has in his favour the history and unvarying character of the Corsicans, who have ever shown themselves in the highest degree incapable of slavery, and Strabo could have pronounced on them no fairer eulogy than in speaking of them as he has done. What Diodorus, who writes as if more largely informed, says of the Corsican sense of justice, is entirely true, and is confirmed by the experience of every age.

Among the epigrams on Corsica ascribed to Seneca, there is one which says of the Corsicans: Their first law is to revenge themselves, their second to live by plunder, their third to lie, and their fourth to deny the gods.

This is all the information of importance we have from the Greeks and Romans on the subject of Corsica.

CHAPTER IV
COMMENCEMENT OF THE
MEDIÆVAL PERIOD

Corsica remained in the possession of the Romans, from whom in later times it received the Christian religion, till the fall of Rome made it once more a prey to the rovers by land and sea. Here, again, we have new inundations of various tribes, and a motley mixture of nations, languages, and customs, as in the earliest period.

Germans, Byzantine Greeks, Moors, Romanized races appear successively in Corsica. But the Romanic stamp, impressed by the Romans and strengthened by bands of fugitive Italians, has already taken its place as an indelible and leading trait in Corsican character. The Vandals came to Corsica under Genseric, and maintained themselves in the island a long time, till they were expelled by Belisarius. After the Goths and Longobards had in their turn invaded the island and been its masters, it fell, along with Sardinia, into the hands of the Byzantines, and remained in their possession nearly two hundred years. It was during this period that numerous Greek names and roots, still to be met with throughout the country and in the language, originated.

The Greek rule was of the Turkish kind. They appeared to look upon the Corsicans as a horde of savages; they loaded them with impossible exactions, and compelled them to sell their very children in order to raise the enormous tribute. A period of incessant fighting now begins for Corsica, and the history of the nation consists for centuries in one uninterrupted struggle for existence and freedom.

The first irruption of the Saracens occurred in 713. Ever since Spain had become Moorish, the Mahommedans had been scouring the Mediterranean, robbing and plundering in all the islands, and founding in many places a dominion of protracted duration. The Greek Emperors, whose hands were full in the East, totally abandoned the West, which found new protectors in the Franks. That Charlemagne had to do with Corsica or with the Moors there, appears from his historian Eginhard, who states that the Emperor sent out a fleet under Count Burkhard, to defend Corsica against the Saracens. His son Charles gave them a defeat at Mariana. These struggles with the Moors are still largely preserved in the traditions of the Corsican people. The Roman noble, Hugo Colonna, a rebel against Pope Stephen IV., who sent him to Corsica with a view to rid himself of him and his two associates, Guido Savelli and Amondo Nasica, figures prominently in the Moorish wars. Colonna's first achievement was the taking of Aleria, after a triple combat of a romantic character, between three chivalrous paladins and as many Moorish knights. He then defeated the Moorish prince Nugalon, near Mariana, and forced all the heathenish people in the island to submit to the rite of baptism. The comrade of this Hugo Colonna was, according to the Corsican chronicler, a nephew of Ganelon of Mayence, also named Ganelon, who had come to Corsica to wipe off the disgrace of his house in Moorish blood.

The Tuscan margrave, Bonifacius, after a great naval victory over the Saracens on the coast of Africa, near Utica, is now said to have landed at the southern extremity of Corsica on his return home, and to have built a fortress on the chalk cliffs there, which received from its founder the name of Bonifazio. This took place in the year 833. Louis the Pious granted him the feudal lordship of Corsica. Etruria thus acquires supremacy over the neighbouring island a second time, and it is certain that the Tuscan margraves continued to govern Corsica till the death of Lambert, the last of their line, in 951.

Berengarius, and after him Adalbert of Friuli, were the next masters of the island; then the Emperor Otto II. gave it to his adherent, the Margrave Hugo of Toscana. No further historical details can be arrived at with any degree of precision till the period when the city of Pisa obtained supremacy in Corsica.

In these times, and up till the beginning of the eleventh century, a fierce and turbulent nobility had been forming in Corsica, as in Italy—the various families of which held sway throughout the island. This aristocracy was only in a very limited degree of native origin. Italian magnates who had fled from the barbarians, Longobard, Gothic, Greek or Frankish vassals, soldiers who had earned for themselves land and feudal title by their exertions in the wars against the Moors, gradually founded houses and hereditary seigniories. The Corsican chronicler makes all the seigniors spring from the Roman knight Hugo Colonna and his companions. He makes him Count of Corsica, and traces to his son Cinarco the origin of the most celebrated family of the old Corsican nobility, the Cinarchesi; to another son, Bianco, that of the Biancolacci; to Pino, a son of Savelli's, the Pinaschi; and in the same way we have Amondaschi, Rollandini, descendants of Ganelon and others. In later times various families emerged into distinction from this confusion of petty tyrants, the Gentili, and Signori da Mare on Cape Corso; beyond the mountains, the seigniors of Leca, of Istria, and Rocca, and those of Ornans and of Bozio.

CHAPTER V
FEUDALISM IN CORSICA—THE
LEGISLATOR SAMBUCUCCIO

For a long period the history of the Corsicans presents nothing but a bloody picture of the tyranny of the barons over the lower orders, and the quarrels of these nobles with each other. The coasts became desolate, the old cities of Aleria and Mariana were gradually forsaken; the inhabitants of the maritime districts fled from the Saracens higher up into the hills, where they built villages, strengthened by nature and art so as to resist the corsairs and the barons. In few countries can the feudal nobility have been so fierce and cruel as in Corsica. In the midst of a half barbarous and quite poor population, Nature around them savage as themselves, unchecked by any counterpoise of social morality or activity, unbridled by the Church, cut off from the world and civilizing intercourse—let the reader imagine these nobles lording it in their rocky fastnesses, and, giving the rein to their restless and unsettled natures in sensuality and violence. In other countries all that was humanizing, submissive to law, positive and not destructive in tendency, collected itself in the cities, organized itself into guilds and corporate bodies, and uniting in a civic league, made head against the aristocracy. But it was extremely difficult to accomplish anything like this in Corsica, where trade and manufactures were unknown, where there were neither cities nor a commercial middle-class. All the more note-worthy is the phenomenon, that a nation of rude peasants should, in a manner reminding us of patriarchal times, have succeeded in forming itself into a democracy of a marked and distinctive character.

The barons of the country, engaged in continual wars with the oppressed population of the villages, and fighting with each other for sole supremacy, had submitted at the beginning of the eleventh century to one of their own number, the lord of Cinarca, who aimed at making himself tyrant of the whole island. Scanty as our materials for drawing a conclusion are, we must infer from what we know, that the Corsicans of the interior had hitherto maintained a desperate resistance to the barons. In danger of being crushed by Cinarca, the people assembled to a general council. It is the first Parliament of the Corsican Commons of which we hear in their history, and it was held in Morosaglia. On this occasion they chose a brave and able man to be their leader, Sambucuccio of Alando, with whom begins the long series of Corsican patriots, who have earned renown by their love of country and heroic courage.

Sambucuccio gained a victory over Cinarca, and compelled him to retire within his own domains. As a means of securing and extending the advantage thus gained, he organized a confederacy, as was done in Switzerland under similar circumstances, though somewhat later. All the country between Aleria, Calvi, and Brando, formed itself into a free commonwealth, taking the title of Terra del Commune, which it has retained till very recently. The constitution of this commonwealth, simple and entirely democratic in its character, was based upon the natural divisions of the country. These arise from its mountain-system, which separates the island into a series of valleys. As a general rule, the collective hamlets in a valley form a parish, called at the present day, as in the earliest times, by the Italian name, *pieve* (plebs). Each *pieve*, therefore, included a certain number of little communities (paese); and each of these, in its popular assembly, elected a presiding magistrate, or *podestà*, with two or more Fathers of the Community (*padri del commune*), probably, as was customary in later times, holding office for a single year. The Fathers of the Community were to be worthy of the name; they were to exercise a fatherly care over the welfare of their respective districts; they were to maintain peace, and shield the defenceless. In a special assembly of their own they chose an official, with the title *caporale*, who seems to have been invested with the functions of a tribune of the Commons, and was expressly intended to defend the rights of the people in every possible way. The podestàs, again, in their assembly, had the right of choosing the *Dodici* or Council of Twelve—the highest legislative body in the confederacy.

However imperfect and confused in point of date our information on the subject of Sambucuccio and his enactments may be, still we gather from it the certainty that the Corsicans, even at that early period, were able by their own unaided energies to construct for themselves a democratic commonwealth. The seeds thus planted could never afterwards be eradicated, but continued to develop themselves under all the storms that assailed them, ennobling the rude vigour of a spirited and warlike people, encouraging through every period an unexampled patriotism, and a heroic love of freedom, and making it possible that, at a time when the great nations in the van of European culture lay prostrate under despotic forms of government, Corsica should have produced the democratic constitution of Pasquale Paoli, which originated before North America freed herself, and when the French Revolution had not begun. Corsica had no slaves, no serfs; every Corsican was free. He shared in the political life of his country through the self-government of his commune, and the popular assemblies — and this, in conjunction with the sense of justice, and the love of country, is the necessary condition of political liberty in general. The Corsicans, as Diodorus mentions to their honour, were not deficient in the sense of justice; but conflicting interests within their island, and the foreign tyrannies to which, from their position and small numbers, they were constantly exposed, prevented them from ever arriving at prosperity as a State.

CHAPTER VI
THE PISANS IN CORSICA

The legislator Sambucuccio fared as many other legislators have done. His death was a sudden and severe blow to his enactments. The seigniors immediately issued from their castles, and spread war and discord over the land. The people, looking round for help, besought the Tuscan margrave Malaspina to rescue them, and placed themselves under his protection. Malaspina landed on the island with a body of troops, defeated the barons, and restored peace. This happened about the year 1020, and the Malaspinas appear to have remained rulers of the Terra del Commune till 1070, while the seigniors bore sway in the rest of the country. At this time, too, the Pope, who pretended to derive his rights from the Frankish kings, interfered in the affairs of the island. It would even seem that he assumed the position of its feudal superior, and that Malaspina was Count of Corsica by the papal permission. The Corsican bishoprics furnished him with another means of establishing his influence in the island. The number of these had in the course of time increased to six, Aleria, Ajaccio, Accia, Mariana, Nebbio, and Sagona.

Gregory VII. sent Landulph, Bishop of Pisa, to Corsica, to persuade the people to put themselves under the power of the Church. This having been effected, Gregory, and then Urban II., in the year 1098, granted the perpetual feudal superiority of the island to the bishopric of Pisa, now raised to an archbishopric. The Pisans, therefore, became masters of the island, and they maintained a precarious possession of it, in the face of continual resistance, for nearly a hundred years.

Their government was wise, just, and benevolent, and is eulogized by all the Corsican historians. They exerted themselves to bring the country under cultivation, and to improve the natural products of the soil. They rebuilt towns, erected bridges, made roads, built towers along the coast, and introduced even art into the island, at least in so far as regarded church architecture. The best old churches in Corsica are of Pisan origin, and may be instantly recognised as such from the elegance of their style. Every two years the republic of Pisa sent as their representative to the island, a Giudice, or judge, who governed and administered justice in the name of the city. The communal arrangements of Sambucuccio were not altered.

Meanwhile, Genoa had been watching with jealous eyes the progress of Pisan ascendency in the adjacent island, and could not persuade herself to allow her rival undisputed possession of so advantageous a station in the Mediterranean, immediately before the gates of Genoa. Even when Urban II. had made Pisa the metropolitan see of the Corsican bishops, the Genoese had protested, and they several times compelled the popes to withdraw the Pisan investiture. At length, in the year 1133, Pope Innocent II. yielded to the urgent solicitations of the Genoese, and divided the investiture, subordinating to Genoa, now also made an archbishopric, the Corsican bishops of Mariana, Accia, and Nebbio, while Pisa retained the bishoprics of Aleria, Ajaccio, and Sagona. But the Genoese were not satisfied with this; they aimed at secular supremacy over the whole island. Constantly at war with Pisa, they seized a favourable opportunity of surprising Bonifazio, when the inhabitants of the town were celebrating a marriage festival. Honorius III. was obliged to confirm them in the possession of this important place in the year 1217. They fortified the impregnable cliff, and made it the fulcrum of their influence in the island; they granted the city commercial and other privileges, and induced a great number of Genoese families to settle there. Bonifazio thus became the first Genoese colony in Corsica.

CHAPTER VII
PISA OR GENOA?—GIUDICE DELLA ROCCA

Corsica was now rent into factions. One section of the inhabitants inclined to Pisa, another to Genoa, many of the seigniors maintained an independent position, and the Terra del Commune kept itself apart. The Pisans, though hard pressed by their powerful foes in Italy, were still unwilling to give up Corsica. They made an islander of the old family of Cinarca, their Lieutenant and Giudice, and committed to him the defence of his country against Genoa.

This man's name was Sinucello, and he became famous under the appellation of Giudice della Rocca. His patriotism and heroic courage, his wisdom and love of justice, have given him a place among those who in barbarous times have distinguished themselves by their individual excellencies. The Cinarchesi, it is said, had been driven by one of the papal margraves to Sardinia. Sinucello was a descendant of the exiled family. He had gone to Pisa and attained to eminence in the service of the republic. The hopes of the Pisans were now centred in him. They made him Count and Judge of the island, gave him some ships, and sent him to Corsica in the year 1280. He succeeded, with the aid of his adherents there, in overpowering the Genoese party among the seigniors, and restoring the Pisan ascendency. The Genoese sent Thomas Spinola with troops. Spinola suffered a severe defeat at the hands of Giudice. The war continued many years, Giudice carrying it on with indefatigable vigour in the name of the Pisan republic; but after the Genoese had won against the Pisans the great naval engagement at Meloria, in which the ill-fated Ugolino commanded, the power of the Pisans declined, and Corsica was no longer to be maintained.

After the victory the Genoese made themselves masters of the east coast of Corsica. They intrusted the subjugation of the island, and the expulsion of the brave Giudice, to their General Luchetto Doria. But Doria too found himself severely handled by his opponent; and for years this able man continued to make an effectual resistance, keeping at bay both the Genoese and the seigniors of the island, which seemed now to have fallen into a state of complete anarchy. Giudice is one of the favourite national heroes of the chroniclers: they throw an air of the marvellous round his noble and truly

Corsican figure, and tell romantic stories of his long-continued struggles. However unimportant these may be in a historical point of view, still they are characteristic of the period, the country, and the men. Giudice had six daughters, who were married to persons of high rank in the island. His bitter enemy, Giovanninello, had also six daughters, equally well married. The six sons-in-law of the latter form a conspiracy against Giudice, and in one night kill seventy fighting men of his retainers. This gives rise to a separation of the entire island into two parties, and a feud like that between the Guelphs and Ghibellines, which lasts for two hundred years. Giovanninello was driven to Genoa: returning, however, soon after, he built the fortress of Calvi, which immediately threw itself into the hands of the Genoese, and became the second of their colonies in the island. The chroniclers have much to say of Giudice's impartial justice, as well as of his clemency, — as, for example, the following. He had once taken a great many Genoese prisoners, and he promised their freedom to all those who had wives, only these wives were to come over themselves and fetch their husbands. They came; but a nephew of Giudice's forced a Genoese woman to spend a night with him. His uncle had him beheaded on the spot, and sent the captives home according to his promise. We see how such a man should have been by preference called Giudice—judge; since among a barbarous people, and in barbarous times, the character of judge must unite in itself all virtue and all other authority.

In his extreme old age Giudice grew blind. A disagreement arose between the blind old man and his natural son Salnese, who, having treacherously got him into his power, delivered him into the hands of the Genoese. When Giudice was being conducted on board the ship that was to convey him to Genoa, he threw himself upon his knees on the shore, and solemnly imprecated a curse on his son Salnese, and all his posterity. Giudice della Rocca was thrown into a miserable Genoese dungeon, and died in Genoa in the tower of Malapaga, in the year 1312. The Corsican historian Filippini, describes him as one of the most remarkable men the island has produced; he was brave, skilful in the use of arms, singularly rapid in the execution of his designs, wise in council, impartial in administering justice, liberal to his friends, and firm in adversity—qualities which almost all distinguished Corsicans have possessed. With Giudice fell the last remains of Pisan ascendency in Corsica.

CHAPTER VIII
COMMENCEMENT OF GENOESE SUPREMACY—CORSICAN COMMUNISTS

Pisa made a formal surrender of the island to Genoa, and thirty years after the death of Giudice, the Terra del Commune, and the greater number of the seigniors submitted to the Genoese supremacy. The Terra sent four messengers to the Genoese Senate, and tendered its submission under the condition, that the Corsicans should pay no further tax than twenty soldi for each hearth. The Senate accepted the condition, and in 1348 the first Genoese governor landed in the island. It was Boccaneria, a man who is praised for his vigour and prudence, and who, during his single year of power, gave the country peace. But he had scarcely returned from his post, when the factions raised their heads anew, and plunged the country into the wildest anarchy. From the first the rights of Genoa had not been undisputed, Boniface VIII. having in 1296, in virtue of the old feudal claims of the papal chair, granted the superiority of Corsica and Sardinia to King James of Arragon. A new foreign power, therefore—Spain, connected with Corsica at a period of hoary antiquity—seemed now likely to seek a footing on the island; and in the meantime, though no overt attempt at conquest had been made, those Corsicans who refused allegiance to Genoa, found a point of support in the House of Arragon.

The next epoch of Corsican history exhibits a series of the most sanguinary conflicts between the seigniors and Genoa. Such confusion had arisen immediately on the death of Giudice, and the people were reduced to such straits, that the chronicler wonders why, in the wretched state of the country, the population did not emigrate in a body. The barons, as soon as they no longer felt the heavy hand of Giudice, used their power most tyrannously, some as independent lords, others as tributary to Genoa—all sought to domineer, to extort. The entire dissolution of social order produced a sect of Communists, extravagant enthusiasts, who appeared contemporaneously in Italy. This sect, an extraordinary phenomenon in the wild Corsica, became notorious and dreaded under the name of the Giovannali. It took its rise in the little district of Carbini, on the other side the hills. Its originators were bastard sons of Guglielmuccio, two brothers, Polo and Arrigo, seigniors of

Attalà. "Among these people," relates the chronicler, "the women were as the men; and it was one of their laws that all things should be in common, the wives and children as well as other possessions. Perhaps they wished to renew that golden age of which the poets feign that it ended with the reign of Saturn. These Giovannali performed certain penances after their fashion, and assembled at night in the churches, where, in going through their superstitious rites and false ceremonies, they concealed the lights, and, in the foulest and the most disgraceful manner, took pleasure the one with the other, according as they were inclined. It was Polo who led this devilish crew of sectaries, which began to increase marvellously, not only on this side the mountains, but also everywhere beyond them."

The Pope, at that time residing in France, excommunicated the sect; he sent a commissary with soldiers to Corsica, who gave the Giovannali, now joined by many seigniors, a defeat in the Pieve Alesani, where they had raised a fortress. Wherever a Giovannalist was found, he was killed on the spot. The phenomenon is certainly remarkable; possibly the idea originally came from Italy, and it is hardly to be wondered at, if among the poor distracted Corsicans, who considered human equality as something natural and inalienable, it found, as the chronicler tells us, an extended reception. Religious enthusiasm, or fanatic extravagance, never at any other time took root among the Corsicans; and the island was never priest-ridden: it was spared at least this plague.

CHAPTER IX
STRUGGLES WITH GENOA—
ARRIGO DELLA ROCCA

The people themselves, driven to desperation after the departure of Boccaneria, begged the assistance of Genoa. The republic accordingly sent Tridano della Torre to the island. He mastered the barons, and ruled seven full years vigorously and in peace.

The second man of mark from the family of Cinarca or Rocca, now appears upon the stage, Arrigo della Rocca—young, energetic, impetuous, born to rule, as stubborn as Giudice, equally inexhaustible in resource and powerful in fight. His father, Guglielmo, had fought against the Genoese, and had been slain. The son took up the contest. Unfortunate at first, he left his native country and went to Spain, offering his services to the House of Arragon, and inciting its then representatives to lay claim to those rights which had already been acknowledged by the Pope. Tridano had been murdered during Arrigo's absence, the seigniors had rebelled, the island had split into two parties—the Caggionacci and the Ristiagnacci, and a tumult of the bloodiest kind had broken out.

In the year 1392, Arrigo della Rocca appeared in Corsica almost without followers, and as if on a private adventure, but no sooner had he shown himself, than the people flocked to his standard. Lionello Lomellino and Aluigi Tortorino were then governors, two at once in those unsettled times. They called a diet at Corte, counselled and exhorted. Meanwhile, Arrigo had marched rapidly on Cinarca, routing the Genoese troops wherever they came in their way; immediately he was at the gates of Biguglia, the residence of the governors; he stormed the place, assembled the people, and had himself proclaimed Count of Corsica. The governors retired in dismay to Genoa, leaving the whole country in the hands of the Corsicans, except Calvi, Bonifazio, and San Columbano.

Arrigo governed the island for four years without molestation— energetically, impartially, but with cruelty. He caused great numbers to be beheaded, not sparing even his own relations. Perhaps some were imbittered by this severity—perhaps it was the inveterate tendency to faction in the

Corsican character, that now began to manifest itself in a certain degree of disaffection.

The seigniors of Cape Corso rose first, with the countenance of Genoa; but they were unsuccessful—with an iron arm Arrigo crushed every revolt. He carried in his banner a griffin over the arms of Arragon, to indicate that he had placed the island under the protection of Spain.

Genoa was embarrassed. She had fought many a year now for Corsica, and had gained nothing. The critical position of her affairs tied the hands of the Republic, and she seemed about to abandon Corsica. Five *Nobili*, however, at this juncture, formed themselves into a sort of joint-stock company, and prevailed upon the Senate to hand the island over to them, the supremacy being still reserved for the Republic. These were the Signori Magnera, Tortorino, Fiscone, Taruffo, and Lomellino; they named their company "The Mahona," and each of them bore the title of Governor of Corsica.

"They appeared in the island at the head of a thousand men, and found the party discontented with Arrigo, awaiting them. They effected little; were, in fact, reduced to such extremity by their energetic opponent, that they thought it necessary to come to terms with him. Arrigo agreed to their proposals, but in a short time again took up arms, finding himself trifled with; he defeated the Genoese Nobili in a bloody battle, and cleared the island of the Mahona. A second expedition which the Republic now sent was more successful. Arrigo was compelled once more to quit Corsica.

He went a second time to Spain, and asked support from King John of Arragon. John readily gave him two galleys and some soldiers, and after an absence of two months the stubborn Corsican appeared once more on his native soil. Zoaglia, the Genoese governor, was not a match for him; Arrigo took him prisoner, and made himself master of the whole island, with the exception of the fortresses of Calvi and Bonifazio. This occurred in 1394. The Republic sent new commanders and new troops. What the sword could not do, poison at last accomplished. Arrigo della Rocca died suddenly in the year 1401. Just at this time Genoa yielded to Charles VI. of France. The fortunes of Corsica seemed about to take a new turn; this aspect of affairs, however, proved, in the meantime, transitory. The French king named Lionello Lomellino feudal count of the island. He is the same who was mentioned as a member of the Mahona, and it is to him Corsica owes the founding of her largest city, Bastia, to which the residence of the Governors was now removed from the neighbouring Castle of Biguglia.

CHAPTER X
VINCENTELLO D'ISTRIA

A man of a similar order began now to take the place of Arrigo della Rocca. Making their appearance constantly at similar political junctures, these bold Corsicans bear an astonishing resemblance to each other; they form an unbroken series of undaunted, indefatigable, even tragic heroes, from Giudice della Rocca, to Pasquale Paoli and Napoleon, and their history—if we except the last notable name—is identical in its general character and final issue, as the struggle of the island against the Genoese rule remains throughout centuries one and the same. The commencement of the career of these men, who all emerge from banishment, has each time a tinge of the romantic and adventurous.

Vincentello d'Istria was a nephew of Arrigo's, son of one of his sisters and Ghilfuccio a noble Corsican. Like his uncle, he had in his youth attached himself to the court of Arragon, had entered into the Arragonese service, and distinguished himself by splendid deeds of arms. Later, having procured the command of some Arragonese ships, he had conducted a successful corsair warfare against the Genoese, and made his name the terror of the Mediterranean. He resolved to take advantage of the favourable position of affairs, and attempt a landing in his native island, where Count Lomellino had drawn odium on himself by his harsh government, and Francesco della Rocca, natural son of Arrigo, who ruled the Terra del Commune in the name of Genoa, as vice-count, was vainly struggling with a formidable opposition.

Vincentello landed unexpectedly in Sagona, marched rapidly to Cinarca, exactly as his uncle had done, took Biguglia, assembled the people, and made himself Count of Corsica. Francesco della Rocca immediately fell by the hand of an assassin; but his sister, Violanta—a woman of masculine energy, took up arms, and made a brave resistance, though at length obliged to yield. Bastia surrendered. Genoa now sent troops with all speed; after a struggle of two years, Vincentello was compelled to leave the island—a number of the selfish seigniors having made common cause with Genoa.

In a short time, Vincentello returned with Arragonese soldiers, and again he wrested the entire island from the Genoese, with the exception of

Calvi and Bonifazio. When he had succeeded thus far, Alfonso, the young king of Arragon, more enterprising than his predecessors, and having equipped a powerful fleet, prepared in his own person to make good the presumed Arragonese rights on the island by force of arms. He sailed from Sardinia in 1420, anchored before Calvi, and forced this Genoese city to surrender. He then sailed to Bonifazio; and while the Corsicans of his party laid siege to the impregnable fortress on the land side, he himself attacked it from the sea. The siege of Bonifazio is an episode of great interest in these tedious struggles, and was rendered equally remarkable by the courage of the besiegers, and the heroism of the besieged. The latter, true to Genoa to the last drop of blood—themselves to a great extent of Genoese extraction—remained immoveable as their own rocks; and neither hunger, pestilence, nor the fire and sword of the Spaniards, broke their spirit during that long and distressing blockade. Every attempt to storm the town was unsuccessful; women, children, monks and priests, stood in arms upon the walls, and fought beside the citizens. For months they continued the struggle, expecting relief from Genoa, till the Spanish pride of Alfonso was at length humbled, and he drew off, weary and ashamed, leaving to Vincentello the prosecution of the siege. Relief came, however, and delivered the exhausted town on the very eve of its fall.

Vincentello retreated; and as Calvi had again fallen into the hands of the Genoese, the Republic had the support of both these strong towns. King Alfonso made no further attempt to obtain possession of Corsica. Vincentello, now reduced to his own resources, gradually lost ground; the intrigues of Genoa effecting more than her arms, and the dissensions among the seigniors rendering a general insurrection impossible.

The Genoese party was specially strong on Cape Corso, where the Signori da Mare were the most powerful family. With their help, and that of the Caporali, who had degenerated from popular tribunes to petty tyrants, and formed now a new order of nobility, Genoa forced Vincentello to retire to his own seigniory of Cinarca. The brave Corsican partly wrought his own fall: libertine as he was, he had carried off a young girl from Biguglia; her friends took up arms, and delivered the place into the hands of Simon da Mare. The unfortunate Vincentello now resolved to have recourse once more to the House of Arragon; but Zacharias Spinola captured the galley which was conveying him to Sicily, and brought the dreaded enemy of Genoa a prisoner to the Senate. Vincentello d'Istria was beheaded on the great stairs of the Palace of Genoa. This was in the year 1434. "He was a glorious man," remarks the old Corsican chronicler.

CHAPTER XI
THE BANK OF ST. GEORGE OF GENOA

After the death of Vincentello, the seigniors contended with each other for the title of Count of Corsica; Simon da Mare, Giudice d'Istria, Renuccio da Leca, Paolo della Rocca, were the chief competitors; now one, now another, assuming the designation. In Genoa, the Fregosi and Adorni had split the Republic into two factions; and both families were endeavouring to secure the possession of Corsica. This occasioned new wars and new miseries. No respite, no year of jubilee, ever came for this unhappy country. The entire population was constantly in arms, attacking or defending. The island was revolt, war, conflagration, blood, from one end to the other.

In the year 1443, some of the Corsicans offered the supremacy to Pope Eugene IV., in the hope that the Church might perhaps be able to restrain faction, and restore peace. The Pope sent his plenipotentiary with troops; but this only increased the embroilment. The people assembled themselves to a diet in Morosaglia, and chose a brave and able man, Mariano da Gaggio, as their Lieutenant-general. Mariano first directed his efforts successfully against the degenerate Caporali, expelled them from their castles, destroyed many of these, and declared their office abolished. The Caporali, on their side, called the Genoese Adorno into the island. The people now placed themselves anew under the protection of the Pope; and as the Fregosi had meanwhile gained the upper hand in Genoa, and Nicholas V., a Genoese Pope, favoured them, he put the government of Corsica into the hands of Ludovico Campo Fregoso in the year 1449. In vain the people rose in insurrection under Mariano. To increase the already boundless confusion, Jacob Imbisora, an Arragonese viceroy, appeared, demanding subjection in the name of Arragon.

The despairing people assembled again to a diet at Lago Benedetto, and adopted the fatal resolution of placing themselves under the Bank of St. George of Genoa. This society had been founded in the year 1346 by a company of capitalists, who lent the Republic money, and farmed certain portions of the public revenue as guarantee for its repayment. At the request of the Corsicans, the Genoese Republic ceded the island to this Bank, and the Fregosi renounced their claims, receiving a sum of money in compensation.

The Company of St. George, under the supremacy of the Senate, entered upon the territory thus acquired in the year 1453, as upon an estate from which they were to draw the highest returns possible.

But years elapsed before the Bank succeeded in establishing its authority in the island. The seigniors beyond the mountains, in league with Arragon, made a desperate resistance. The governors of the Bank acted with reckless severity; many heads fell; various nobles went into exile, and collected around Tomasin Fregoso, a man of a restless disposition, whose remembrance of his family's claims upon Corsica had been greatly quickened, since his uncle Lodovico had become Doge. He came, accompanied by the exiles, routed the forces of the Bank, and put himself in possession of a large portion of the island, after the people had proclaimed him Count.

In 1464, Genoa fell into the hands of Francesco Sforza of Milan, and a power with which Corsica had never had anything to do, began to look upon the island as its own. The Corsicans, who preferred all other masters to the Genoese, gladly took the oath of allegiance to the Milanese general, Antonio Cotta, at the diet of Biguglia. But on the same day a slight quarrel again kindled the flames of war over all Corsica. Some peasants of Nebbio had fallen out with certain retainers of the seigniors from beyond the mountains, and blood had been shed. The Milanese commandant forthwith inflicted punishment on the guilty parties. The haughty nobles, considering their seigniorial rights infringed on, immediately mounted their horses and rode off to their homes without saying a word. Preparations for war commenced. To avert a new outbreak, the inhabitants of the Terra del Commune held a diet, named Sambucuccio d'Alando—a descendant of the first Corsican legislator—their vicegerent, and empowered him to use every possible means to establish peace. Sambucuccio's dictatorship dismayed the insurgents; they submitted to him and remained quiet. A second diet despatched him and others as ambassadors to Milan, to lay the state of matters before the Duke, and request the withdrawal of Cotta.

Cotta was replaced by the certainly less judicious Amelia, who occasioned a war that lasted for years. In all these troubles the democratic Terra del Commune appears as an island in the island, surrounded by the seigniories; it remains always united, and true to itself, and represents, it may be said, the Corsican people. For almost two hundred years we have seen nothing decisive happen without a popular Diet (*veduta*), and we have several times remarked that the people themselves have elected their counts or vicegerents.

The war between the Corsicans and the Milanese was still raging with great fury when Thomas Campo Fregoso again appeared upon the island, trying his fortunes there once more. The Milanese sent him to Milan a prisoner. Singular to relate, he returned from that city in the year 1480, furnished with documents entitling him to have his claims acknowledged. His government, and that of his son Janus, were so cruel, that it was impossible the rule of the Fregoso family could last long, though they had connected themselves by marriage with one of the most influential men in the island, Giampolo da Leca.

The people, meanwhile, chose Renuccio da Leca as their leader, who immediately addressed himself to the Prince of Piombino, Appian IV., and offered to place Corsica under his protection, provided he sent sufficient troops to clear the island of all tyrants. How unhappy the condition of this poor people must have been, seeking help thus on every side, beseeching the aid now of one powerful despot, now of another, adding by foreign tyrants to the number of its own! The Prince of Piombino thought proper to see what could be done in Corsica, more especially as part of Elba already belonged to him. He sent his brother Gherardo di Montagnara with a small army. Gherardo was young, handsome, of attractive manners, and he lived in a style of theatrical splendour. He came sumptuously dressed, followed by a magnificent retinue, with beautiful horses and dogs, with musicians and jugglers. It seemed as if he were going to conquer the island to music. The Corsicans, who had scarcely bread to eat, gazed on him in astonishment, as if he were some supernatural visitant, conducted him to their popular assembly at the Lago Benedetto, and amid great rejoicings, proclaimed him Count of Corsica, in the year 1483. The Fregosi lost courage, and, despairing of their sinking cause, sold their claim to the Genoese Bank for 2000 gold scudi. The Bank now made vigorous preparations for war with Gherardo and Renuccio. Renuccio lost a battle. This frightened the young Prince of Piombino to such a degree, that he quitted the island with all the haste possible, somewhat less theatrically than he had come to it. Piombino desisted from all further attempts.

CHAPTER XII
PATRIOTIC STRUGGLES—GIAMPOLO DA LECA—RENUCCIO DELLA ROCCA

Two bold men now again rise in succession to oppose Genoa. Giampolo da Leca had, as we have seen, become connected with the Fregosi. Although these nobles had resigned their title in favour of the Bank, they were exceedingly uneasy under the loss of influence they had sustained. Janus, accordingly, without leaving Genoa, incited his relative to revolt against the governor, Matias Fiesco. Giampolo rose. But beaten and hard pressed by the troops of the Bank, he saw himself compelled, after a vain attempt to obtain aid from Florence, to lay down his arms, and to emigrate to Sardinia with wife, child, and friends, in the year 1487.

A year had scarcely passed, when he again appeared at the call of his adherents. A second time unfortunate, he made his escape again to Sardinia. The Genoese now punished the rebels with the greatest severity—with death, banishment, and the confiscation of their property. More and more fierce grew the Corsican hatred towards Genoa. For ten years they nursed its smouldering glow. All this while Giampolo remained in exile, meditating revenge—his watchful eye never lifted from his oppressed and prostrate country. At last he came back. He had neither money nor arms; four Corsicans and six Spaniards were all his troops, and with these he landed. He was beloved by the people, for he was noble, brave, and of great personal beauty. The Corsicans crowded to him from Cinarca, from Vico, from Niolo, and from Morosaglia. He was soon at the head of a body of seven thousand foot and two hundred horse—a force which made the Bank of Genoa tremble for its power. It accordingly despatched to the island Ambrosio Negri, an experienced general. Negri, by intrigue and fair promises, contrived to detach a part of Giampolo's followers, and particularly to draw over to himself Renuccio della Rocca, a nobleman of activity and spirit. Giampolo, with forces sensibly diminished, came to an engagement with the Genoese commander at the Foce al Sorbo, and suffered a defeat, in which his son Orlando was taken prisoner. He concluded a treaty with Negri, the terms of which allowed him to leave the island unmolested. He returned to Sardinia in 1501, with fifty Corsicans, there to waste his life in inconsolable grief.

Giampolo's fall was mainly owing to Renuccio della Rocca. This man, the head of the haughty family of Cinarca, saw that the Genoese Bank had adopted a particular line of policy, and was pursuing it with perseverance; he saw that it was resolved to crush completely and for ever the power of the seigniors, more especially of those whose lands lay beyond the mountains, and that his own turn would come. Convinced of this, he suddenly rose in arms in the year 1502. The contest was short, and the issue favourable for Genoa, whose governor in the island was at that time one of the Doria family. All the Dorias, as governors, distinguished themselves by their energy and by their reckless cruelty, and it was to them alone that Genoa owed her gratitude for the important service of at length crushing the Corsican nobility. Nicolas Doria forced Renuccio to come to terms; and one of the conditions imposed on the Corsican noble was that he and his family were henceforth to reside in Genoa.

Giampolo was, still living in Sardinia, more than all other Corsican patriots a source of continual anxiety to the Genoese, who made several attempts to come to an amicable agreement with him. His son Orlando, who had newly escaped to Rome from his prison in Genoa, sent pressing solicitations from that city to his father to rouse himself from his dumb and prostrate inactivity. But Giampolo continued to maintain his heartbroken silence, and listened as little to the suggestions of his son as to those of the Genoese.

Suddenly Renuccio disappeared from Genoa in the year 1504; he left wife and child in the hands of his enemies, and went secretly to Sardinia to seek an interview with the man whom he had plunged into misfortune. Giampolo refused to see him. He was equally deaf to the entreaties of the Corsicans, who all eagerly awaited his arrival. His own relations had in the meantime murdered his son. The viceroy caught the murderers, and was about to execute them, in order to show a favour to Giampolo. But the generous man forgave them, and begged their liberation.

Renuccio had meanwhile gathered eighteen resolute men about him, and, undeterred by the fate of his children, who had been thrown into a dungeon immediately after his flight, he landed again in Corsica. Nicolas Doria, however, lost no time in attacking him before the insurrection became formidable, and he gained a victory. To daunt Renuccio, he had his eldest son beheaded, and he threatened the youngest with a like fate, but allowed himself to be moved by the boy's entreaties and tears. The unhappy father, defeated at every point, fled to Sardinia, and then to Arragon. Doria took ample revenge on all who had shown him countenance, laid whole districts of the island waste, burned the villages, and dispersed the inhabitants.

Renuccio della Rocca returned in the year 1507. This unyielding man was entirely the reverse of the moody and sorrow-laden Giampolo. He set foot on his native soil with only twenty companions. Another of the Dorias met him this time, Andreas, afterwards the famous Doge, who had served under his cousin Nicolò. The Corsican historian Filippini, a Genoese partisan, admits the cruelties committed by Andreas during this short campaign. He succeeded in speedily crushing the revolt; and compelled Renuccio a second time to accept a safe conduct to Genoa. When the Corsican arrived, the people would have torn him to pieces, had not the French governor carried him off with all speed to his castle.

Three years elapsed. Suddenly Renuccio again showed himself in Corsica. He had escaped from Genoa, and after in vain imploring the aid of the European princes, once more bidding defiance to fortune, he had landed in his native country with eight friends. Some of his former vassals received him in Freto, weeping, deeply moved by the accumulated misfortunes of the man, and his unexampled intrepidity of soul. He spoke to them, and conjured them once more to draw the sword. They were silent, and went away. He remained some days in Freto, in concealment. Nicolo Pinello, a captain of Genoese troops in Ajaccio, accidentally passed by upon his horse. The sight of him proved so intolerable to Renuccio, that he attacked him at night and killed him, took his horse, and now showed himself in public. As soon us his presence in the island became known, the soldiers of Ajaccio were sent out to capture him. Renuccio fled into the hills, hunted like a bandit or wild beast. The peasantry, who were put to the torture by his pursuers, as a means of inducing them to discover his lurking-places, at last resolved to end their own miseries and his life. In the month of May 1511, Renuccio della Rocca was found miserably slain in the hills. He was one of the stoutest hearts of the noble house of Cinarca. "They tell," says the Corsican chronicler, "that Renuccio was true to himself till the last, and that he showed no less heroism in his death than in his life; and this is, of a truth, much to his honour, for a brave man should never lose his nobleness of soul, even when fate brings him to an ignominious end."

Giampolo had meanwhile gone to Rome, to ask the aid of the Pope, but, unsuccessful in his exertions, he died there in the year 1515.

CHAPTER XIII
STATE OF CORSICA UNDER THE
BANK OF ST. GEORGE

With Giampolo and Renuccio ended the resistance of the Corsican seigniors. The noble families of the island decayed, their strong keeps fell into ruin, and at present we hardly distinguish here and there upon the rocks of Corsica the blackened walls of the castles of Cinarca, Istria, Leca, and Ornano. But Genoa, in crushing one dreaded foe, had raised against herself another far more formidable—the Corsican people.

During this era of the iron rule of the Genoese Bank, many able men emigrated, and sought for themselves name and fame in foreign countries. They entered into military service, and became famous as generals and Condottieri. Some were in the service of the Medici, others in that of the Spozzi; or they were among the Venetians, in Rome, with the Gonzagas, or with the French. Filippini names a long array of them; among the rest, Guglielmo of Casabianca, Baptista of Leca, Bartelemy of Vivario, with the surname of Telamon, Gasparini, Ceccaldi, and Sampiero of Bastelica. Fortune was especially kind to a Corsican of Bastia, named Arsano; turning renegade, he raised himself to be King of Algiers, under the appellation of Lazzaro. This is the more singular, that precisely at this time Corsica was suffering dreadfully from the Moors, and the Bank had surrounded the whole island with a girdle of beacons and watch-towers, and fortified Porto Vecchio on the southern coast.

After the wars with Giampolo and Renuccio, the government of the Bank was at first mild and paternal, and Corsica enjoyed the blessings of order and peace. So says the Corsican chronicler.

The administration of public affairs, on which very slight alteration was made after the Republic took it out of the hands of the Bank, was as follows:—

The Bank sent a governor to Corsica yearly, who resided in Bastia. He brought with him a vicario, or vicegerent, and a doctor of laws. The entire executive was in his hands; he was the highest judicial and military authority. He had his lieutenants (*luogotenenti*) in Calvi, Algajola, San Fiorenzo, Ajaccio, Bonifazio, Sartena, Vico, Cervione, and Corte. An appeal lay from them to the governor. All these officials were changed once a year, or once in two years. To protect the people from an oppressive exercise of power on their part, a Syndicate had been established, before which a complaint against any particular magistrate could be lodged. If the complaint was found to be well grounded, the procedure of the magistrate concerned could be reversed, and he himself punished with removal from his office. The governor himself was responsible to the Syndics. They were six in number—three from the people, and three from the aristocracy; and might be either Corsicans or Genoese. In particular cases, commissaries came over, charged with the duty of instituting inquiries.

Besides all this, the people exercised the important right of naming the Dodici, or Council of Twelve; and they did this each time a change took place in the highest magistracy. Strictly speaking, twelve were chosen for the districts this side the mountains, six for those beyond. The Dodici represented the people's voice in the deliberations of the governor; and without their consent no law could be enacted, abolished, or modified. One of their number went to Genoa, with the title of Oratore, to act as representative of the Corsican people in the Senate there.

The democratic basis of the constitution of the communes and *pievi*, with their Fathers of the Community and their *podestàs*, was not altered, and the popular assembly (*veduta* or *consulta*) was still permitted. The governor usually summoned it in Biguglia, when anything of general importance was to be done with the consent of the people.

It is clear that these arrangements were of a democratic nature— that they allowed the people free political movement, and a share in the government; gave them a hold on the protection of the law, and checked the arbitrary tendencies of officials. The Corsican people was, therefore, well entitled to congratulate itself, and consider itself favoured far beyond the other nations of Europe, if such laws were really allowed their due force, and did not become an empty show. How they did become an empty show, and how the Genoese rule passed into an abominable despotism—Genoa, like Venice, committing the fatal error of alienating her foreign provinces by a tyrannous, instead of attaching them to herself by a benevolent treatment—we shall see in the following chapters. For now Corsica brings forward her bravest man, and one of the most remarkable characters of the century, against Genoa.

CHAPTER XIV
THE PATRIOT SAMPIERO

Sampiero was born in Bastelica, a spot lying above Ajaccio, in one of the wildest regions of the Corsican mountains, not of an ancient family, but of unknown parents. Guglielmo, grandson of Vinciguerra, has been named as his father; others say he was of the family of the Porri.

Like other Corsican youths, Sampiero had betaken himself to the Continent, and foreign service, at an early age. We find him in the service of the Cardinal Hippolyto de Medici, among the Black Bands at Florence; and he was still young when the world was already talking of his bold deeds, noble disposition, and great force of character. He was the sword and shield of the Medici in their struggle with the Pazzi. Thirsting for action and a wider field, he left his position of Condottiere with these princes, and entered the army of Francis I. of France. The king made him colonel of a Corsican regiment which he had formed. Bayard became his friend, and Charles of Bourbon honoured his impetuous bravery and military skill. "On a day of battle," said Bourbon, "the Corsican colonel is worth ten thousand men." Sampiero distinguished himself on many fields and before many fortresses, and his reputation was equally great with friend and foe.

Entirely devoted to the interests of his master, who was now prosecuting the war with Spain, he had still ear and eye for his native island, from which voices reached him now and then that moved him deeply. He came to Corsica in the year 1547, to take a wife from among his own countrywomen. He chose a daughter of one of the oldest houses beyond the mountains—the house of Ornano. Though he was himself without ancestry, Sampiero's fame and well-known manly worth were a patent of nobility which Francesco Ornano could not despise; and he gave him the hand of his only daughter, the beautiful Vannina, the heiress of Ornano.

No sooner did the governor of the Genoese Bank learn the presence of Sampiero—in whom he foreboded an implacable foe—within the bounds of his authority, than, in defiance of all justice, he had him seized and thrown into prison. Francesco Ornano, fearing for his son-in-law's life, hastened to Genoa to the French ambassador. The latter instantly demanded Sampiero's liberation. The demand was complied with; but the insult done him was now for Sampiero another and a personal spur to give relief in action to his long-cherished hatred of Genoa, and ardent wish to free his native country.

The posture of continental affairs, the war between France and Charles V., soon gave him opportunity.

Henry II., husband of Catherine de Medici, deeply involved in Italian politics, in active war with the Emperor, and in alliance with the Turks, who were on the point of sending a fleet into the Western Mediterranean, agreed to the proposal of an enterprise against Corsica. A double end seemed attainable by this: for first, in threatening Corsica, Genoa was menaced; and secondly, as the Republic, since Andreas Doria had freed her from the French yoke, had become the close ally of Charles V., carrying the war into Corsica was carrying it on against the Emperor himself. And besides, the island offered an excellent position in the Mediterranean, and a basis for the operations of the combined French and Turkish fleets. Marshal Thermes, therefore, at that time in Italy, and besieging Siena, received orders to prepare for the conquest of Corsica.

He held a council of war in Castiglione. Sampiero was overjoyed at the turn affairs had taken; all his wishes were centred in the liberation of his country. He represented to Thermes the necessary and important consequences of the undertaking, and it was forthwith set on foot. Its success could not be doubted. The French only needed to land, and the Corsican people would that moment rise in arms. The hatred of the rule of the Genoese merchants had reached, since the fall of Renuccio, the utmost pitch of intensity; and it had its ground not merely in the ineradicable passion of the people for liberty, but in the actual state of affairs in the island. For, as soon as the Bank saw its power secured, it began to rule despotically. The Corsicans had been stripped of all their political rights: they had lost their Syndicate, the Dodici, their old communal magistracies; justice was venal, murder permitted—at least the murderer was protected in Genoa, and furnished with letters-patent for his personal safety. The horrors of the Vendetta, therefore, of the implacable revenge that insists on blood for blood, took root firm and fast. All writers on Corsican history are unanimous, that the demoralization of the courts of justice was the deepest wound which the Bank of Genoa inflicted on Corsica.

Sampiero had sent a Corsican, named Altobello de Gentili, into the island, to ascertain the state of the popular feeling; his letters, and the hope of his coming kindled the wildest joy; the people trembled with eagerness for the arrival of the fleet. Thermes, and Admiral Paulin, whose squadron had effected a junction with the Turkish fleet at Elba, now sailed for Corsica in August 1553. The brave Pietro Strozzi and his company was with them, though not long; Sampiero, the hope of the Corsicans, was with them; Johann Ornano, Rafael Gentili, Altobello, and other exiles, all burning for revenge, and impatient to drench their swords in Genoese blood.

They landed on the Renella near Bastia. Scarcely had Sampiero shown himself on the city walls, which the invaders ascended by means of scaling ladders, when the people threw open the gates. Bastia surrendered. Without delay they proceeded to reduce the other strong towns, and the interior. Paulin anchored before Calvi, the Turk Dragut before Bonifazio, Thermes marched on San Fiorenzo, Sampiero on Corte, the most important of the inland fortresses. Here too he had no sooner shown himself than the gates were opened. The Genoese fled in every direction, the cause of liberty was triumphant throughout the island; only Ajaccio, Bonifazio, and Calvi, trusting to the natural strength of their situation, still held out. Neither Paulin from the sea, nor Sampiero from the land, could make any impression on Calvi. The siege was raised, and Sampiero hastened to Ajaccio. The Genoese under Lamba Doria prepared for an obstinate defence, but the people opened the gates to their deliverer. The houses of the Genoese were plundered; yet, even here, in the case of their country's enemies, the Corsicans showed how sacred in their eyes were the natural laws of generosity and hospitality; many Genoese, fleeing to the villages for an asylum, found shelter with their foes. Francesco Ornano took Lamba Doria into his own house.

CHAPTER XV
SAMPIERO—FRANCE AND CORSICA

Meanwhile the Turk was besieging Bonifazio with furious vigour, ravaging at the same time the entire surrounding country. Dragut was provoked by the heroic resistance of the inhabitants, who showed themselves worthy descendants of those earlier Bonifazians that so bravely held the town against Alfonso of Arragon. Night and day, despite of hunger and weariness, they manned the walls, successfully repelling all attacks, the women showing equal courage with the men. Sampiero came to the assistance of the Turks; the assaults of the besiegers continued without intermission, but the town remained steadfast. The Bonifazians were in hopes of relief, hourly expecting Cattaciolo, one of their fellow-citizens, from Genoa. The messenger came, bearing news of approaching succours; but he fell into the hands of the French. They made a traitor of him, inducing him to carry forged letters into the city, which advised the commandant to give up all hope of being relieved. He accordingly concluded a treaty, and surrendered the unconquered town under the condition that the garrison should be allowed to embark for Genoa with military honours. The brave defenders had scarcely left the protection of their walls, when the barbarous Turk, trampling under foot at once his oath and common humanity, fell upon them, and began to cut them in pieces. Sampiero with difficulty rescued all that it was still possible to rescue. Not content with this revenge, Dragut demanded to be allowed to plunder the city, and, when this was refused, a large sum in compensation, which Thermes could not pay, but promised to pay. Dragut, exasperated, instantly embarked, and set sail for Asia—he had been corrupted by Genoese gold.

After the fall of Bonifazio, Genoa had not a foot of land left in Corsica, except the "ever-faithful" Calvi. No time was to be lost, therefore, if the island was not to be entirely relinquished. The Emperor had promised help, and placed some thousands of Germans and Spaniards at the disposal of the Genoese, and Cosmo de Medici sent an auxiliary corps. A very considerable force had thus been collected, and, to put success beyond question, the leadership of the expedition was intrusted to their most celebrated general, Andreas Doria, while Agostino Spinola was made second in command.

Andreas Doria was at that time in his eighty-sixth year; but the aspect of affairs seemed so critical, that the old man could not but comply with the call of his fellow-citizens. He received the banner of the enterprise in the Cathedral of Genoa, from the senators, protectors of the Bank, the clergy, and the people.

On the 20th November 1553, Doria landed in the Gulf of San Fiorenzo, and, in a short time, the star of Genoa was once more in the ascendant. San Fiorenzo, which had been strongly fortified by Thermes, fell; Bastia surrendered; the French gave way on every side. Sampiero had about this time, in consequence of a quarrel with Thermes, been obliged to proceed to the French court; but after putting his calumniators there to silence, he returned in higher credit than before, and as the alone heart and soul of the war, which the incapable Thermes had proved himself unfit to conduct. He was indefatigable in attack, in resistance, in guerilla warfare. Spinola met with a sharp repulse on the field of Golo, but a wound which Sampiero received in the fight rendering him for some time inactive, the Corsicans suffered a bloody defeat at Morosaglia. Sampiero now gave his wound no more time to heal; he again appeared on the field, and defeated the Spaniards and Germans in the battle of Col di Tenda, in the year 1554.

The war was carried on with unabated fury for five years. Corsica seemed to be certain of the perpetual protection of France, and in general to regard herself as an independently organized section of that kingdom. Francis II. had named Jourdan Orsini his viceroy, and the latter, at a general diet, had, in the name of his king, pronounced Corsica incorporated with France, declaring that it was now for all time impossible to separate the island from the French crown—that the one could be abandoned only with the other. The fate of Corsica seemed, therefore, already linked to the French monarchy, and the island to be detached from the general body of the Italian states, to which it naturally belongs. But scarcely had the king made the solemn announcement above referred to, when the treaty of Cateau Cambresis, in the year 1559, shattered at a single blow all the hopes of the Corsicans.

France concluded a peace with Philip of Spain and his allies, and engaged to surrender Corsica to the Genoese. The French, accordingly, immediately put all the places they had garrisoned into the hands of Genoa, and embarked their troops. A desperate struggle had been maintained for six years to no purpose, diplomacy now lightly gamed away the earnings of that long war's bloody toil, and the Corsican saw himself hurled back into his old misery, and abandoned, defenceless, to Genoese vengeance, by a rag of paper, a pen-and-ink peace. This breach of faith was a crushing blow, and extorted from the country a universal cry of despair, but it was not listened to.

CHAPTER XVI
SAMPIERO IN EXILE—HIS WIFE VANNINA

It was now that Sampiero began to show himself in all his greatness; for the man must be admitted to be really great whom adversity does not bend, but who gathers double strength from misfortune. He had quitted Corsica as an outlaw. The peace had taken the sword out of his hand; the island, ravaged and desolate from end to end, could not venture a new struggle on its own resources—a new war needed fresh support from a foreign power. For four years Sampiero wandered over Europe seeking help at its most distant courts; he travelled to France to Catherine, hoping to find her mindful of old services that he had done the house of Medici; he went to Navarre; to the Duke of Florence; to the Fregosi; to one Italian court after another; he sailed to Algiers to Barbarossa; he hastened to Constantinople to the Sultan Soliman. His stern, imposing demeanour, the emphatic sincerity of his speech, his powerful intellect, his glowing patriotism, everywhere commanded admiration and respect, among the barbarians not less than among the Christians; but they comforted him with vain hopes and empty promises.

While Sampiero was thus wandering with unwearied perseverance from court to court, inciting the princes to an enterprise in behalf of Corsica, Genoa had not lost sight of him; Genoa was alarmed to think what might one day be the result of his exertions. It was clearly necessary, by some means or other, to cripple once for all the dreaded arm of Sampiero. Poison and assassination, it is said, had been tried, but had failed. It was resolved to crush his spirit, by bringing his natural affection as a father and a husband into conflict with his passionate love of country. It was resolved to break his heart.

Sampiero's wife Vannina lived in her own house at Marseilles, under the protection of France. She had her youngest son, Francesco, beside her; the elder, Alfonso, was at the court of Catherine. The Genoese surrounded her with their agents and spies. It was their aim, and it was important to them, to allure Sampiero's wife and child to Genoa. To effect this, they employed a certain Michael Angelo Ombrone, who had been tutor to the young sons of Sampiero, and enjoyed his entire confidence; a cunning villain of the name of Agosto Bazzicaluga was another of their tools. Vannina was of a susceptible and credulous nature, proud of the ancient name of Ornano. These Genoese traitors represented to her the fate that necessarily awaited the children of her proscribed husband. Heirs of their father's outlawry, robbed of the seigniory of their renowned ancestors, poor—their very lives not safe, what might they not come to? They pictured to her alarmed imagination these, her beloved children, in the wretchedness of exile, eating the bread of dependence, or what was worse, if they trod in the footsteps of their father, hunted in the mountains, at last captured, and loaded with the chains of galley-slaves.

Vannina was deeply moved—her fidelity began to waver; the thought of going to Genoa grew gradually less foreign to her—less and less repulsive. There, said Ombrone and Bazzicaluga, they will restore to your children the seigniory of Ornano, and your own gentle persuasions will at length succeed in reconciling even Sampiero with the Republic. The poor mother's heart was not proof against this. Vannina was thoroughly a woman; her natural feeling at last spoke with imperious decision, refusing to comprehend or sympathize with the grand, rugged, terrible character of her husband, who only lived because he loved his country, and hated its oppressors; and who nourished with his own being the all-consuming fire of his sole passion— remorselessly flinging in all his other possessions like faggots to feed the flames. Her blinded heart extorted from Vannina the resolution to go to Genoa. One day, she said to herself, we shall all be happy, peaceful, and reconciled.

Sampiero was in Algiers, where the bold renegade Barbarossa, as Sultan of the country, had received him with signal marks of respect, when a ship arrived from Marseilles, and brought the tidings that his wife was on the point of escaping to Genoa with his boy. When Sampiero began to comprehend the possibility of this flight, his first thought was to throw himself instantly into the vessel, and hasten to Marseilles; he became calmer, and bade his noble friend, Antonio of San Fiorenzo, go instead, and prevent the escape—if prevention were still possible. He himself, restraining his sorrow within his innermost heart, remained, negotiated with Barbarossa about an expedition against Genoa, and subsequently sailed for Constantinople, to try what could be effected with the Sultan, not till then proposing to return to Marseilles to ascertain the position of his private affairs.

Antonio of San Fiorenzo had made all possible haste upon his mission. Rushing into Vannina's house, he found it empty and silent. She was away with her child, and Ombrone, and Bazzicaluga, in a Genoese ship, secretly, the day before. Hurriedly Antonio collected friends, Corsicans, armed men, threw himself into a brigantine, and made all sail in the direction which the fugitives ought to have taken. He sighted the Genoese vessel off Antibes, and signalled for her to shorten sail. When Vannina saw that she was pursued, knowing too well who her pursuers were likely to be, in an agony of terror she begged to be put ashore, scarcely knowing what she did. But Antonio reached her as she landed, and took possession of her person in the name of Sampiero and the King of France.

He brought her to the house of the Bishop of Antibes, that the lady, quite prostrate with grief, might enjoy the consolations of religion, and might have a secure asylum in the dwelling of a priest. Horrible thoughts, to which he gave no expression, made this advisable. But the Bishop of Antibes was afraid of the responsibility he might incur, and refusing to run any risk, he gave Vannina into the hands of the Parliament of Aix. The Parliament declared its readiness to take her under its protection, and to permit none, whoever he might be, to do her violence. But Vannina wished nothing of all this, and declined the offer. She was, she said, Sampiero's wife, and whatever sentence her husband might pronounce on her, to that sentence she would submit. The guilty consciousness of her fatal step lay heavy on her heart, and while she wept bitterest tears of repentance, she imposed on herself a noble and silent resignation to the consequences.

And now Sampiero, leaving the Turkish court, where Soliman had for a while wonderingly entertained the famous Corsican, returned to Marseilles, giving himself up to his own personal anxieties. At Marseilles, he found Antonio, who related to him what had occurred, and endeavoured to restrain his friend's gathering wrath. One of Sampiero's relations, Pier Giovanni of Calvi, let fall the imprudent remark that he had long foreseen Vannina's flight. "And you concealed what you foresaw?" cried Sampiero, and stabbed him dead with a single thrust of his dagger. He threw himself on horseback, and rode in furious haste to Aix, where his trembling wife waited for him in the castle of Zaisi. Antonio hurried after him, agonized with the fear that all efforts of his to avert some dreadful catastrophe might be unavailing.

Sampiero waited beneath the windows of the castle till morning. He then went to his wife, and took her away with him to Marseilles. No one could read his silent purposings in his stern face. As he entered his house with her, and saw it standing desolate and empty, the whole significance of the affront—the full consciousness of her treason and its possible results, sank upon his heart; once more the intolerable thought shot through him that it was his own wife who had basely sold herself and his child into the detested hands of his country's enemies; the demon of phrenzy took possession of his soul, and he slew her with his own hand.

Sampiero, says the Corsican historian, loved his wife passionately, but as a Corsican—that is, to the last Vendetta.

He buried his dead in the Church of St. Francis, and did not spare funereal pomp. He then went to show himself at the court of Paris. This occurred in the year 1562.

CHAPTER XVII
RETURN OF SAMPIERO—STEPHEN DORIA

Sampiero was coldly received at the French court; the courtiers whispered, avoided him, sneered at him from behind their virtuous mask. Sampiero was not the man to be dismayed by courtiers, nor was the court of Catherine de Medici a tribunal before which the fearful deed of one of the most remarkable men of his time could be tried. Catherine and Henry II. forgot that Sampiero had murdered his wife, but they would do no more for Corsica than willingly look on while it was freed by the exertions of others.

Now that he had done all that was possible as a diplomatist, and saw no prospect of foreign aid, Sampiero fell back upon himself, and resolved to trust to his own and his people's energies. He accordingly wrote to his friends in Corsica that he would come to free his country or die. "It lies with us now," he said, "to make a last effort to attain the happiness and glory of complete freedom. We have applied to the cabinets of France, of Navarre, and of Constantinople; but if we do not take up arms till the day when the aid of France or Tuscany shall be with us in the fight, there is a long period of oppression yet in store for our country. And at any rate, would a national independence obtained with the assistance of foreigners be a prize worth contending for? Did the Greeks seek help of their neighbours to rescue their independence from the yoke of the Persians? The Italian Republics are recent examples of what the strong will of a people can do, combined with the love of country. Doria could free his native city from the oppression of a tyrannous aristocracy; shall we forbear to rise till the soldiers of the King of Navarre come to fight in our ranks?"

On the 12th of June 1564, Sampiero landed in the Gulf of Valinco, with a band of twenty Corsicans, and five-and-twenty Frenchmen. He sank the galley which had brought him. When he was asked why he had done so, and where he would find refuge if the Genoese were now suddenly to attack him, he answered, "In my sword!" He assaulted the castle of Istria with this handful of men, took it, and marched rapidly upon Corte. The Genoese drew out to meet him before the walls of the town, with a much superior force, as Sampiero had still not above a hundred men. But such was the terror inspired by his mere name, that he no sooner appeared in sight than they fled without drawing sword. Corte opened its gates, and Sampiero had thus gained one important position. The Terra del Commune immediately made common cause with him.

Sampiero now advanced on Vescovato, the richest district of the island, on the slopes of the mountains where they sink towards the beautiful plain of Mariana. The people of Vescovato assembled at his approach, alarmed for the safety of their harvest, which was threatened by this new storm of war. They were urgently counselled by the Archdeacon Filippini, the Corsican historian, to remain neutral, and take no notice of Sampiero, whatever he might do. When Sampiero entered Vescovato, he found it ominously quiet, and the people all within their houses; at last, yielding to curiosity or sympathy, they came out. Sampiero spoke to them, accusing them, as he justly might, of a want of patriotism. His words made a deep impression. Offers of entertainment in some of their houses were made; but Sampiero punished the inhabitants of Vescovato with his contempt, and passed the night in the open air.

The place became nevertheless the scene of a bloody battle. Nicolas Negri led his Genoese against it, as a position held by Sampiero. It was a murderous struggle; the more so that as the number engaged on both sides was comparatively small, it was mainly a series of single combats. Corsicans, too, were here fighting against Corsicans—for a company of the islanders had remained in the service of Genoa. These fell back, however, when Sampiero upbraided them for fighting against their country. Victory was inclining to the side of Genoa—for Bruschino, one of the bravest of the Corsican captains, had fallen, when Sampiero, rallying his men for one last effort, succeeded in finally repulsing the Genoese, who fled in disorder towards Bastia.

The victory of Vescovato brought new additions to the forces of Sampiero, and another at Caccia, in which Nicolas Negri was among the killed, spread the insurrection through the whole interior. Sampiero now hoped to be assisted in earnest by Tuscany, and even by the Turks; for in winning battle after battle over the Spaniards and Genoese, with such inconsiderable means at his command, he had shown what Corsican patriotism might do if it were supported.

On the death of Negri, the Genoese without delay despatched their best general to the island, in the person of Stephen Doria, whose bravery, skill, and unscrupulous severity rendered him worthy of the name. He was at the head of a force of four thousand German and Italian mercenaries. The war broke out, therefore, with fresh fury. The Corsicans suffered some reverses; but the Genoese, weakened by important defeats, were once more thrown back upon Bastia. Doria had made an attack on Bastelica, Sampiero's birthplace, had laid it in ashes, and made the patriot's house level with the ground. Houses and property were little to the man whose own hand had sacrificed his wife to his country; noticeable, however, is this Genoese policy of constantly bringing the patriotism of the Corsicans into tragic conflict with their personal affections. What they tried in vain with Sampiero, succeeded with Campocasso—a man of unusual heroism, of an influential family of old Caporali. His mother had been seized and placed in confinement. Her son did not hesitate a moment—he threw away his sword, and hastened into the Genoese camp to save his mother from the torture. He left it again when they proposed to him to become the murderer of Sampiero, and remained quiet at home. Powerful friends were becoming fewer and fewer round Sampiero; now that Bruschino had fallen, Campocasso gone over to the enemy, and the brave Napoleon of Santa Lucia, the first of his name who distinguished himself as a military leader, had suffered a severe defeat.

If the whole hatred of the Corsicans and Genoese could be put into two words, these two are Sampiero and Doria. Both names, suggestive of the deadliest personal feud, at the same time completely represent their respective nationalities. Stephen Doria exceeded all his predecessors in cruelty. He had sworn to annihilate the Corsican people. His openly expressed opinions are these:—"When the Athenians became masters of the principal town in Melos, after it had held out for seven months, they put all the inhabitants above fourteen years of age to death, and sent a colony to people the place anew, and keep it in obedience. Why do we not imitate this example? Is it because the Corsicans deserve punishment less than those ancient rebels? The Athenians saw in these terrible chastisements the means of conquering the Peloponnese, the whole of Greece, Africa, and Sicily. By putting all their enemies to the sword, they restored the reputation and terror of their arms. It will be said that this procedure is contrary to the law of nations, to humanity, to the progress of civilisation. What does it matter, provided we only make ourselves feared?—that is all I ask. I care more for what Genoa says than for the judgment of posterity, which has no terrors for me. This empty word posterity checks none but the weak and irresolute.

Our interest is to extend on every side the circle of conquered country, and to take from the insurgents everything that can support a war. Now, I see but two ways of doing this—first, by destroying the crops, and secondly, by burning the villages, and pulling down the towers in which they fortify themselves when they dare not venture into the field."

The advice of Doria sufficiently shows how fierce the Genoese hatred of this indomitable people had become, and indicates but too plainly the unspeakable miseries the Corsicans had to endure. Stephen Doria laid half the island desolate with fire and sword; and Sampiero was still unconquered. The Corsican patriot had held an assembly of the people in Bozio to strengthen the general cause by the adoption of suitable measures, to regulate anew the council of the Dodici and the other popular magistracies, and to organize, if possible, an insurrection of the entire people. Sampiero was not a mere soldier, he was a far-seeing statesman. He wished to give his country, with its independence, a free republican constitution, founded on the ancient enactments of Sambucuccio of Alando. He wished to draw, from the situation of the island, from its forests and its products in general, such advantages as might enable it to become a naval power; he wished to make Corsica, in alliance with France, powerful and formidable, as Rhodes and Tyre had once been. Sampiero did not aim at the title of Count of Corsica; he was the first who was called Father of his country. The times of the seigniors were past.

He sent messengers to the continental courts, particularly to France, asking assistance; but the Corsicans were left to their fate. Antonio Padovano returned from France empty-handed; he only brought Sampiero's young son Alfonso, ten thousand dollars in money, and thirteen standards with the inscription—*Pugna pro patria*. This was, nevertheless, enough to raise the spirits of the Corsicans; and the standards, which Sampiero divided among the captains, became the occasion of envy and dangerous heartburnings.

Here are two letters of Sampiero's.

To Catherine of France.—"Our affairs have hitherto been prosperous. I can assure your Majesty, that unless the enemy had received both secret and open help from the Catholic King of Spain, at first twenty-two galleys and four ships, with a great number of Spaniards, we should have reduced them to such extremity, that by this time they would have been no longer able to maintain a footing in the island. Nevertheless, and come what will, we will never abandon the resolution we have taken, to die sooner than acknowledge in any way whatever the supremacy of the Republic. I pray of your Majesty, therefore, in these circumstances, not to forget my devotion to your person, and that of my country to France. If his Catholic Majesty shows himself so friendly to the Genoese, who are, even without him, so formidable to us—a people forsaken by all the world—will your Majesty suffer us to be destroyed by our cruel foes?"

To the Duke of Parma.—"Although we should become tributary to the Ottoman Porte, and thus run the risk of offending all the Princes of Christendom, nevertheless this is our unalterable resolution—A hundred times rather the Turks than the supremacy of the Republic. France herself has not respected the treaty, which, as they said, was to be the guarantee of our rights and the end of our miseries. If I take the liberty of troubling you with the affairs of the island, it is that your Highness may, if need be, take our part at the court of Rome against the attacks of our enemies. I desire that my words may at least remain a solemn protest against the indifference of the Catholic Princes, and an appeal to the Divine justice."

CHAPTER XVIII
THE DEATH OF SAMPIERO

Once more ambassadors set out for France, five in number; but the Genoese intercepted them off the coast. Three leapt into the sea to save themselves by swimming, one of whom was drowned; the two who were captured were first put to the torture, and then executed. The war assumed the frightful character of a merciless Vendetta on both sides. Doria, however, effected nothing. Sampiero defeated him again and again; and at last, in the passes of Luminanda, almost annihilated the Genoese forces. It required the utmost exertion of Doria's great skill and personal bravery to extricate himself on the latter occasion. He arrived in San Fiorenzo, bleeding, exhausted, and in despair, and soon after left the island. The Republic replaced him by Vivaldi, and afterwards by the artful and intriguing Fornari; but the Genoese had lost all hope of crushing Sampiero by war and open force. Against this man, who had come to the island as an outlaw with a few outlawed followers, they had gradually sent their whole force into the field — their own and a Spanish fleet, their mercenaries, Germans, fifteen thousand Spaniards, their greatest generals, Doria, Centurione, and Spinola; yet, the same Genoa that had conquered Pisa and Venice had proved unable to subdue a poor people, forsaken by the whole world, who came into the ranks of battle starving, in rags, unshod, badly armed, and who, when they returned home, found nothing but the ashes of their villages.

It was therefore decided that Sampiero must be murdered.

Dissensions, fomented by the Genoese, had long existed between him and the descendants of the old seigniors. Some, like Hercules of Istria, had deserted him from lust of Genoese gold, or because their pride revolted at the thought of obeying a man who had risen from the dust. Others had a Vendetta with Sampiero; they had a debt of blood to exact from him. These were the nobles of the Ornano family, three brothers — Antonio, Francesco, and Michael Angelo, cousins of Vannina. Genoa had won them with gold, and the promise of the seigniory of Ornano, of which Vannina's children were the rightful heirs. The Ornanos, again, gained the monk Ambrosius of Bastelica, and Sampiero's own servant Vittolo, a trusted follower, with whose help it was agreed to take Sampiero in an ambuscade. The governor,

Fornari, approved of the plan, and committed its execution to Rafael Giustiniani.

Sampiero was in Vico when the monk brought him forged letters, urgently requesting him to come to Rocca, where a rebellion, it was said, had broken out against the popular cause. Sampiero instantly despatched Vittolo with twenty horse to Cavro, and himself followed soon after. He was accompanied by his son Alfonso, Andrea de' Gentili, Antonio Pietro of Corte, and Battista da Pietra. Vittolo, in the meantime, instructed the brothers Ornano, and Giustiniani, that Sampiero would pass through the defile of Cavro; on receiving which intelligence, they immediately set out for the spot indicated with a considerable force of foot and horse, and formed the ambuscade. Sampiero and his little band were riding unsuspectingly through the pass, when they suddenly found themselves assailed on every side, and the defile swarming with armed men. He saw that his hour was come. Yielding now to those impulses of natural affection which he had once so signally disowned, he ordered his son Alfonso to leave him, to flee, and save himself for his country. The son obeyed, and escaped. Most of his friends had fallen bravely fighting by his side, when Sampiero rushed into the *mêlée*, to hew his way through if it were possible. The day was just dawning. The three Ornanos had kept their eyes constantly upon him, at first afraid to assail the terrible man; but at length, spurred on by revenge, they pressed in upon him, some Genoese soldiery at their back. Sampiero fought desperately. He had thrown himself upon Antonio Ornano, and wounded him with a pistol-shot in the throat. But his carbine missed fire; Vittolo, in loading it, had put in the bullet first. Sampiero's face was streaming with blood; freeing his eyes from it with his left, his right hand still grasped his sword, and kept all at bay, when Vittolo, from behind, shot him through the back, and he fell. The Ornanos now rushed in upon the dying man, and finished their work. They cut off Sampiero's head, and carried it to the Governor.

It was on the 17th of January in the year 1567 that Sampiero fell. He had reached his sixty-ninth year, his vigour unimpaired by age or military toil. The stern grandeur of his soul, and his pure and heroic patriotism, have made his name immortal. He was great in the field, inexhaustible in council; owing all to his own extraordinary nature, without ancestry, he inherited nothing from fortune, which usually favours the *parvenu*, but from misfortune everything, and he yielded, like Viriathus, only to the assassin. He has shown, by his elevating example, what a noble man can do, when he remains unyieldingly true to a great passion.

Sampiero was above the middle height, of proud and martial bearing, dark and stern, with black curly hair and beard. His eye was piercing, his words few, firm, and impressive. Though a son of nature, and without education, he possessed acute perceptions and unerring judgment. His friends accused him of seeking the sovereignty of his native island; he sought only its freedom. He lived as simply as a shepherd, wore the woollen blouse of his country, and slept on the naked earth. He had lived at the most luxurious courts of his time, at those of Florence and Versailles, but he had contracted none of their hollowness of principle, or corrupt morality. The rugged patriot could murder his wife because she had betrayed herself and her child to her country's enemies, but he knew nothing of those crimes that pervert nature, and those principles that would refine the vile abuse into a philosophy of life. He was simple, rugged, and grand, headlong and terrible in anger, a whole man, and fashioned in the mightiest mould of primitive nature.

CHAPTER XIX
SAMPIERO'S SON, ALFONSO—
TREATY WITH GENOA

At the news of Sampiero's fall, the bells were rung in Genoa, and the city was illuminated. The murderers quarrelled disgracefully over their Judas-hire; that of Vittolo amounted to one hundred and fifty gold scudi.

Sorrow and dismay fell upon the Corsican nation; its father was slain. The people assembled in Orezza; three thousand armed men, many weeping, all profoundly sad, filled the square before the church. Leonardo of Casanova, Sampiero's friend and fellow-soldier, broke the silence. He was about to pronounce the patriot's funeral oration.

This man was at the time labouring under the severest personal affliction. Unheard-of misfortunes had overtaken him. He had shortly before escaped from prison, by the aid of a heroic youth, his own son. Leonardo had been made prisoner by the Genoese, who had thrown him into a dungeon in Bastia. His son, Antonio, meditated plans of rescue night and day. Disguised in the dress of the woman who brought the prisoners their food, he made his way into his father's cell. He conjured his father to make his escape and leave him behind; though they should put him to death, he said, he was but a stripling, and his death would do him honour, while it preserved his father's arm and wisdom for his country; their duty as patriots pointed out this course. Long and terrible was the struggle in the father's mind. At last he saw that he ought to do as his son had said; he tore himself from his arms, and, wrapped in the female dress, passed safely out. When the youth was discovered, he gave himself up without resistance, proud and happy. They led him to the governor, and, at his command, he was hung from the window of his father's castle of Fiziani.

Leonardo, the generous victim's fate written in stern characters on his face, rose now like a prophet before the assembled people—

"Slaves weep," he said, "free men avenge themselves! No weak-spirited lamenting! Our mountains should re-echo nothing but shouts of war. Let us show, by the vigour of our measures, that he is not all dead. Has he not left us the example of his life? The Fornari and the Vittoli cannot rob us of that. It has escaped their ambuscades and their treacherous balls. Why did he cry to his son, Save thyself? Doubtless that there might still remain a hero for our country, a head for our soldiers, a dreaded foe for the Genoese. Yes, countrymen, Sampiero has left to his murderers the stain of his death, and to the young Alfonso the duty of vengeance. Let us aid in accomplishing the noble work. Close the ranks! The spirit of the father returns to us in the son. I know the youth. He is worthy of the name he bears, and of the country's confidence. He has nothing of youth but its glow—the ripeness of the judgment is sometimes in advance of the time of life, and a ripe judgment is a gift that Heaven has not denied him. He has long shared the dangers and toils of his father. All the world knows he is master of the rough craft of arms. Our soldiers are eager to march under his command, and you may be sure their instinct is true—it never deceives them. The masses guess their men. They are seldom mistaken in their choice of those whom they think fit to lead them. And, moreover, what higher tribute could you pay to the memory of Sampiero, than to choose his son? Those who hear me have set their hearts too high to be within the reach of fear.

"Are there men among us base enough to prefer the shameful security of slavery to the storms and dangers of freedom? Let them go, and separate themselves from the rest of the people. But let them leave us their names. When we have engraved these names on a pillar of eternal shame, which we shall erect on the spot where Sampiero was assassinated, we will send their owners off, covered with disgrace, to keep company with Vittolo and Angelo at the court of Fornari. But they are fools not to know that arms and battle, which are the honourable resource of free and brave men, are also the safest recourse of the weak. If they still hesitate, let me say to them—On the one side stand renown for our standard, liberty for ourselves, independence for our country; on the other, the galleys, infamy, contempt, and all the other miseries of slavery. Choose!"

After this speech of Leonardo's, the people elected by acclamation Alfonso d'Ornano to be Chief and General of the Corsicans. Alfonso was seventeen years old, but he was Sampiero's son. The Corsicans thus, far from being broken and cast down by the death of Sampiero, as their enemies had hoped, set up a stripling against the proud Republic of Genoa, mocking the veteran Genoese generals, and the name of Doria; and for two years the youth, victorious in numerous conflicts, held the Genoese at bay.

Meanwhile the long war had exhausted both sides. Genoa was desirous of peace; the island, at that time divided by the factions of the Rossi and Negri, was critically situated, and, like its enemy, disposed for a cessation of hostilities. The Republic, which had already, in 1561, resumed Corsica from the Bank of St. George, now recalled the detested Fornari, and sent George Doria to the island—the only man of the name of whom the Corsicans have preserved a grateful memory. The first measure of this wise and temperate nobleman was to proclaim a general amnesty. Many districts tendered allegiance; many captains laid down their arms. The Bishop of Sagona succeeded in persuading even the young Alfonso to a treaty, which was concluded between him and Genoa on the following terms:—1. Complete amnesty for Alfonso and his adherents. 2. Liberty for them and their families to embark for the Continent. 3. Liberty to dispose of their property by sale, or by leaving it in trust. 4. Restoration of the seigniory of Ornano to Alfonso. 5. Assignment of the Pieve Vico to the partisans of Alfonso till their embarkation. 6. A space of sixty days for the settlement of their affairs. 7. Liberty for each man to take a horse and some dogs with him. 8. Cancelling of the liabilities of those who were debtors to the public treasury; for all others, five years' grace, in consideration of the great distress prevailing in the country. 9. Liberation of certain persons then in confinement.

Alfonso left his native island with three hundred companions in the year 1569; he went to France, where he was honourably received by King Charles IX., who made him colonel of the Corsican regiment he was at that time forming. Many Corsicans went to Venice, great numbers took service with the Pope, who organized from them the famous Corsican Guard of the Eight Hundred.

BOOK II
HISTORY

CHAPTER I
STATE OF CORSICA IN THE SIXTEENTH CENTURY—A GREEK COLONY ESTABLISHED ON THE ISLAND

It was not till the close of the war of Sampiero that the wretched condition of the island became fully apparent. It had become a mere desert, and the people, decimated by the war, and by voluntary or compulsory emigration, were plunged in utter destitution and savagery. To make the cup of their sorrows full, the plague several times visited the country, and famine compelled the inhabitants to live on acorns and roots. Besides all this, the corsairs roved along the coasts, plundered the villages, and carried off men and women into slavery. It was in this state George Doria found the island, when he came over as governor; and so long as he was at the head of its affairs, Corsica had reason to rejoice in his paternal care, his mildness and clemency, and his conscientious observance of the stipulations of the treaty, by which the statutes and privileges of the Terra del Commune had been specially guaranteed.

Scarcely had George Doria made way for another governor, when Genoa returned to her old mischievous policy. People in power are usually so obstinate and blind, that they see neither the past nor the future. Gradually the Corsicans were again extruded from all offices, civil, military, and ecclesiastical—the meanest posts filled with Genoese, the old institutions suppressed, and a one-sided administration of justice introduced. The island was considered in the light of a Government domain. Impoverished

Genoese *nobili* had places given them there to restore their finances. The Corsicans were involved in debt, and they now fell into the hands of the usurers—mostly priests—to whom they had recourse, in order to muster money for the heavy imposts. The governor himself was to be looked on as a satrap. On his arrival in Bastia, he received a sceptre as a symbol of his power; his salary, paid by the country, was no trifle; and in addition, his table had to be furnished by payments in kind—every week a calf, and a certain quantity of fruits and vegetables. He received twenty-five per cent. of all fines, confiscations, and prizes of smuggled goods. His lieutenants and officials were cared for in proportion. For he brought to the island with him an attorney-general, a master of the ceremonies, a secretary-general, and a private secretary, a commandant of the ports, a captain of cavalry, a captain of police, a governor-general of the prisons. All these officials were vampires; Genoese writers themselves confess it. The imposts became more and more oppressive; industry was at a stand-still; commerce in the same condition—for the law provided that all products of the country, when exported, should be carried to the port of Genoa.

All writers who have treated of this period in Corsican history, agree in saying that of all the countries in the world, she was at that time the most unhappy. Prostrate under famine, pestilence, and the ravages of war; unceasingly harassed by the Moors; robbed of her rights and her liberty by the Genoese; oppressed, plundered; the courts of justice venal; torn by the factions of the Blacks and Reds; bleeding at a thousand places from family feuds and the Vendetta; the entire land one wound—such is the picture of Corsica in those days—an island blessed by nature with all the requisites for prosperity. Filippini counted sixty-one fertile districts which now lay desolate and forsaken—house and church still standing—a sight, as he says, to make one weep. Destitute of any other pervading principle of social cohesion, the Corsican people must have utterly broken up, and scattered into mere hordes, unless it had been penetrated by the sentiment of patriotism, to an extent so universal and with a force so intense. The virtue of patriotism shows itself here in a grandeur almost inconceivable, if we consider what a howling wilderness it was to which the Corsicans clung with hearts so tender and true; a wilderness, but drenched with their blood, with the blood of their fathers, of their brothers, and of their children, and therefore dear. The Corsican historian says, in the eleventh book of his history, "If patriotism has ever been known at any time, and in any country of the world, to exercise power over men, truly we may say that in the island of Corsica it has been mightier than anywhere else; for I am altogether amazed and astounded that the love of the inhabitants of this island for their country has been so great, as at all times to prevent them from coming to a firm and voluntary determination to emigrate. For if we pursue the course of their history, from the earliest inhabitants down to the present time, we see that throughout so many centuries this people has never had peace and quiet for so much as a hundred years together; and that, nevertheless, they have never resolved to quit their native island, and so avoid the unspeakable ruin that has followed so many and so cruel wars, that were accompanied with dearth, with conflagration, with feuds, with murders, with inward dissensions, with tyrannous exercise of power by so many different nations, with plundering of their goods, with frequent attacks of those cruel barbarians—the corsairs, and with endless miseries besides, that it would be tedious to reckon up." Within a period of thirty years, twenty-eight thousand assassinations were committed in Corsica.

"A great misfortune for Corsica," says the same historian, "is the vast number of those accursed machines of arquebuses." The Genoese Government drew a considerable revenue from the sale of licenses to carry these. "There are," remarks Filippini, "more than seven thousand licenses at present issued; and, besides, many carry fire-arms without any license, and especially in the mountains, where you see nothing but bands of twenty and thirty men, or more, all armed with arquebuses. These licenses bring seven thousand lire out of poor, miserable Corsica every year; for every new governor that comes annuls the licenses of his predecessor, in order forthwith to confirm them afresh. But the buying of the fire-arms is the worst. For you will find no Corsican so poor that he has not his gun—in value at least from five to six scudi, besides the outlay for powder and ball; and those that have no money sell their vineyard, their chestnuts, or other possessions, that they may be able to buy one, as if it were impossible to exist unless they did so. In truth, it is astonishing, for the greater part of these people have not a coat upon their back that is worth a half scudo, and in their houses nothing to eat; and yet they hold themselves for disgraced, if they appear beside their neighbours without a gun. And hence it comes that the vineyards and the fields are no longer under cultivation, and lie useless, and overgrown with brushwood, and the owners are compelled to betake themselves to highway robbery and crime; and if they find no convenient opportunity for this, then they violently make opportunity for themselves, in order to deprive those who go quietly about their business, and support their poor families, of their oxen, their kine, and other cattle. From all this arises such calamity, that the pursuit of agriculture is quite vanished out of Corsica, though it was the sole means of support the people had—the only kind of industry still left to these islanders. They who live in such a mischievous manner, hinder the others from doing so well as they might be disposed to do: and the evil does not end here; for we hear every day of murders done now in one village, now in another, because of the easiness with which life can be taken by means of the arquebuses. For formerly, when such weapons were not in use, when foes met upon the streets, if the one was two or three times stronger than the other, an attack was not ventured. But now-a-days, if a man has some trifling quarrel with another, although perhaps with a different sort of weapon he would not dare to look him in the face, he lies down behind a bush, and without the least scruple murders him, just as you shoot down a wild beast, and nobody cares anything about it afterwards; for justice dares not intermeddle. Moreover, the Corsicans have come to handle their pieces so skilfully, that I pray God may shield us from war; for their enemies will have to be upon their guard, because from the children of eight and ten years, who can hardly carry a gun, and never let the trigger lie still, they are day and night at the target, and if the mark be but the size of a scudo, they hit it."

Filippini, the contemporary of Sampiero, saw fire-arms introduced into Corsica, which were quite unknown on the island, as he informs us, till the year 1553. Marshal Thermes—the French, therefore—first brought fire-arms into Corsica. "And," says Filippini, "it was laughable to see the clumsiness of the Corsicans at first, for they could neither load nor fire; and when they discharged, they were as frightened as the savages." What the Corsican historian says as to the fearful consequences of the introduction of the musket into Corsica is as true now, after the lapse of three hundred years, as it was then, and a chronicler of to-day could not alter an iota of what Filippini has said.

In the midst of all this Corsican distress, we are surprised by the sudden appearance of a Greek colony on their desolate shores. The Genoese had striven long and hard to denationalize the Corsican people by the introduction of foreign and hostile elements. Policy of this nature had probably no inconsiderable share in the plan of settling a Greek colony in the island, which was carried into execution in the year 1676. Some Mainotes of the Gulf of Kolokythia, weary of the intolerable yoke of the Turks, like those ancient Phocæans who refused to submit to the yoke of the Persians, had resolved to migrate with wife, child, and goods, and found for themselves a new home. After long search and much futile negotiation for a locality, their ambassador, Johannes Stefanopulos, came at length to Genoa, and expressed to the Senate the wishes of his countrymen. The Republic listened to them most gladly, and proposed for the acceptance of the Greeks the district of Paomia, which occupies the western coast of Corsica from the Gulf of Porto to the Gulf of Sagona. Stefanopulos convinced himself of the suitable nature of the locality, and the Mainotes immediately contracted an agreement with the Genoese Senate, in terms of which the districts of

Paomia, Ruvida, and Salogna, were granted to them in perpetual fief, with a supply of necessaries for commencing the settlement, and toleration for their national religion and social institutions; while they on their part swore allegiance to Genoa, and subordinated themselves to a Genoese official sent to reside in the colony. In March 1676, these Greeks, seven hundred and thirty in number, landed in Genoa, where they remained two months, previously to taking possession of their new abode. Genoa planted this colony very hopefully; she believed herself to have gained, in the brave men composing it, a little band of incorruptible fidelity, who would act as a permanent forepost in the enemy's country. It was, in fact, impossible that the Greeks could ever make common cause with the Corsicans. These latter gazed on the strangers when they arrived—on the new Phocæans—with astonishment. Possibly they despised men who seemed not to love their country, since they had forsaken it; without doubt they found it a highly unpleasant reflection that these intruders had been thrust in upon their property in such an altogether unceremonious manner. The poor Greeks were destined to thrive but indifferently in their new rude home.

CHAPTER II
INSURRECTION AGAINST GENOA

For half a century the island lay in a state of exhaustion—the hatred of Genoa continuing to be fostered by general and individual distress, and at length absorbing into itself every other sentiment. The people lived upon their hatred; their hatred alone prevented their utter ruin.

Many circumstances had been meanwhile combining to bring the profound discontent to open revolt. It appeared to the sagacious Dodici— for this body still existed, at least in form—that a main source of the miseries of their country was the abuse in the matter of licensing fire-arms. Within thirty years, as was noticed above, twenty-eight thousand assassinations had been committed in Corsica. The Twelve urgently entreated the Senate of the Republic to forbid the granting of these licenses. The Senate yielded. It interdicted the selling of muskets, and appointed a number of commissaries to disarm the island. But as this interdict withdrew a certain amount of yearly revenue from the exchequer, an impost of twelve scudi was laid upon each hearth, under the name of the *due seini*, or two sixes. The people paid, but murmured; and all the while the sale of licenses continued, both openly and secretly.

In the year 1724, another measure was adopted which greatly annoyed the Corsicans. The Government of the country was divided—the lieutenant of Ajaccio now receiving the title of Governor—and thus a double burden and twofold despotism henceforth pressed upon the unfortunate people. In the hands of both governors was lodged irresponsible power to condemn to the galleys or death, without form or procedure of any kind; as the phrase went—*ex informata conscientia* (from informed conscience). An administration of justice entirely arbitrary, lawlessness and murder were the results.

Special provocations—any of which might become the immediate occasion of an outbreak—were not wanting. A punishment of a disgraceful kind had been inflicted on a Corsican soldier in a small town of Liguria. Condemned to ride a wooden horse, he was surrounded by a jeering crowd who made mirth of his shame. His comrades, feeling their national honour insulted, attacked the mocking rabble, and killed some. The authorities beheaded them for this. When news of the occurrence reached Corsica, the pride of the nation was roused, and, on the day for lifting the tax of the *due seini*, a spark fired the powder in the island itself.

The Lieutenant of Corte had gone with his collector to the Pieve of Bozio; the people were in the fields. Only an old man of Bustancio, Cardone by name, was waiting for the officer, and paid him his tax. Among the coin he tendered was a gold piece deficient in value by the amount of half a soldo. The Lieutenant refused to take it. The old man in vain implored him to have pity on his abject poverty; he was threatened with an execution on his goods, if he did not produce the additional farthing on the following day; and he went away musing on this severity, and talking about it to himself, as old men will do. Others met him, heard him, stopped, and gradually a crowd collected on the road. The old man continued his complaints; then passing from himself to the wrongs of the country, he worked his audience into fury, forcibly picturing to them the distress of the people, and the tyranny of the Genoese, and ending by crying out—"It is time now to make an end of our oppressors!" The crowd dispersed, the words of the old man ran like wild-fire through the country, and awakened everywhere the old gathering-cry *Evviva la libertà!—Evviva il popolo!* The conch[A] blew and the bells tolled the alarm from village to village. A feeble old man had thus preached the insurrection, and half a sou was the immediate occasion of a war destined to last for forty years. An irrevocable resolution was adopted—to pay no further taxes of any kind whatever. This occurred in October of the year 1729.

On hearing of the commotion among the people of Bozio, the governor, Felix Pinelli, despatched a hundred men to the Pieve. They passed the night in Poggio de Tavagna, having been quietly received into the houses of the place. One of the inhabitants, however, named Pompiliani, conceived the plan of disarming them during the night. This was accomplished, and the defenceless soldiers permitted to return to Bastia. Pompiliani was henceforth the declared head of the insurgents. The people armed themselves with axes, bills, pruning-knives, threw themselves on the fort of Aleria, stormed it, cut the garrison in pieces, took possession of the arms and ammunition, and marched without delay upon Bastia. More than five thousand men encamped before the city, in the citadel of which Pinelli had shut himself up. To gain time he sent the Bishop of Mariana into the camp of the insurgents to open negotiations with them. They demanded the removal of all the burdens of the Corsican people. The bishop, however, persuaded them to conclude a truce of four-and-twenty days, to return into the mountains, and to wait for the Senate's answer to their demands. Pinelli employed the time he thus gained in procuring reinforcements, strengthening forts in his neighbourhood, and fomenting dissensions. When the people saw themselves merely trifled with and deceived, they came down from the mountains, this time ten thousand strong, and once more encamped before Bastia. A general insurrection was now no longer to be prevented; and Genoa in vain sent her commissaries to negotiate and cajole.

An assembly of the people was held in Furiani. Pompiliani, chosen commander under the urgent circumstances of the commencing outbreak, had shown himself incapable, and was now set aside, making room for two men of known ability—Andrea Colonna Ceccaldi of Vescovato, and Don Luis Giafferi of Talasani—who were jointly declared generals of the people. Bastia was now attacked anew and more fiercely, and the bishop was again sent among the insurgents to sooth them if possible. A truce was concluded for four months. Both sides employed it in making preparations; intrigues of the old sort were set on foot by the Genoese Commissary Camillo Doria; but an attempt to assassinate Ceccaldi failed. The latter had meanwhile travelled through the interior along with Giafferi, adjusting family feuds, and correcting abuses; subsequently they had opened a legislative assembly in Corte. Edicts were here issued, measures for a general insurrection taken, judicial authorities and a militia organized. A solemn oath was sworn, never more to wear the yoke of Genoa. The insurrection, thus regulated, became legal and universal. The entire population, this side as well as on the other side the mountains, now rose under the influence of one common sentiment. Nor was the voice of religion unheard. The clergy of the island held a convention in Orezza, and passed a unanimous resolution—that if the Republic refused the people their rights, the war was a measure of necessary self-defence, and the people relieved from their oath of allegiance.

CHAPTER III
SUCCESSES AGAINST GENOA, AND GERMAN MERCENARIES—PEACE CONCLUDED

The canon Orticoni had been sent to the Continent to seek the protection of the foreign powers, and Giafferi to Tuscany to procure arms and ammunition, which were much needed; and meanwhile the truce had expired. Genoa, refusing all concessions, demanded unconditional submission, and the persons of the two leaders of the revolt; but when the war was found to break out simultaneously all over the island, and the Corsicans had taken numbers of strong places, and formed the sieges of Bastia, of Ajaccio, and of Calvi, the Republic began to see her danger, and had recourse to the Emperor Charles VI. for aid.

The Emperor granted them assistance. He agreed to furnish the Republic with a corps of eight thousand Germans, making a formal bargain and contract with the Genoese, as one merchant does with another. It was the time when the German princes commenced the practice of selling the blood of their children to foreign powers for gold, that it might be shed in the service of despotism. It was also the time when the nations began to rouse themselves; the presence of a new spirit—the spirit of the freedom and power and progress of the masses—began to be felt throughout the world. The poor people of Corsica have the abiding honour of opening this new era.

The Emperor disposed of the eight thousand Germans under highly favourable conditions. The Republic pledged herself to support them, to pay thirty thousand gulden monthly for them, and to render a compensation of one hundred gulden for every deserter and slain man. It became customary, therefore, with the Corsicans, whenever they killed a German, to call out, "A hundred gulden, Genoa!"

The mercenaries arrived in Corsica on the 10th of August 1731; not all however, but in the first instance, only four thousand men—a number which the Senate hoped would prove sufficient for its purposes. This body of Germans was under the command of General Wachtendonk. They had scarcely landed when they attacked the Corsicans, and compelled them to raise the siege of Bastia.

The Corsicans saw the Emperor himself interfering as their oppressor, with grief and consternation. They were in want of the merest necessaries. In their utter poverty they had neither weapons, nor clothing, nor shoes. They ran to battle bareheaded and barefoot. To what side were *they* to turn for aid? Beyond the bounds of their own island they could reckon on none but their banished countrymen. It was resolved, therefore, at one of the diets, to summon these home, and the following invitation was directed to them:—

"Countrymen! our exertions to obtain the removal of our grievances have proved fruitless, and we have determined to free ourselves by force of arms—all hesitation is at an end. Either we shall rise from the shameful and humiliating prostration into which we have sunk, or we know how to die and drown our sufferings and our chains in blood. If no prince is found, who, moved by the narrative of our misfortunes, will listen to our complaints and protect us from our oppressors, there is still an Almighty God, and we stand armed in the name and for the defence of our country. Hasten to us, children of Corsica! whom exile keeps at a distance from our shores, to fight by the side of your brethren, to conquer or die! Let nothing hold you back—take your arms and come. Your country calls you, and offers you a grave and immortality!"

They came from Tuscany, from Rome, from Naples, from Marseilles. Not a day passed but parties of them landed at some port or another, and those who were not able to bear arms sent what they could in money and weapons. One of these returning patriots, Filician Leoni of Balagna, hitherto a captain in the Neapolitan service, landed near San Fiorenzo, just as his father was passing with a troop to assault the tower of Nonza. Father and son embraced each other weeping. The old man then said: "My son, it is well that you have come; go in my stead, and take the tower from the Genoese." The son instantly put himself at the head of the troop; the father awaited the issue. Leoni took the tower of Nonza, but a ball stretched the young soldier on the earth. A messenger brought the mournful intelligence to his father. The old man saw him approaching, and asked him how matters stood. "Not well," cried the messenger; "your son has fallen!" "Nonza is taken?" "It is taken." "Well, then," cried the old man, "evviva Corsica!"

Camillo Doria was in the meantime ravaging the country and destroying the villages; General Wachtendonk had led his men into the interior to reduce the province of Balagna. The Corsicans, however, after inflicting severe losses on him, surrounded him in the mountains near San Pellegrino. The imperial general could neither retreat nor advance, and was, in fact, lost. Some voices loudly advised that these foreigners should be cut down to a man. But the wise Giafferi was unwilling to rouse the wrath of the Emperor against his poor country, and permitted Wachtendonk and his army to return unharmed to Bastia, only exacting the condition, that the General should endeavour to gain Charles VI.'s ear for the Corsican grievances. Wachtendonk gave his word of honour for this—astonished at the magnanimity of men whom he had come to crush as a wild horde of rebels. A cessation of hostilities for two months was agreed on. The grievances of the Corsicans were formally drawn up and sent to Vienna; but before an answer returned, the truce had expired, and the war commenced anew.

The second half of the imperial auxiliaries was now sent to the island; but the bold Corsicans were again victorious in several engagements; and on the 2d of February 1732, they defeated and almost annihilated the Germans under Doria and De Vins, in the bloody battle of Calenzana. The terrified Republic hereupon begged the Emperor to send four thousand men more. But the world was beginning to manifest a lively sympathy for the brave people who, utterly deserted and destitute of aid, found in their patriotism alone, resources which enabled them so gloriously to withstand such formidable opposition.

The new imperial troops were commanded by Ludwig, Prince of Würtemberg, a celebrated general. He forthwith proclaimed an amnesty under the condition that the people should lay down their arms, and submit to Genoa. But the Corsicans would have nothing to do with conditions of this kind. Würtemberg, therefore, the Prince of Culmbach, Generals Wachtendonk, Schmettau, and Waldstein, advanced into the country according to a plan of combined operation, while the Corsicans withdrew into the mountains, to harass the enemy by a guerilla warfare. Suddenly the reply of the imperial court to the Corsican representation of grievances arrived, conveying orders to the Prince of Würtemberg to proceed as leniently as possible with the people, as the Emperor now saw that they had been wronged.

On the 11th of May 1732, a peace was concluded at Corte on the following terms—1. General amnesty. 2. That Genoa should relinquish all claims of compensation for the expenses of the war. 3. The remission of all unpaid taxes. 4. That the Corsicans should have free access to all offices, civil, military, and ecclesiastical. 5. Permission to found colleges, and unrestricted liberty to teach therein. 6. Reinstatement of the Council of Twelve, and of the Council of Six, with the privilege of an Oratore. 7. The right of defence for accused persons. 8. The appointment of a Board to take cognizance of the offences of public officials.

The fulfilment of this—for the Corsicans—advantageous treaty, was to be personally guaranteed by the Emperor; and accordingly, most of the German troops left the island, after more than three thousand of their number had found a grave in Corsica. Only Wachtendonk remained some time longer to see the terms of the agreement carried into effect.

CHAPTER IV
RECOMMENCEMENT OF HOSTILITIES—
DECLARATION OF INDEPENDENCE—
DEMOCRATIC CONSTITUTION OF COSTA

The imperial ratification was daily expected; but before it arrived, the Genoese Senate allowed the exasperation of defeat and the desire of revenge to hurry it into an action which could not fail to provoke the Corsican people to new revolt. Ceccaldi, Giafferi, the Abbé Aitelli, and Rafaelli, the leaders of the Corsicans who had signed the treaty in the name of their nation, were suddenly seized, and dragged off to Genoa, under the pretext of their entertaining treasonable designs against the state. A vehement cry of protest arose from the whole island: the people hastened to Wachtendonk, and urged upon him that his own honour was compromised in this violent act of the Genoese; they wrote to the Prince of Würtemberg, to the Emperor himself, demanding protection in terms of the treaty. The result was that the Emperor without delay ratified the conditions of peace, and demanded the liberation of the prisoners. All four were set at liberty, but the Senate endeavoured to extract a promise from them never again to return to their country. Ceccaldi went to Spain, where he entered into military service; Rafaelli to Rome; Aitelli and Giafferi to Leghorn, in the vicinity of their native island; where they could observe the course of affairs, which to all appearance could not remain long in their present posture.

On the 15th of June 1733, Wachtendonk and the last of the German troops left the island, which, with the duly ratified instrument of treaty in its possession, now found itself face to face with Genoa. The two deadly foes had hardly exchanged glances, when both were again in arms. Nothing but war to the knife was any longer possible between the Corsicans and the Genoese. In the course of centuries, mutual hate had become a second nature with both. The Genoese citizen came to the island rancorous, intriguing, cunning; the Corsican was suspicious, irritable, defiant, exultingly conscious of his individual manliness, and his nation's tried powers of self-defence.

Two or three arrests and attempts at assassination, and the people instantly rose, and gathered in Rostino, round Hyacinth Paoli, an active, resolute, and intrepid burgher of Morosaglia. This was a man of unusual talent, an orator, a poet, and a statesman; for among the rugged Corsicans, men had ripened in the school of misfortune and continual struggle, who were destined to astonish Europe. The people of Rostino named Hyacinth Paoli and Castineta their generals. They had now leaders, therefore, though they were to be considered as provisional.

No sooner had the movement broken out in Rostino, and the struggle with Genoa been once more commenced, than the brave Giafferi threw himself into a vessel, and landed in Corsica. The first general diet was held in Corte, which had been taken by storm. War was unanimously declared against Genoa, and it was resolved to place the island under the protection of the King of Spain, whose standard was now unfurled in Corte. The canon, Orticoni, was sent to the court of Madrid to give expression to this wish on the part of the Corsican people.

Don Luis Giafferi was again appointed general, and this talented commander succeeded, in the course of the year 1734, in depriving the Genoese of all their possessions in the island, except the fortified ports. In the year 1735, he called a general assembly of the people in Corte. On this occasion he demanded Hyacinth Paoli as his colleague, and this having been agreed to, the advocate, Sebastiano Costa, was appointed to draw up the scheme of a constitution. This remarkable assembly affirmed the independence of the Corsican people, and the perpetual separation of Corsica from Genoa; and announced as leading features in the new arrangements— the self-government of the people in its parliament; a junta of six, named by parliament, and renewed every three months, to accompany the generals as the parliament's representatives; a civil board of four, intrusted with the oversight of the courts of justice, of the finances, and of commercial interests. The people in its assemblies was declared the alone source of law. A statute-book was to be composed by the highest junta.

Such were the prominent features of a constitution sketched by the Corsican Costa, and approved of in the year 1735, when universal political barbarism still prevailed upon the Continent, by a people in regard to which the obscure rumour went that it was horribly wild and uncivilized. It appears, therefore, that nations are not always educated for freedom and independence by science, wealth, or brilliant circumstances of political prominence; oftener perhaps by poverty, misfortune, and love for their country. A little people, without literature, without trade, had thus in obscurity, and without assistance, outstripped the most cultivated nations of Europe in political wisdom and in humanity; its constitution had not sprung from the hot-bed of philosophical systems—it had ripened upon the soil of its material necessities.

Giafferi, Ceccaldi, and Hyacinth Paoli had all three been placed at the head of affairs. Orticoni had returned from his mission to Spain, with the answer that his catholic Majesty declined taking Corsica under his special protection, but declared that he would not support Genoa with troops. The Corsicans, therefore, as they could reckon on no protection from any earthly potentate, now did as some of the Italian republics had done during the Middle Ages, placed themselves by general consent under the guardian care of the Virgin Mary, whose picture henceforth figured on the standards of the country; and they chose Jesus Christ for their *gonfaloniere*, or standard-bearer.

Genoa—which the German Emperor, involved in the affairs of Poland, could not now assist—was meanwhile exerting itself to the utmost to reduce the Corsicans to subjection. The republic first sent Felix Pinelli, the former cruel governor, and then her bravest general, Paul Battista Rivarola, with all the troops that could be raised. The situation of the Corsicans was certainly desperate. They were destitute of all the necessaries for carrying on the war; the country was completely exhausted, and the Genoese cruisers prevented importation from abroad. Their distress was such that they even made proposals for peace, to which, however, Genoa refused to listen. The whole island was under blockade; all commercial intercourse was at an end; vessels from Leghorn had been captured; there was a deficiency of arms, particularly of fire-arms, and they had no powder. Their embarrassments had become almost insupportable, when, one day, two strange vessels came to anchor in the gulf of Isola Rossa, and began to discharge a heavy cargo of victuals and warlike stores—gifts for the Corsicans from unknown and mysterious donors. The captains of the vessels scorned all remuneration, and only asked the favour of some Corsican wine in which to drink the brave nation's welfare. They then put out to sea again amidst the blessings of the multitude who had assembled on the shore to see their foreign benefactors. This little token of foreign sympathy fairly intoxicated the poor Corsicans. Their joy was indescribable; they rang the bells in all the villages; they said to one another that Divine Providence, and the Blessed Virgin, had sent their rescuing angels to the unhappy island, and their hopes grew lively that some foreign power would at length bestow its protection on the Corsicans. The moral impression produced by this event was so powerful, that the Genoese feared what the Corsicans hoped, and immediately commenced treating for peace. But it was now the turn of the Corsicans to be obstinate.

Generous Englishmen had equipped these two ships, friends of liberty, and admirers of Corsican heroism. Their magnanimity was soon to come into conflict with their patriotism, through the revolt of North America. The English supply of arms and ammunition enabled the Corsicans to storm Aleria, where they made a prize of four pieces of cannon. They now laid siege to Calvi and Bastia. But their situation was becoming every moment more helpless and desperate. All their resources were again spent, and still no foreign power interfered. In those days the Corsicans waited in an almost religious suspense; they were like the Jews under the Maccabees, when they hoped for a Messiah.

CHAPTER V
BARON THEODORE VON NEUHOFF

Early in the morning of the 12th of March 1736, a vessel under British colours was seen steering towards Aleria. The people who crowded to the shore greeted it with shouts of joy; they supposed it was laden with arms and ammunition. The vessel cast anchor; and soon afterwards, some of the principal men of the island went on board, to wait on a certain mysterious stranger whom she had brought. This stranger was of kingly appearance, of stately and commanding demeanour, and theatrically dressed. He wore a long caftan of scarlet silk, Moorish trowsers, yellow shoes, and a Spanish hat and feather; in his girdle of yellow silk were a pair of richly inlaid pistols, a sabre hung by his side, and in his right hand he held a long truncheon as sceptre. Sixteen gentlemen of his retinue followed him with respectful deference as he landed—eleven Italians, two French officers, and three Moors. The enigmatical stranger stepped upon the Corsican shore with all the air of a king,—and with the purpose to be one.

The Corsicans surrounded the mysterious personage with no small astonishment. The persuasion was general that he was—if not a foreign prince—at least the ambassador of some monarch now about to take Corsica under his protection. The ship soon began to discharge her cargo before the eyes of the crowd; it consisted of ten pieces of cannon, four thousand muskets, three thousand pairs of shoes, seven hundred sacks of grain, a large quantity of ammunition, some casks of zechins, and a considerable sum in gold coins of Barbary. It appeared that the leading men of the island had expected the arrival of this stranger. Xaverius Matra was seen to greet him with all the reverence due to a king; and all were impressed by the dignity of his princely bearing, and the lofty composure of his manner. He was conducted in triumph to Cervione.

This singular person was a German, the Westphalian Baron Theodore von Neuhoff—the cleverest and most fortunate of all the adventurers of his time. In his youth he had been a page at the court of the Duchess of Orleans, had afterwards gone into the Spanish service, and then returned to France. His brilliant talents had brought him into contact with all the remarkable personages of the age; among others, with Alberoni, with Ripperda, and Law, in whose financial speculations he had been involved. Neuhoff had experienced everything, seen everything, thought, attempted, enjoyed, and suffered everything. True to the dictates of a romantic and adventurous nature, he had run through all possible shapes in which fortune can appear, and had at length taken it into his head, that for a man of a powerful mind like him, it must be a desirable thing to be a king. And he had not conceived this idea in the vein of the crackbrained Knight of La Mancha, who, riding errant into the world, persuaded himself that he would at least be made emperor of Trebisonde in reward for his achievements; on the contrary, accident threw the thought into his quite unclouded intellect, and he resolved to be a king, to become so in a real and natural way,—and he became a king.

In the course of his rovings through Europe, Neuhoff had come to Genoa just at the time when Giafferi, Ceccaldi, Aitelli, and Rafaelli were brought to the city as prisoners. It seems that his attention was now for the first time drawn to the Corsicans, whose obstinate bravery made a deep impression on him. He formed a connexion with such Corsicans as he could find in Genoa, particularly with men belonging to the province of Balagna; and after gaining an insight into the state of affairs in the island, the idea of playing a part in the history of this romantic country gradually ripened in his mind. He immediately went to Leghorn, where Orticoni, into whose hands the foreign relations of the island had been committed, was at the time residing. He introduced himself to Orticoni, and succeeded in inspiring him with admiration, and with confidence in his magnificent promises. For, intimately connected, as he said he was, with all the courts, he affirmed that, within the space of a year, he would procure the Corsicans all the necessary means for driving the Genoese for ever from the island. In return, he demanded nothing more than that the Corsicans should crown him as their king. Orticoni, carried away by the extraordinary genius of the man, by his boundless promises, by the cleverness of his diplomatic, economic, and political ideas, and perceiving that Neuhoff really might be able to do his country good service, asked the opinion of the generals of the island. In their desperate situation, they gave him full power to treat with Neuhoff. Orticoni, accordingly, came to an agreement with the baron, that he should be proclaimed king of Corsica as soon as he put the islanders in a position to free themselves completely from the yoke of Genoa.

As soon as Theodore von Neuhoff saw this prospect before him, he began to exert himself for its realisation with an energy which is sufficient of itself to convince us of his powerful genius. He put himself in communication with the English consul at Leghorn, and with such merchants as traded to Barbary; he procured letters of recommendation for that country; went to Africa; and after he had moved heaven and earth there in person, as in Europe by his agents, finding himself in possession of all necessary equipments, he suddenly landed in Corsica in the manner we have described.

He made his appearance when the misery of the island had reached the last extreme. In handing over his stores to the Corsican leaders, he informed them that they were only a small portion of what was to follow. He represented to them that his connexions with the courts of Europe, already powerful, would be placed on a new footing the moment that the Genoese had been overcome; and that, wearing the crown, he should treat as a prince with princes. He therefore desired the crown. Hyacinth Paoli, Giafferi, and the learned Costa, men of the soundest common sense, engaged upon an enterprise the most pressingly real in its necessities that could possibly be committed to human hands—that of liberating their country, and giving its liberty a form, and secure basis, nevertheless acceded to this desire. Their engagements to the man, and his services; the novelty of the event, which had so remarkably inspirited the people; the prospects of further help; in a word, their necessitous circumstances, demanded it. Theodore von Neuhoff, king-designate of the Corsicans, had the house of the Bishop of Cervione appointed him for his residence; and on the 15th of April, the people assembled to a general diet in the convent of Alesani, in order to pass the enactment converting Corsica into a kingdom. The assembly was composed of two representatives from every commune in the country, and of deputies from the convents and clergy, and more than two thousand people surrounded the building. The following constitution was laid before the Parliament: The crown of the kingdom of Corsica is given to Baron Theodore von Neuhoff and his heirs; the king is assisted by a council of twenty-four, nominated by the people, without whose and the Parliament's consent no measures can be adopted or taxes imposed. All public offices are open to the Corsicans only; legislative acts can proceed only from the people and its Parliament.

These articles were read by Gaffori, a doctor of laws, to the assembled people, who gave their consent by acclamation; Baron Theodore then signed them in presence of the representatives of the nation, and swore, on the holy gospels, before all the people, to remain true to the constitution. This done, he was conducted into the church, where, after high mass had been said, the generals placed the crown upon his head. The Corsicans were too poor to have a crown of gold; they plaited one of laurel and oak-leaves, and crowned therewith their first and last king. And thus Baron Theodore von Neuhoff, who already styled himself Grandee of Spain, Lord of Great Britain, Peer of France, Count of the Papal Dominions, and Prince of the Empire, became King of the Corsicans, with the title of Theodore the First.

Though this singular affair may be explained from the then circumstances of the island, and from earlier phenomena in Corsican history, it still remains astonishing. So intense was the patriotism of this people, that to obtain their liberty and rescue their country, they made a foreign adventurer their king, because he held out to them hopes of deliverance; and that their brave and tried leaders, without hesitation and without jealousy, quietly divested themselves of their authority.

CHAPTER VI
THEODORE I., KING OF CORSICA

Now in possession of the kingly title, Theodore wished to see himself surrounded by a kingly court, and was, therefore, not sparing in his distribution of dignities. He named Don Luis Giafferi and Hyacinth Paoli his prime ministers, and invested them with the title of Count. Xaverius Matra became a marquis, and grand-marshal of the palace; Giacomo Castagnetta, count and commandant of Rostino; Arrighi, count and inspector-general of the troops. He gave others the titles of barons, margraves, lieutenants-general, captains of the Royal Guard, and made them commandants of various districts of the country. The advocate Costa, now Count Costa, was created grand-chancellor of the kingdom, and Dr. Gaffori, now Marquis Gaffori, cabinet-secretary to his Majesty the constitutional king.

Ridiculous as all these pompous arrangements may appear, King Theodore set himself in earnest to accomplish his task. In a short time he had established order in the country, settled family feuds, and organized a regular army, with which, in April 1736, he took Porto Vecchio and Sartene from the Genoese. The Senate of Genoa had at first viewed the enigmatic proceedings that were going on before its eyes with astonishment and fear, imagining that the intentions of some foreign power might be concealed behind them. But when obscurities cleared away, and Baron Theodore stood disclosed, they began to lampoon him in pamphlets, and brand him as an unprincipled adventurer deep in debt. King Theodore replied to the Genoese manifestoes with kingly dignity, German bluntness, and German humour. He then marched in person against Bastia, fought like a lion before its walls, and when he found he could not take the city, blockaded it, making, meanwhile, expeditions into the interior of the island, in the course of which he punished rebellious districts with unscrupulous severity, and several times routed the Genoese troops.

The Genoese were soon confined to their fortified towns on the sea. In their embarrassment at this period they had recourse to a disgraceful method of increasing their strength. They formed a regiment, fifteen hundred strong, of their galley-slaves, bandits, and murderers, and let loose this refuse upon Corsica. The villanous band made frequent forays into the country, and perpetrated numberless enormities. They got the name of Vittoli, from Sampiero's murderer, or of Oriundi.

King Theodore made great exertions for the general elevation of the country. He established manufactories of arms, of salt, of cloth; he endeavoured to introduce animation into trade, to induce foreigners to settle in the island, by offering them commercial privileges, and, by encouraging privateering, to keep the Genoese cruisers in check. The Corsican national flag was green and yellow, and bore the motto: *In te Domine speravi.* Theodore had also struck his own coins—gold, silver, and copper. These coins showed on the obverse a shield wreathed with laurel, and above it a crown with the initials, T. R.; on the reverse were the words: *Pro bono et libertate.* On the Continent, King Theodore's money was bought up by the curious for thirty times its value. But all this was of little avail; the promised help did not come, the people began to murmur. The king was continually announcing the immediate appearance of a friendly fleet; the friendly fleet never appeared, because its promise was a fabrication. The murmurs growing louder, Theodore assembled a Parliament on the 2d of September, in Casacconi; here he declared that he would lay down his crown, if the expected help did not appear by the end of October, or that he would then go himself to the Continent to hasten its appearance. He was in the same desperate position in which, as the story goes, Columbus was, when the land he had announced would not appear.

On the dissolution of the Parliament, which, at the proposal of the king, had agreed to a new measure of finance—a tax upon property, Theodore mounted his horse, and went to view his kingdom on the other side the mountains. This region had been the principal seat of the Corsican seigniors, and the old aristocratic feeling was still strong there. Luca Ornano received the monarch with a deputation of the principal gentlemen, and conducted him in festal procession to Sartene. Here Theodore fell upon the princely idea of founding a new order of knighthood; it was a politic idea, and, in fact, we observe, in general, that the German baron and Corsican king knows how to conduct himself in a politic manner, as well as other upstarts of greater dimensions who have preceded and followed him. The name of the new order was The Order of the Liberation (*della Liberazione*). The king was grand-master, and named the cavaliers. It is said that in less than two months the Order numbered more than four hundred members, and that upwards of a fourth of these were foreigners, who sought the honour of membership, either for the mere singularity of the thing, or to indicate their good wishes for the brave Corsicans. The membership was dear, for it had been enacted that every cavalier should pay a thousand scudi as entry-money, from which he was to draw an annuity of ten per cent. for life. The

Order, then, in its best sense, was an honour awarded in payment for a loan—a financial speculation. During his residence in Sartene, the king, at the request of the nobles of the region, conferred with lavish hand the titles of Count, Baron, and Baronet, and with these the representatives of the houses of Ornano, Istria, Rocca, and Leca, went home comforted.

While the king thus acted in kingly fashion, and filled the island with counts and cavaliers, as if poor Corsica had overnight become a wealthy empire, the bitterest cares of state were preying upon him in secret. For he could not but confess to himself that his kingdom was after all but a painted one, and that he had surrounded himself with phantoms. The long-announced fleet obstinately refused to appear, because it too was a painted fleet. This chimera occasioned the king greater embarrassment than if it had been a veritable fleet of a hundred well-equipped hostile ships. Theodore began to feel uncomfortable. Already there was an organized party of malcontents in the land, calling themselves the Indifferents. Aitelli and Rafaelli had formed this party, and Hyacinth Paoli himself had joined it. The royal troops had even come into collision with the Indifferents, and had been repulsed. It seemed, therefore, as if Theodore's kingdom were about to burst like a soap-bubble; Giafferi alone still kept down the storm for a while.

In these circumstances, the king thought it might be advisable to go out of the way for a little; to leave the island, not secretly, but as a prince, hastening to the Continent to fetch in person the tardy succours. He called a parliament at Sartene, announced that he was about to take his departure, and the reason why; settled the interim government, at the head of which he put Giafferi, Hyacinth Paoli, and Luca Ornano; made twenty-seven Counts and Baronets governors of provinces; issued a manifesto; and on the 11th of November 1736, proceeded, accompanied by an immense retinue, to Aleria, where he embarked in a vessel showing French colours, taking with him Count Costa, his chancellor, and some officers of his household. He would have been captured by a Genoese cruiser before he was out of sight of his kingdom, and sent to Genoa, if he had not been protected by the French flag. King Theodore landed at Leghorn in the dress of an abbé, wishing to remain incognito; he then travelled to Florence, to Rome, and to Naples, where he left his chancellor and his officers, and went on board a vessel bound for Amsterdam, from which city, he said, his subjects should speedily hear good news.

CHAPTER VII
GENOA IN DIFFICULTIES—AIDED BY FRANCE—
THEODORE EXPELLED HIS KINGDOM

The Corsicans did not believe in the return of their king, nor in the help he promised to send them. Under the pressure of severe necessity, the poor people, intoxicated with their passion for liberty, had gone so far as even to expose themselves to the ridicule which could not fail to attach to the kingship of an adventurer. In their despair they had caught at a phantom, at a straw, for rescue; what would they not have done out of hatred to Genoa, and love of freedom? Now, however, they saw themselves no nearer the goal they wished to reach. Many showed symptoms of discontent. In this state of affairs, the Regents attempted to open negotiations with Rivarola, but without result, as the Genoese demanded unconditional submission, and surrender of arms. An assembly of the people was called, and its voice taken. The people resolved unhesitatingly that they must remain true to the king to whom they had sworn allegiance, and acknowledge no other sovereign.

Theodore had meanwhile travelled through part of Europe, formed new connexions, opened speculations, raised money, named cavaliers, enlisted Poles and Germans; and although his creditors at Amsterdam threw him into a debtors' prison, the fertile genius of the wonderful man succeeded in raising supplies to send to Corsica. From time to time a ship reached the island with warlike stores, and a proclamation encouraging the Corsicans to remain steadfast.

This, and the fear that the unwearying and energetic Theodore might at length actually win some continental power to his side, made the Republic of Genoa anxious. The Senate had set a price of two thousand genuini on the head of the Corsican king, and the agents of Genoa dogged his footsteps at every court. Herself in pecuniary difficulties, Genoa had drawn upon the Bank for three millions, and taken three regiments of Swiss into her pay. The guerilla warfare continued. It was carried on with the utmost ferocity; no quarter was given now on either side. The Republic, seeing no end of the exhausting struggle, resolved to call in the assistance of France. She had hitherto hesitated to have recourse to a foreign power, as her treasury was exhausted, and former experiences had not been of the most encouraging kind.

The French cabinet willingly seized an opportunity, which, if properly used, would at least prevent any other power from obtaining a footing on an island whose position near the French boundaries gave it so high an importance. Cardinal Fleury concluded a treaty with the Genoese on the 12th of July 1737, in virtue of which France pledged herself to send an army into Corsica to reduce the "rebels" to subjection. Manifestoes proclaimed this to the Corsican people. They produced the greatest sorrow and consternation, all the more so, that a power now declared her intention of acting against the Corsicans, which, in earlier times, had stood in a very different relation to them. The Corsican people replied to these manifestoes, by the declaration that they would never again return under the yoke of Genoa, and by a despairing appeal to the compassion of the French king.

In February of the year 1738, five French regiments landed under the command of Count Boissieux. The General had strict orders to effect, if possible, a peaceable settlement; and the Genoese hoped that the mere sight of the French would be sufficient to disarm the Corsicans. But the Corsicans remained firm. The whole country had risen as one man at the approach of the French; beacons on the hills, the conchs in the villages, the bells in the convents, called the population to arms. All of an age to carry arms took the field furnished with bread for eight days. Every village formed its little troop, every pieve its battalion, every province its camp. The Corsicans stood ready and waiting. Boissieux now opened negotiations, and these lasted for six months, till the announcement came from Versailles that the Corsicans must submit unconditionally to the supremacy of Genoa. The people replied in a manifesto addressed to Louis XV., that they once more implored him to cast a look of pity upon them, and to bear in mind the friendly interest which his illustrious ancestors had taken in Corsica; and they declared that they would shed their last drop of blood before they would return under the murderous supremacy of Genoa. In their bitter need, they meanwhile gave certain hostages required, and expressed themselves willing to trust the French king, and to await his final decision.

In this juncture, Baron Droste, nephew of Theodore, landed one day at Aleria, bringing a supply of ammunition, and the intelligence that the king would speedily return to the island. And on the 15th of September this remarkable man actually did land at Aleria, more splendidly and regally equipped than when he came the first time. He brought three ships with him; one of sixty-four guns, another of sixty, and the third of fifty-five, besides gunboats, and a small flotilla of transports. They were laden with munitions of war to a very considerable amount—27 pieces of cannon, 7000 muskets with bayonets, 1000 muskets of a larger size, 2000 pistols, 24,000 pounds of coarse and 100,000 pounds of fine powder, 200,000 pounds of lead, 400,000 flints, 50,000 pounds of iron, 2000 lances, 2000 grenades and bombs. All this had been raised by the same man whom his creditors in Amsterdam threw into a debtors' prison. He had succeeded by his powers of persuasion in interesting the Dutch for Corsica, and convincing them that a connexion with this island in the Mediterranean was desirable. A company of capitalists—the wealthy houses of Boom, Tronchain, and Neuville—had agreed to lend the Corsican king vessels, money, and the materials of war. Theodore thus landed in his kingdom under the Dutch flag. But he found to his dismay that affairs had taken a turn which prostrated all his hopes; and that he had to experience a fate tinged with something like irony, since, when he came as an adventurer he obtained a crown, but now could not be received as king though he came as a king, with substantial means for maintaining his dignity. He found the island split into conflicting parties, and in active negotiation with France. The people, it is true, led him once more in triumph to Cervione, where he had been crowned; but the generals, his own counts, gave him to understand that circumstances compelled them to have nothing more to do with him, but to treat with France. Immediately on Theodore's arrival, Boissieux had issued a proclamation, which declared every man a rebel, and guilty of high treason, who should give countenance to the outlaw, Baron Theodore von Neuhoff; and the king thus saw himself forsaken by the very men whom he had, not long before, created counts, margraves, barons, and cavaliers. The Dutchmen, too, disappointed in their expectations, and threatened by French and Genoese ships, very soon made up their minds, and in high dudgeon steered away for Naples. Theodore von Neuhoff, therefore, also saw himself compelled to leave the island; and vexed to the heart, he set sail for the Continent.

CHAPTER VIII
THE FRENCH REDUCE CORSICA—NEW INSURRECTION—THE PATRIOT GAFFORI

In the end of October, the expected decisive document arrived from Versailles in the form of an edict issued by the Doge and Senate of Genoa, and signed by the Emperor and the French king. The edict contained a few concessions, and the express command to lay down arms and submit to Genoa. Boissieux gave the Corsicans fifteen days to comply with this. They immediately assembled in the convent of Orezza to deliberate, and to rouse the nation; and they declared in a manifesto—"We shall not lose courage; arming ourselves with the manly resolve to die, we shall prefer ending our lives nobly with our weapons in our hands, to remaining idle spectators of the sufferings of our country, living in chains, and bequeathing slavery to our posterity. We think and say with the Maccabees: *Melius est mori in bello, quam videre mala gentis nostræ*—Better to die in war, than see the miseries of our nation."

Hostilities instantly commenced. The haughty and impetuous Boissieux had even sent four hundred men to Borgo to disarm the population in that quarter, before the expiry of the time he had himself allowed. The people were still holding their diet at Orezza. When the news came that the French had entered Borgo, the old cry arose, *Evviva la libertà! Evviva il popolo!* They rushed upon Borgo, attacked the French, and shut them up in the town. The officer in command of the corps sent messengers to Boissieux, who immediately marched to the rescue with two thousand men. The Corsicans, however, repulsed Boissieux, and drove his battalions in confusion to the walls of Bastia. The French general now sent despatches to France, asking reinforcements, and begging to be relieved from his command on account of sickness. Boissieux, a nephew of the celebrated Villars, died in Bastia on the 2d of February 1739. His successor was the Marquis of Maillebois, who landed in Corsica in spring with a large force.

Maillebois, severe and just, swift and sure in action, was precisely the man fitted to accomplish the task assigned to him. He allowed the Corsicans a certain time to lay down their arms, and on its expiry, advanced his troops at once in several different directions. Hyacinth Paoli, attacked in the Balagna, was obliged to retire, and, more a politician than a soldier, despairing of any successful resistance, he surrendered. The result was that Giafferi did the same. Maillebois now invited the leaders of the Corsicans to an interview with him in Morosaglia, and represented to them that the peace of the country required their leaving it. They yielded; and in the summer of the year 1739, twenty-two of the leading patriots left Corsica. Among these were Hyacinth Paoli, with his son Pasquale, then fourteen years old, Giafferi, with his son, Castineta and Pasqualini.

The country this side the mountains was therefore to be considered as reduced; but on the other side, two brave kinsmen of King Theodore still maintained themselves—his nephews, the Baron von Droste, and Baron Frederick von Neuhoff. After a courageous resistance—Frederick having wandered about for some time in the woods and mountains as guerilla—they laid down their arms on honourable terms, and received passes to quit the island.

It was Maillebois who now, properly speaking, ruled the island. He kept the Genoese governor in check, and, by his vigorous, just, and wise management, restored and preserved order. He formed all those Corsicans who were deeply compromised—and, fearing the vengeance of Genoa, wished to serve under the French standard—into a regiment, which received the name of the Royal-Corse. Events on the Continent rendering his recall necessary, he left Corsica in 1741, and was followed soon after by the whole of the French troops.

The island was scarcely clear of the French, when the hatred of Genoa again blazed forth. It had become a national characteristic, and was destined to pervade the entire history of Corsica's connexion with Genoa. The Governor, Domenico Spinola, made an attempt to collect the impost of the *due seini*. That instant, insurrection, fighting, and overthrow of the Genoese. Guerilla warfare covered the whole island.

Suddenly, in January 1743, the forgotten King Theodore once more appeared. He landed one day in Isola Rossa with three English men-of-war, and well furnished, as before, with warlike stores. Though ignominiously driven from his kingdom, Theodore had not given up the wish and plan of again being king; he had gone to England, and his zeal and energy there again effected what they had accomplished in Amsterdam. He now anchored off the Corsican coast, distributed his arms and ammunition, and issued proclamations, in which he assumed the tone of an injured and angry monarch, threatened traitors, and summoned his faithful subjects to rally round his person. The people received these in silence; and all that he learned convinced the unhappy ex-king that his realm was lost for ever. With a heavy heart, he weighed anchor and sailed away, never more to return to his island kingdom. He went back to England.

Both Corsicans and Genoese had meanwhile become inclined for a new treaty. An agreement was come to on favourable conditions, which allowed the country those rights already so often demanded and so often infringed on. During two years things remained quiet, and there seemed some faint prospect of a permanent peace, though the island was torn by family feuds and the Vendetta. In order to remove these evils, the people named three men—Gaffori, Venturini, and Alexius Matra—protectors of the country, and these triumvirs now appear as the national leaders. Others, however—exiled, enterprising men—saw the smouldering glow beneath its thin covering, and resolved to make a new assault upon the Genoese supremacy.

Count Domenico Rivarola was at this time in the service of the King of Sardinia; he was a Genoese of Bastia by birth, but at deadly enmity with the Republic. He collected a number of Corsicans about himself, represented to King Charles Emanuel the probable success of an enterprise in behalf of Corsica, obtained some ships, and with English aid made himself master of Bastia. The Corsicans declared for him, and the war became general. Giampetro Gaffori, a man of unusual heroism, marched upon Corte and attacked the citadel, which occupies a strong position on a steep crag. The Genoese commandant saw that it must necessarily fall, if the heavy fire of the Corsicans continued long enough to make another breach. He therefore had Gaffori's young son, who had been made prisoner, bound to the wall of the citadel, in order to stop the firing. The Corsicans were horror-struck to see Gaffori's son hanging on the wall, and their cannon instantly became silent: not another shot was fired. Giampetro Gaffori shuddered; then breaking the deep silence, he shouted, "Fire!" and with redoubled fury the artillery again began to ply upon the wall. A breach was made and stormed, but the boy remained uninjured, and the heroic father enjoyed the reward of clasping his son living to his breast.

On the fall of Corte, the whole interior of the island rose; and on the 10th of August 1746, a general assembly once more affirmed the independence of Corsica. Gaffori, Venturini, and Matra were declared Generals and Protectors of the nation; and an invitation was issued, calling on all Corsicans beyond the seas to return home. The hopes of material aid from Sardinia were, however, soon disappointed; its assistance was found insufficient, Bastia fell again into the hands of the Genoese, and Rivarola had been obliged to flee to Turin. The Genoese Senate again betook itself to France, and begged the minister to send a corps of auxiliaries against the Corsicans.

In 1748, two thousand French troops came to Corsica under the command of General Cursay. Their appearance again threw the unhappy people into the utmost consternation. As the peace of Aix-la-Chapelle had extinguished every hope of help from Sardinia, the Corsicans agreed to accept the mediation of the King of France. Cursay himself was a man of the noblest character—humane, benevolent, and just; he gained the attachment of the Corsicans as soon as they came to know him, and they willingly committed their affairs into his hands. Accordingly, through French mediation, a treaty was effected in July 1751, highly favourable to the Corsicans, allowing them more privileges than they had hitherto enjoyed, and above all, protecting their nationality. But this treaty made Cursay incur the hatred of the Genoese; the Republic and the French general became open enemies. Tumult and bloodshed resulted; and the favourite of the Corsican people would have lost his life in a disturbance at Ajaccio, if the brave Gaffori had not hastened to his rescue. The Genoese calumniated him at his court, asserted that he was the cause of continual disturbances, that he neglected his proper duties, and intrigued for his own ends—in short, that he had views upon the crown of Corsica. This had the desired effect; the noble Cursay was deprived of his command and thrown into the Tower of Antibes as prisoner of state, there to remain till his case had been tried, and sentence pronounced.

The fate of Cursay infuriated the Corsicans; the entire population on both sides of the mountains rose in arms. A diet was held in Orezza, and Giampetro Gaffori created sole General and Governor of the nation.

Gaffori now became the terror of Genoa. Sampiero himself seemed to have risen again to life in this indomitable and heroic spirit. He was no sooner at the head of the people, than he collected and skilfully organized their forces, threw himself like lightning on the enemy, routed them in every direction, and speedily was in possession of the entire island except the strong seaports. Grimaldi was at this time governor; wily and unscrupulous as Fornari had once shown himself, he could see no safety for Genoa except in the murder of her powerful foe. He formed a plot against his life. Gaffori was, in Corsican fashion, involved in a Vendetta; he had some deadly enemies, men of Corte, by name Romei. The governor gained these men; and, to make his deed the more abominable, he won Gaffori's own brother, Anton-Francesco, for the plot. The conspirators inveigled Gaffori into an ambuscade, and murdered him on the third of October 1753. Vengeance overtook only the unnatural brother: captured a few days after the nefarious act, he was broken on the wheel; but the Romei found refuge with the governor. It is said that Giampetro's wife—a woman whose heroism had already made her famous—after the death of her husband, led her son, a boy of twelve, to the altar, and made him swear to avenge the murder of his father. The Corsican people had lost in him their noblest patriot. Giampetro Gaffori, doctor of laws, and a man of learning, possessed of the already advanced cultivation of his century, generous, of high nobility of soul, ready to sacrifice everything for his country—was one of the bravest of the Corsican heroes, and worthy to be named in the history of his country along with Sampiero. But a nation that could, time after time, produce such men, was invincible. Gaffori had fallen; Pasquale Paoli stood ready to take his place.

After Giampetro's death, the people assembled as after the death of Sampiero, to do honour to the hero by public funeral obsequies. They then, with one voice, declared war to the knife against Genoa, and pronounced all those guilty of capital crime who should ever venture to propose a treaty with the hereditary foe. Five individuals were placed at the head of the government—Clemens Paoli, Hyacinth's eldest son, Thomas Santucci, Simon Pietro Frediani, and Doctor Grimaldi.

These five conducted the affairs of the island and the war against the Republic for two years, but it was felt necessary that the forces of the nation should be united in one strong hand; and a man destined to be not only an honour to his country, but an ornament to humanity, was called home for that purpose.

CHAPTER IX
PASQUALE PAOLI

Pasquale Paoli was the youngest son of Hyacinth. His father had taken him at the age of fourteen to Naples, when he went there to live in exile. The unusual abilities of the boy already promised a man likely to be of service to his country. His highly cultivated father had him educated with great care, and procured him the instructions of the most celebrated men of the city. Naples was at that time, and throughout the whole of the eighteenth century, in a remarkable degree, the focus of that great Italian school of humanistic philosophers, historians, and political economists, which could boast such names as those of Vico, Giannone, Filangieri, Galiani, and Genovesi. The last mentioned, the great Italian political economist, was Pasquale's master, and bore testimony to the genius of his pupil. From this school issued Pasquale Paoli, one of the greatest and most practical of those humanistic philosophers of the eighteenth century, who sought to realize their opinions in legislation and the ordering of society.

It was Clemens Paoli who, when the government of the Five was found not to answer the requirements of the country, directed the attention of the Corsicans to his brother Paoli. Pasquale was then an officer in the Neapolitan service; he had distinguished himself during the war in Calabria, and his noble character and cultivated intellect had secured him the esteem of all who knew him. His brother Clemens wrote to him, one day, that he must return to his native island, for it was the will of his countrymen that he should be their head. Pasquale, deeply moved, hesitated. "Go, my son," said old Hyacinth to him, "do your duty, and be the deliverer of your country."

On the 29th of April 1755, the young Pasquale landed at Aleria, on the same spot where, nineteen years before, Baron Theodore had first set foot on Corsican soil. Not many years had elapsed since then, but the aspect of things had greatly changed. It was now a native Corsican who came to rule his country—a young man who had no brilliant antecedents, nor splendid connexions, on the strength of which he could promise foreign aid; who was not a maker of projects, seeking to produce an impression by theatrical show, but who came with empty hands, without pretensions, modest almost to timidity, bringing nothing with him but his love for his country, his own force of character, and his humanistic philosophy, as the means by which he was to transform a primitive people, reduced to a state of savagery by family feuds, banditti-life, and the Vendetta, to an orderly and peaceable community. The problem was extraordinary, nay, in history unexampled; and the success with which, before the eyes of all Europe, Paoli wrought at its solution, at a time when similar attempts on the cultured nations of the Continent signally failed, affords a proof that the rude simplicity of nature is more susceptible of democratic freedom than the refined corruption of polished society.

Pasquale Paoli was now nine-and-twenty, of graceful and vigorous make, with an air of natural dignity; his calm, composed, unobtrusive manners, the mild and firm expression of his features, the musical tones of his voice, his simple but persuasive words, inspired instant confidence, and bespoke the man of the people, and the great citizen. When the nation, assembled in San Antonio della Casabianca, had declared Pasquale Paoli its sole General, he at first declined the honour, pleading his youth and inexperience; but the people would not even give him a colleague. On the 15th of July 1755, Pasquale Paoli placed himself at the helm of his country.

He found his country in this condition: the Genoese, confined to their fortified towns, making preparations for war; the greater part of the island free; the people grown savage, torn by faction and family feud; the laws obsolete; agriculture, trade, science, neglected or non-existent; the material everywhere raw and in confusion, but full of the germs of a healthy life, implanted by former centuries, and in the subsequent course of events not stifled, but strengthened and encouraged; finally, he had to deal with a people whose noblest qualities—love of country and love of freedom—had been stimulated to very madness.

Paoli's very first measures struck at the root of abuses. A law was enacted punishing the Vendetta with the pillory, and death at the hands of the public executioner. Not only fear, but the sense of honour, and the moral sentiment, were called into action. Priests—missionaries against the Vendetta—travelled over the country, and preached in the fields, inculcating the forgiveness of enemies. Paoli himself made a journey through the island to reconcile families at feud with each other. One of his relations had, in spite of the law, committed a murderous act of vengeance. Paoli did not hesitate a moment; he let the law take its course upon his relative, and he was executed. This firm and impartial administration of justice made a deep impression, and produced wholesome results.

In the midst of activity of this kind, Paoli was surprised by the intelligence that Emanuel Matra had collected his adherents, raised the standard of revolt, and was marching against him. Matra, who belonged to an ancient family of Caporali from beyond the mountains, had been driven to this course by ambition and envy. He had himself reckoned on obtaining the highest position in the state, and it was to wrest it from his rival that he was now in arms. He was a dangerous opponent. Paoli wished to save his country from a civil war, and proposed to Matra that the sword should remain sheathed, and that an assembly of the people should decide which of them was to be General of the nation. The haughty Matra of course rejected this proposal, boastfully intimating his reliance on his own abilities, military experience, and even on support from Genoa. He defeated the troops of Paoli in several engagements, but was afterwards repulsed with serious loss. In the spring of 1756, he again took the field with Genoese auxiliaries, and made a sudden and fierce attack on Paoli in Bozio. Pasquale, who had only a few men with him, hastily entrenched himself in the convent. A furious assault was made upon the cloister; the danger was imminent; already the doors were on fire, and the flames penetrating to the interior. Paoli gave himself up for lost. Suddenly conchs were heard from the hills, and a band of brave friends, led by his brother Clemens, and Thomas Carnoni, hitherto at deadly feud with Pasquale, and armed by his own mother for the rescue of his foe, rushed down upon the besiegers. The fight became desperate. It is said that Matra fought with unheard of ferocity after all his men had fallen or fled, and that he continued the struggle even when a ball had brought him upon his knee, until another shot stretched him on the earth. Paoli wept over the body of his enemy, to see a man of such heroic energy dead among traitors, and lost to his country's cause. The danger was now happily over, and the party of the Matras annihilated; a few of them had reached Bastia, and waited there in safety with the Genoese, till a favourable opportunity should occur for again emerging.

It was apparent, however, that Genoa was now exhausted. This once powerful Republic had grown old, and was on the eve of its fall. Alarmed at the progress of the Corsicans, she indeed made some attempts to check it by force of arms, but these no longer made such impression as in the days of the Dorias and Spinolas. The Republic several times took Swiss and Germans into her service; and on one occasion attacked Paoli's head-quarters at Furiani in the neighbourhood of Bastia, but without success. She had recourse again to France. The French cabinet, to prevent the English from throwing a garrison into some of the seaports, garrisoned the fortified towns in 1756. But the French remained otherwise neutral, doing no more than keeping possession of these cities, which they again evacuated in the year 1759.

Genoa lost heart. She saw Corsica rapidly becoming a compact and well-regulated state, and exhibiting the most marked signs of increased prosperity. The finances, and the administration generally, were managed with skill; agriculture was advancing, manufactories, even powder-mills, were in operation; the new city of Isola Rossa had risen under the very eyes of the foe; Paoli had actually fitted out a fleet, and the Corsican cruisers made the sea unsafe for Genoese vessels. The whole of Corsica, cleared of family broils, stood completely prepared for defence and offence; the last of the strong towns still in the possession of the Republic were more and more closely blockaded, and their fall seemed now at least not impossible. So rapidly had the Corsican people developed its resources under a wise government, that it now no longer stood in need of foreign aid. Genoa would willingly have made peace, but the Corsicans declared that they would only do this when the Genoese had entirely quitted the island.

Once more the Republic tried war. She again had recourse to the Matra family—to Antonio and Alexius Matra, the latter of whom had once been Regent along with Gaffori. These men, who were, one after the other, made Genoese marshals, and furnished with troops, excited revolts, which were crushed after a short struggle. The Genoese began to see that the Corsicans were no longer to be subdued unless by a serious attack on the part of France, and on the 7th of August 1764, they concluded a new treaty with the French king at Compiègne, according to which the latter pledged himself to hold the seaports for four years. Six battalions of French soldiery now landed in Corsica, under command of Count Marbœuf, who announced to the Corsicans that it was his purpose to observe strict neutrality between them and the Genoese, as he should give effect to the treaty if he merely garrisoned the seaports. It was, however, itself an act of hostility towards the Corsicans, to garrison these towns—a procedure which they were not in a position to hinder; and a neutrality which bound their hands, and forced them to raise sieges already far advanced towards success, did not deserve the name. They complained and protested, but they raised the siege of San Fiorenzo, which was near its fall.

Affairs continued in this undetermined state for four years; the Genoese inactive; the French maintaining an independent position in relation to their allies—occupying the fortified towns, and on terms of friendly intercourse with the Corsicans; these latter in full activity, strengthening their constitution, rejoicing in their independence, and indulging the fond hope that they would come into complete possession of their island after the lapse of the four years of the treaty, and thus at length attain the goal of their heroic national struggles.

All Europe was full of admiration for them, and praised the Corsican constitution as the model of a free and popular form of government. Certainly it was praiseworthy in its simplicity and thorough practical efficiency; the political wisdom of the century of the Humanists has raised for itself no nobler monument.

CHAPTER X
PAOLI'S LEGISLATION

Pasquale Paoli, in giving form to the Corsican Republic, proceeded on the simple principle that the people are the alone source of authority and law, and that the whole design of the latter is to effect and preserve the people's welfare. His idea as to the government was that it should form a kind of national jury, subdivided into as many branches as there were branches of the administration, and that the entire system ought to resemble an edifice of crystal, in which all could see what was going on, as it appeared to him that mystery and concealment favoured arbitrary exercise of power, and engendered distrust in the nation.

As the basis of his constitution, Paoli adopted the old popular arrangements of the Terra del Commune, with its Communes, Pieves, Podestàs, and Fathers of Communities.

All citizens above the age of twenty-five had a vote in the election of a member for the General Assembly (*consulta*). They met under the presidency of the Podestà of the place, and gave an oath that they would only elect such men as they held worthiest.

Every thousand of the population sent a representative to the Consulta. The sovereign power was vested in the Consulta in the name of the people. It was composed of the deputies of the Communes, and clergy; the magistrates of each province also sent their president as deputy. The Consulta imposed taxes, decided on peace or war, and enacted the laws. A majority of two-thirds was required to give a measure legal force.

The Consulta nominated from among its own numbers the Supreme Council (*consiglio supremo*)—a body of nine men, answering to the nine free provinces of Corsica—Nebbio, Casinca, Balagna, Campoloro, Orezza, Ornano, Rogna, Vico, and Cinarca. In the Supreme Council was vested the executive power; it summoned the Consulta, represented it in foreign affairs, regulated public works, and watched in general over the security of the country. In cases of unusual importance it was the last appeal, and was privileged to interpose a veto on the resolutions of the Consulta till the matter in question had been reconsidered. Its president was the General of the nation, who could do nothing without the approval of this council.

Both powers, however—the council as well as the president—were responsible to the people, or their representatives, and could be deposed and punished by a decree of the nation. The members of the Supreme Council held office for one year; they were required to be above thirty-five years of age, and to have previously been representatives of the magistracy of a province.

The Consulta also elected the five syndics, or censors. The duty of the Syndicate was to travel through the provinces, and hear appeals against the general or the judicial administration of any particular district; its sentence was final, and could not be reversed by the General. The General named persons to fill the public offices, and the collectors of taxes, all of whom were subject to the censorship of the Syndicate.

Justice was administered as follows:—Each Podestà could decide in cases not exceeding the value of ten livres. In conjunction with the Fathers of the Community, he could determine causes to the value of thirty livres. Cases involving more than thirty livres were tried before the tribunal of the province, where the court consisted of a president and two assessors named by the Consulta, and of a fiscal named by the Supreme Council. This tribunal was renewed every year.

An appeal lay from it to the Rota Civile, the highest court of justice, consisting of three doctors of laws, who held office for life. The same courts administered criminal justice, assisted always by a jury consisting of six fathers of families, who decided on the merits of the case from the evidence furnished by the witnesses, and pronounced a verdict of guilty or not guilty.

The members of the supreme council, of the Syndicate, and of the provincial tribunals, could only be re-elected after a lapse of two years. The Podestàs and Fathers of the Communities were elected annually by the citizens of their locality above twenty-five years of age.

In cases of emergency, when revolt and tumult had broken out in some part of the island, the General could send a temporary dictatorial court into the quarter, called the War Giunta (*giunta di osservazione o di guerra*), consisting of three or more members, with one of the supreme councillors at their head. Invested with unlimited authority to adopt whatever measures seemed necessary, and to punish instantaneously, this swiftly-acting "court of high commission" could not fail to strike terror into the discontented and evil-disposed; the people gave it the name of the *Giustizia Paolina*. Having fulfilled its mission, it rendered an account of its proceedings to the Censors.

Such is an outline of Paoli's legislation, and of the constitution of the Corsican Republic. When we consider its leading ideas—self-government of the people, liberty of the individual citizen protected and regulated on every side by law, participation in the political life of the country, publicity and simplicity in the administration, popular courts of justice—we cannot but confess that the Corsican state was constructed on principles of a wider and more generous humanity than any other in the same century. And if we look at the time when it took its rise, many years before the world had seen the French democratic legislation, or the establishment of the North American republic under the great Washington, Pasquale Paoli and his people gain additional claims to our admiration.

Paoli disapproved of standing armies. He himself said:—"In a country which desires to be free, each citizen must be a soldier, and constantly in readiness to arm himself for the defence of his rights. Paid troops do more for despotism than for freedom. Rome ceased to be free on the day when she began to maintain a standing army; and the unconquerable phalanxes of Sparta were drawn immediately from the ranks of her citizens. Moreover, as soon as a standing army has been formed, *esprit de corps* is originated, the bravery of this regiment and that company is talked of—a more serious evil than is generally supposed, and one which it is well to avoid as far as possible. We ought to speak of the intrepidity of the particular citizen, of the resolute bravery displayed by this commune, of the self-sacrificing spirit which characterizes the members of that family; and thus awaken emulation in a free people. When our social condition shall have become what it ought to be, our whole people will be disciplined, and our militia invincible."

Necessity compelled Paoli to yield so far in this matter, as to organize a small body of regular troops to garrison the forts. These consisted of two regiments of four hundred men each, commanded by Jacopo Baldassari and Titus Buttafuoco. Each company had two captains and two lieutenants; French, Prussian, and Swiss officers gave them drill. Every regular soldier was armed with musket and bayonet, a pair of pistols, and a dagger. The uniform was made from the black woollen cloth of the country; the only marks of distinction for the officers were, that they wore a little lace on the coat-collar, and had no bayonet in their muskets. All wore caps of the skin of the Corsican wild-boar, and long gaiters of calf-skin reaching to the knee. Both regiments were said to be highly efficient.

The militia was thus organized: All Corsicans from sixteen to sixty were soldiers. Each commune had to furnish one or more companies, according to its population, and chose its own officers. Each pieve, again, formed a camp, under a commandant named by the General. The entire militia was divided into three levies, each of which entered for fifteen days at a time. It was a generally-observed rule to rank families together, so that the soldiers of a company were mostly blood-relations. The troops in garrison received yearly pay, the others were paid only so long as they kept the field. The villages furnished bread.

The state expenses were met from the tax of two livres on each family, the revenues from salt, the coral-fishery, and other indirect imposts.

Nothing that can initiate or increase the prosperity of a people was neglected by Paoli. He bestowed special attention on agriculture; the Consulta elected two commissaries yearly for each province, whose business it was to superintend and foster agriculture in their respective districts. The cultivation of the olive, the chestnut, and of maize, was encouraged; plans for draining marshes and making roads were proposed. With one hand, at that period, the Corsican warded off his foe, as soldier; with the other, as husbandman, he scattered his seed upon the soil.

Paoli also endeavoured to give his people mental cultivation—the highest pledge and the noblest consummation of all freedom and all prosperity. The iron times had hitherto prevented its spread. The Corsicans had remained children of nature; they were ignorant, but rich in mother-wit. Genoa, it is said, had intentionally neglected the schools; but now, under Paoli's government, their numbers everywhere increased, and the Corsican clergy, brave and liberal men, zealously instructed the youth. A national printing-house was established in Corte, from which only books devoted to the instruction and enlightenment of the people issued. The children found it written in these books, that love of his native country was a true man's highest virtue; and that all those who had fallen in battle for liberty had died as martyrs, and had received a place in heaven among the saints.

On the 3d of January 1765, Paoli opened the Corsican university. In this institution, theology, philosophy, mathematics, jurisprudence, philology, and the belles-lettres were taught. Medicine and surgery were in the meantime omitted, till Government was in a position to supply the necessary instruments. All the professors were Corsicans; the leading names were Guelfucci of Belgodere, Stefani of Benaco, Mariani of Corbara, Grimaldi of Campoloro, Ferdinandi of Brando, Vincenti of Santa Lucia. Poor scholars were supported at the public expense. At the end of each session, an examination took place before the members of the Consulta and the Government. Thus the presence of the most esteemed citizens of the island heightened both praise and blame. The young men felt that they were regarded by them, and by the people in general, as the hope of their country's future, and that they would soon be called upon to join or succeed them in their patriotic endeavours. Growing up in the midst of the weighty events of their own nation's stormy history, they had the one high ideal constantly and vividly before their eyes. The spirit which accordingly animated these youths may readily be imagined, and will be seen from the following fragment of one of the orations which it was customary for some student of the Rhetoric class to deliver in presence of the representatives and Government of the nation.

"All nations that have struggled for freedom have endured great vicissitudes of fortune. Some of them were less powerful and less brave than our own; nevertheless, by their resolute steadfastness they at last overcame their difficulties. If liberty could be won by mere talking, then were the whole world free; but the pursuit of freedom demands an unyielding constancy that rises superior to all obstacles—a virtue so rare among men that those who have given proof of it have always been regarded as demigods. Certainly the privileges of a free people are too valuable—their condition too fortunate, to be treated of in adequate terms; but enough is said if we remember that they excite the admiration of the greatest men. As regards ourselves, may it please Heaven to allow us to follow the career on which we have entered! But our nation, whose heart is greater than its fortunes, though it is poor and goes coarsely clad, is a reproach to all Europe, which has grown sluggish under the burden of its heavy chains; and it is now felt to be necessary to rob us of our existence.

"Brave countrymen! the momentous crisis has come. Already the storm rages over our heads; dangers threaten on every side; let us see to it that we maintain ourselves superior to circumstances, and grow in strength with the number of our foes; our name, our freedom, our honour, are at stake! In vain shall we have exhibited heroic endurance up till the present time—in vain shall our forefathers have shed streams of blood and suffered unheard-of miseries; if *we* prove weak, then all is irremediably lost. If we prove weak! Mighty shades of our fathers! ye who have done so much to bequeath to us liberty as the richest inheritance, fear not that we shall make you ashamed of your sacrifices. Never! Your children will faithfully imitate your example; they are resolved to live free, or to die fighting in defence of their inalienable and sacred rights. We cannot permit ourselves to believe that the King of France will side with our enemies, and direct his arms against our island; surely this can never happen. But if it is written in the book of fate, that the most powerful monarch of the earth is to contend against one of the smallest peoples of Europe, then we have new and just cause to be proud, for we are certain either to live for the future in honourable freedom, or to make our fall immortal. Those who feel themselves incapable of such virtue need not tremble; I speak only to true Corsicans, and their feelings are known.

"As regards us, brave youths, none—I swear by the manes of our fathers!—not one will wait a second call; before the face of the world we must show that we deserve to be called brave. If foreigners land upon our coasts ready to give battle to uphold the pretensions of their allies, shall we who fight for our own welfare—for the welfare of our posterity—for the maintenance of the righteous and magnanimous resolutions of our fathers—shall we hesitate to defy all dangers, to risk, to sacrifice our lives? Brave fellow-citizens! liberty is our aim—and the eyes of all noble souls in Europe are upon us; they sympathize with us, they breathe prayers for the triumph of our cause. May our resolute firmness exceed their expectations! and may our enemies, by whatever name called, learn from experience that the conquest of Corsica is not so easy as it may seem! We who live in this land are freemen, and freemen can die!"

CHAPTER XI
CORSICA UNDER PAOLI—TRAFFIC IN
NATIONS—VICTORIES OVER THE FRENCH

All the thoughts and wishes of the Corsican people were thus directed towards a common aim. The spirit of the nation was vigorous and buoyant; ennobled by the purest love of country, by a bravery that had become hereditary, by the sound simplicity of the constitution, which was no artificial product of foreign and borrowed theorizings, but the fruit of sacred, native tradition. The great citizen, Pasquale Paoli, was the father of his country. Wherever he showed himself, he was met by the love and the blessings of his people, and women and gray-haired men raised their children and children's children in their arms, that they might see the man who had made his country happy. The seaports, too, which had hitherto remained in the power of Genoa, became desirous of sharing the advantages of the Corsican constitution. Disturbances occurred; Carlo Masseria and his son undertook to deliver the castle of Ajaccio into the hands of the Nationalists by stratagem. The attempt failed. The son was killed, and the father, who had already received his death-wound, died without a complaint, upon the rack.

The Corsican people had now become so much stronger that, far from turning anxiously to some foreign power for aid, they found in themselves, not only the means of resistance, but even of attack and conquest. Their flag already waved on the waters of the Mediterranean. De Perez, a knight of Malta, was the admiral of their little fleet, which was occasioning the Genoese no small alarm. People said in Corsica that the position of the island might well entitle it to become a naval power—such as Greek islands in the eastern seas had formerly been; and a landing of the Corsicans on the coast of Liguria was no longer held impossible.

The conquest of the neighbouring island of Capraja gave such ideas a colour of probability; while it astonished the Genoese, and showed them that their fears were well grounded. This little island had in earlier times been part of the seigniory of the Corsican family of Da Mare, but had passed into the hands of the Genoese. It is not fertile, but an important and strong position in the Genoese and Tuscan waters. A Corsican named Centurini conceived the idea of surprising it. Paoli readily granted his consent, and in February 1765 a little expedition, consisting of two hundred regular troops and a body of militia, ran out from Cape Corso. They attacked the town of Capraja, which at first resisted vigorously, but afterwards made common cause with them. The Genoese commandant, Bernardo Ottone, held the castle, however, with great bravery; and Genoa, as soon as it heard of the occurrence, hastily despatched her fleet under Admiral Pinelli, who thrice suffered a repulse. In Genoa, such was the shame and indignation at not being able to rescue Capraja from the handful of Corsicans who had effected a lodgment in the town, that the whole Senate burst into tears. Once more they sent their fleet, forty vessels strong, against the island. The five hundred Corsicans under Achille Murati maintained the town, and drove the Genoese back into the sea. Bernardo Ottone surrendered in May 1767, and Capraja, now completely in possession of the Corsicans, was declared their province.

The fall of Capraja was a heavy blow to the Senate, and accelerated the resolution totally to relinquish the now untenable Corsica. But the enfeebled Republic delayed putting this painful determination into execution, till a blunder she herself committed forced her to it. It was about this time that the Jesuits were driven from France and Spain; the King of Spain had, however, requested the Genoese Senate to allow the exiles an asylum in Corsica. Genoa, to show him a favour, complied, and a large number of the Jesuit fathers one day landed in Ajaccio. The French, however, who had pronounced sentence of perpetual banishment on the Jesuits, regarded it as an insult on the part of Genoa, that the Senate should have opened to the fathers the Corsican seaports which they, the French, garrisoned. Count Marbœuf immediately received orders to withdraw his troops from Ajaccio, Calvi, and Algajola; and scarcely had this taken place, when the Corsicans exultingly occupied the city of Ajaccio, though the citadel was still in possession of a body of Genoese troops.

Under these circumstances, and considering the irritated state of feeling between France and Genoa, the Senate foresaw that it would have to give way to the Corsicans; it accordingly formed the resolution to sell its presumed claims upon the island to France.

The French minister, Choiseul, received the proposal with joy. The acquisition of so important an island in the Mediterranean seemed no inconsiderable advantage, and in some degree a compensation for the loss of Canada. The treaty was concluded at Versailles on the 15th of May 1768, and signed by Choiseul on behalf of France, and Domenico Sorba on behalf of Genoa. The Republic thus, contrary to all national law, delivered a nation, on which it had no other claim than that of conquest—a claim, such as it was, long since dilapidated—into the hands of a foreign despotic power, which had till lately treated with the same nation as with an independent people; and a free and admirably constituted state was thus bought and sold like some brutish herd. Genoa had, moreover, made the disgraceful stipulation that she should re-enter upon her rights, as soon as she was in a position to reimburse the expenses which France had incurred by her occupation of the island.

Before the French expedition quitted the harbours of Provence, rumours of the negotiations, which were at first kept secret, had reached Corsica. Paoli called a Consulta at Corte; and it was unanimously resolved to resist France to the last and uttermost, and to raise the population *en masse*. Carlo Bonaparte, father of Napoleon, delivered a manly and spirited speech on this occasion.

Meanwhile, Count Narbonne had landed with troops in Ajaccio; and the astonished inhabitants saw the Genoese colours lowered, and the white flag of France unfurled in their stead. The French still denied the real intention of their coming, and amused the Corsicans with false explanations, till the Marquis Chauvelin landed with all his troops in Bastia, as commander-in-chief.

The four years' treaty of occupation was to expire on the 7th August of the same year, and on that day it was expected hostilities would commence. But on the 30th of July, five thousand French, under the command of Marbœuf, marched from Bastia towards San Fiorenzo, and after some unsuccessful resistance on the part of the Corsicans, made themselves masters of various points in Nebbio. It thus became clear that the doom of the Corsicans had been pronounced. Fortune, always unkind to them, had constantly interposed foreign despots between them and Genoa; and regularly each time, as they reached the eve of complete deliverance, had hurled them back into their old misery.

Pasquale Paoli hastened to the district of Nebbio with some militia. His brother Clemens had already taken a position there with four thousand men. But the united efforts of both were insufficient to prevent Marbœuf from making himself master of Cape Corso. Chauvelin, too, now made his appearance with fifteen thousand French, sent to enslave the freest and bravest people in the world. He marched on the strongly fortified town of Furiani, accompanied by the traitor, Matias Buttafuoco of Vescovato—the first who loaded himself with the disgrace of earning gold and title from the enemy. Furiani was the scene of a desperate struggle. Only two hundred Corsicans, under Carlo Saliceti and Ristori, occupied the place; and they did not surrender even when the cannon of the enemy had reduced the town to a heap of ruins, but, sword in hand, dashed through the midst of the foe during the night, and reached the coast.

Conflicts equally sanguinary took place in Casinca, and on the Bridge of Golo. The French were repulsed at every point, and Clemens Paoli covered himself with glory. History mentions him and Pietro Colle as the heroes of this last struggle of the Corsicans for freedom.

The remains of the routed French threw themselves into Borgo, an elevated town in the mountains of Mariana, and reinforced its garrison. Paoli was resolved to gain the place, cost what it might; and he commenced his assault on the 1st of October, in the night. It was the most brilliant of all the achievements of the Corsicans. Chauvelin, leaving Bastia, moved to the relief of Borgo; he was opposed by Clemens, while Colle, Grimaldi, Agostini, Serpentini, Pasquale Paoli, and Achille Murati led the attack upon Borgo. Each side expended all its energies. Thrice the entire French army made a desperate onset, and it was thrice repulsed. The Corsicans, numerically so much inferior, and a militia, broke and scattered here the compact ranks of an army which, since the age of Louis XIV., had the reputation of being the best organized in Europe. Corsican women in men's clothes, and carrying musket and sword, were seen mixing in the thickest of the fight. The French at length retired upon Bastia. They had suffered heavily in killed and wounded — among the latter was Marbœuf; and seven hundred men, under Colonel Ludre, the garrison of Borgo, laid down their arms and surrendered themselves prisoners.

The battle of Borgo showed the French what kind of people they had come to enslave. They had now lost all the country except the strong seaports. Chauvelin wrote to his court, reported his losses, and demanded new troops. Ten fresh battalions were sent.

CHAPTER XII
THE DYING STRUGGLE

The sympathy for the Corsicans had now become livelier than ever. In England especially, public opinion spoke loudly for the oppressed nation, and called upon the Government to interfere against such shameless and despotic exercise of power on the part of France. It was said Lord Chatham really entertained the idea of intimating England's decided disapproval of the French policy. Certainly the eyes of the Corsicans turned anxiously towards the free and constitutional Great Britain; they hoped that a great and free nation would not suffer a free people to be crushed. They were deceived. The British cabinet forbade, as in the year 1760, all intercourse with the Corsican "rebels." The voice of the English people became audible only here and there in meetings, and with these and private donations of money, the matter rested. The cabinets, however, were by no means sorry that a perilous germ of democratic freedom should be stifled along with a heroic nationality.

Pasquale Paoli saw well how dangerous his position was, notwithstanding the success that had attended the efforts of his people. He made proposals for a treaty, the terms of which acknowledged the authority of the French king, left the Corsicans their constitution, and allowed the Genoese a compensation. His proposals were rejected; and preparations continued to be made for a final blow. Chauvelin meanwhile felt his weakness. It has been affirmed that he allowed the Genoese to teach him intrigue; Paoli, like Sampiero and Gaffori, was to be removed by the hand of the assassin. Treachery is never wanting in the history of brave and free nations; it seems as if human nature could not dispense with some shadow of baseness where its nobler qualities shine with the purest light. A traitor was found in the son of Paoli's own chancellor, Matias Maffesi; letters which he lost divulged his secret purpose. Placed at the bar of the Supreme Council, he confessed, and was delivered over to the executioner. Another complot, formed by the restless Dumouriez, at that time serving in Corsica, to carry off Paoli during the night from his own house at Isola Rossa, also failed.

Chauvelin had brought his ten new battalions into the field, but they had met with a repulse from the Corsicans in Nebbio. Deeply humiliated, the haughty Marquis sent new messengers to France to represent the difficulty of subduing Corsica. The French government at length recalled Chauvelin from his post in December 1768, and Marbœuf was made interim commander, till Chauvelin's successor, Count de Vaux, should arrive.

De Vaux had served in Corsica under Maillebois; he knew the country, and how a war in it required to be conducted. Furnished with a large force of forty-five battalions, four regiments of cavalry, and considerable artillery, he determined to end the conflict at a single blow. Paoli saw how heavily the storm was gathering, and called an assembly in Casinca on the 15th of April 1769. It was resolved to fight to the last drop of blood, and to bring every man in Corsica into the field. Lord Pembroke, Admiral Smittoy, other Englishmen, Germans, and Italians, who were present, were astonished by the calm determination of the militia who flocked into Casinca. Many foreigners joined the ranks of the Corsicans. A whole company of Prussians, who had been in the service of Genoa, came over to their side. No one, however, could conceal from himself the gloominess of the Corsican prospects; French gold was already doing its work; treachery was rearing its head; even Capraja had fallen through the treasonable baseness of its commandant, Astolfi.

Corsica's fatal hour was at hand. England did not, as had been hoped, interfere; the French were advancing in full force upon Nebbio. This mountain province, traversed by a long, narrow valley, had frequently already been the scene of decisive conflicts. Paoli, leaving Saliceti and Serpentini in Casinca, had established his head-quarters here; De Vaux, Marbœuf, and Grand-Maison entered Nebbio to annihilate him at once. The attack commenced on the 3d of May. After the battle had lasted three days, Paoli was driven from his camp at Murati. He now concluded to cross the Golo, and place that river between himself and the enemy. He fixed his head-quarters in Rostino, and committed to Gaffori and Grimaldi the defence of Leuto and Canavaggia, two points much exposed to the French. Grimaldi betrayed his trust; and Gaffori, for what reason is uncertain, also failed to maintain his post.

The French, finding the country thus laid open to them, descended from the heights, and pressed onwards to Ponte Nuovo, the bridge over the Golo. The main body of the Corsicans was drawn up on the further bank; above a thousand of them, along with the company of Prussians, covered the bridge. The French, whose descent was rapid and unexpected, drove in the militia, and these, thrown into disorder and seized with panic, crowded towards the bridge and tried to cross. The Prussians, however, who had received orders to bring the fugitives to a halt, fired in the confusion on their own friends, while the French fired upon their rear, and pushed forward with the bayonet. The terrible cry of "Treachery!" was heard. In vain did Gentili attempt to check the disorder; the rout became general, no position was any longer tenable, and the militia scattered themselves in headlong flight among the woods, and over the adjacent country. The unfortunate battle of Ponte Nuovo was fought on the 9th of May 1769, and on that day the Corsican nation lost its independence.

Paoli still made an attempt to prevent the enemy from entering the province of Casinca. But it was too late. The whole island, this side the mountains, fell in a few days into the hands of the French; and that instinctive feeling of being lost beyond help, which sometimes, in moments of heavy misfortune, seizes on the minds of a people with overwhelming force, had taken possession of the Corsicans. They needed a man like Sampiero. Paoli despaired. He had hastened to Corte, almost resolved to leave his country. The brave Serpentini still kept the field in Balagna, with Clemens Paoli at his side, who was determined to fight while he drew breath; and Abatucci still maintained himself beyond the mountains with a band of bold patriots. All was not yet lost; it was at least possible to take to the fastnesses and guerilla fighting, as Renuccio, Vincentello, and Sampiero had done. But the stubborn hardihood of those men of the iron centuries, was not and could not be part of Paoli's character; nor could he, the lawgiver and Pythagoras of his people, lower himself to range the hills with guerilla bands. Shuddering at the thought of the blood with which a protracted struggle would once more deluge his country, he yielded to destiny. His brother Clemens, Serpentini, Abatucci, and others joined him. The little company of fugitives hastened to Vivario, then, on the 11th of June, to the Gulf of Porto Vecchio. There they embarked, three hundred Corsicans, in an English ship, given them by Admiral Smittoy, and sailed for Tuscany, from which they proceeded to England, which has continued ever since to be the asylum of the fugitives of ruined nationalities, and has never extended her hospitality to nobler exiles.

Not a few, comparing Pasquale Paoli with the old tragic Corsican heroes, have accused him of weakness. Paoli's own estimate of himself appears from the following extract from one of his letters:—"If Sampiero had lived in my day, the deliverance of my country would have been of less difficult accomplishment. What we attempted to do in constituting the nationality, he would have completed. Corsica needed at that time a man of bold and enterprising spirit, who should have spread the terror of his name to the very *comptoirs* of Genoa. France would not have mixed herself in the struggle, or, if she had, she would have found a more terrible adversary than any I was able to oppose to her. How often have I lamented this! Assuredly not courage nor heroic constancy was wanting in the Corsicans; what they wanted was a leader, who could combine and conduct the operations of the war in the face of experienced generals. We should have shared the noble work; while I laboured at a code of laws suitable to the traditions and requirements of the island, his mighty sword should have had the task of giving strength and security to the results of our common toil."

On the 12th of June 1769, the Corsican people submitted to French supremacy. But while they were yet in all the freshness of their sorrow, that centuries of unexampled conflict should have proved insufficient to rescue their darling independence; and while the warlike din of the French occupation still rang from end to end of the island, the Corsican nation produced, on the 15th of August, in unexhausted vigour, one hero more, Napoleon Bonaparte, who crushed Genoa, who enslaved France, and who avenged his country. So much satisfaction had the Fates reserved for the Corsicans in their fall; and such was the atoning close they had decreed to the long tragedy of their history.

BOOK III
WANDERINGS IN THE
SUMMER OF 1852

"Nel mezzo del cammin di nostra vita
Mi ritrovai per una selva oscura,
Che la diritta via era smarrita.
Ahi quanto a dir qual era è cosa dura.
Questa selva selvaggia, ed aspra, e forte—
Ma per trattar del ben, ch' ivi trovai
Dirò dell' altre cose, ch' io v'ho scorte."

Dante.

CHAPTER I
ARRIVAL IN CORSICA

Lasciate ogni speranza voi ch' entrate.—Dante.

The voyage across to Corsica from Leghorn is very beautiful, and more interesting than that from Leghorn to Genoa. We have the picturesque islands of the Tuscan Channel constantly in view. Behind us lies the Continent, Leghorn with its forest of masts at the foot of Monte Nero; before us the lonely ruined tower of Meloria, the little island-cliff, near which the Pisans under Ugolino suffered that defeat from the Genoese, which annihilated them as a naval power, and put their victorious opponents in possession of Corsica; farther off, the rocky islet of Gorgona; and near it in the west, Capraja. We are reminded of Dante's verses, in the canto where he sings the fate of Ugolino—

"O Pisa! the disgrace of that fair land
Where Si is spoken: since thy neighbours round

Take vengeance on thee with a tardy hand,—
To dam the mouth of Arno's rolling tide
Let Capraja and Gorgona raise a mound
That all may perish in the waters wide."

The island of Capraja conceals the western extremity of Corsica; but behind it rise, in far extended outline, the blue hills of Cape Corso. Farther west, and off Piombino, Elba heaves its mighty mass of cliff abruptly from the sea, descending more gently on the side towards the Continent, which we could faintly descry in the extreme distance. The sea glittered in the deepest purple, and the sun, sinking behind Capraja, tinged the sails of passing vessels with a soft rose-red. A voyage on this basin of the Mediterranean is in reality a voyage through History itself. In thought, I saw these fair seas populous with the fleets of the Phœnicians and the Greeks, with the ships of those Phocæans, whose roving bands were once busy here;—then Hasdrubal, and the fleets of the Carthaginians, the Etruscans, the Romans, the Moors, and the Spaniards, the Pisans, and the Genoese. But still more impressively are we reminded, by the constant sight of Corsica and Elba, of the greatest drama the world's history has presented in modern times— the drama which bears the name of Napoleon. Both islands lie in peaceful vicinity to each other; as near almost as a man's cradle and his grave— broad, far-stretching Corsica, which gave Napoleon birth, and the little Elba, the narrow prison in which they penned the giant. He burst its rocky bonds as easily as Samson the withes of the Philistines. Then came his final fall at Waterloo. After Elba, he was merely an adventurer; like Murat, who, leaving Corsica, went, in imitation of Napoleon, to conquer Naples with a handful of soldiers, and met a tragic end.

The view of Elba throws a Fata Morgana into the excited fancy, the picture of the island of St. Helena lying far off in the African seas. Four islands, it seems, strangely influenced Napoleon's fate—Corsica, England, Elba, and St. Helena. He himself was an island in the ocean of universal history—*unico nel mondo*, as the stout Corsican sailor said, beside whom I stood, gazing on Corsica, and talking of Napoleon. "*Ma Signore*," said he, "I know all that better than you, for I am his countryman;" and now, with the liveliest gesticulations, he gave me an abridgment of Napoleon's history, which interested me more in the midst of this scenery than all the volumes of Thiers. And the nephew?—"I say the *Napoleone primo* was also the *unico*." The sailor was excellently versed in the history of his island, and was as well acquainted with the life of Sampiero as with those of Pasquale Paoli, Saliceti, and Pozzo di Borgo.

Night had fallen meanwhile. The stars shone brilliantly, and the waves phosphoresced. High over Corsica hung Venus, the *stellone* or great star, as the sailors call it, now serving us to steer by. We sailed between Elba and Capraja, and close past the rocks of the latter. The historian, Paul Diaconus, once lived here in banishment, as Seneca did, for eight long years, in Corsica. Capraja is a naked granite rock. A Genoese tower stands picturesquely on a cliff, and the only town in the island, of the same name, seems to hide timidly behind the gigantic crag which the fortress crowns. The white walls and white houses, the bare, reddish rocks, and the wild and desolate seclusion of the place, give the impression of some lonely city among the cliffs of Syria. Capraja, which the bold Corsicans made a conquest of in the time of Paoli, remained in possession of the Genoese when they sold Corsica to France; with Genoa it fell to Piedmont.

Capraja and its lights had vanished, and we were nearing the coast of Corsica, on which fires could be seen glimmering here and there. At length we began to steer for the lighthouse of Bastia. Presently we were in the harbour. The town encircles it; to the left the old Genoese fort, to the right the Marina, high above it in the bend a background of dark hills. A boat came alongside for the passengers who wished to go ashore.

And now I touched, for the first time, the soil of Corsica—an island which had attracted me powerfully even in my childhood, when I saw it on the map. When we first enter a foreign country, particularly if we enter it during the night, which veils everything in a mysterious obscurity, a strange expectancy, a burden of vague suspense, fills the mind, and our first impressions influence us for days. I confess my mood was very sombre and uneasy, and I could no longer resist a certain depression.

In the north of Europe we know little more of Corsica than that Napoleon was born there, that Pasquale Paoli struggled heroically there for freedom, and that the Corsicans practise hospitality and the Vendetta, and are the most daring bandits. The notions I had brought with me were of the gloomiest cast, and the first incidents thrown in my way were of a kind thoroughly to justify them.

Our boat landed us at the quay, on which the scanty light of some hand-lanterns showed a group of doganieri and sailors standing. The boatman sprang on shore. I have hardly ever seen a man of a more repulsive aspect. He wore the Phrygian cap of red wool, and had a white cloth tied over one eye; he was a veritable Charon, and the boundless fury with which he screamed to the passengers, swearing at them, and examining the fares by the light of his lantern, gave me at once a specimen of the ungovernably passionate temperament of the Corsicans.

The group on the quay were talking eagerly. I heard them tell how a quarter of an hour ago a Corsican had murdered his neighbour with three thrusts of a dagger (*ammazzato, ammazzato*—a word never out of my ears in Corsica; *ammazzato con tre colpi di pugnale*). "On what account?" "Merely in the heat of conversation; the sbirri are after him; he will be in the *macchia* by this time." The *macchia* is the bush. I heard the word *macchia* in Corsica just as often as *ammazzato* or *tumbato*. He has taken to the *macchia*, is as much as to say, he has turned bandit.

I was conscious of a slight shudder, and that suspense which the expectation of strange adventures creates. I was about to go in search of a locanda—a young man stepped up to me and said, in Tuscan, that he would take me to an inn. I followed the friendly Italian—a sculptor of Carrara. No light was shed on the steep and narrow streets of Bastia but by the stars of heaven. We knocked in vain at four locandas; none opened. We knocked at the fifth; still no answer. "We shall not find admittance here," said the Carrarese; "the landlord's daughter is lying on her bier." We wandered about the solitary streets for an hour; no one would listen to our appeals. Is this the famous Corsican hospitality? I thought; I seem to have come to the City of the Dead; and to-morrow I will write above the gate of Bastia: "All hope abandon, ye who enter here!"

However, we resolved to make one more trial. Staggering onwards, we came upon some other passengers in the same unlucky plight as myself; they were two Frenchmen, an Italian emigrant, and an English convert. I joined them, and once more we made the round of the locandas. This first night's experience was by no means calculated to inspire one with a high idea of the commercial activity and culture of the island; for Bastia is the largest town in Corsica, and has about fifteen thousand inhabitants. If this was the stranger's reception in a city, what was he to expect in the interior of the country?

A band of sbirri met us, Corsican gendarmes, dusky-visaged fellows with black beards, in blue frock-coats, with white shoulder-knots, and carrying double-barrelled muskets. We made complaint of our unfortunate case to them. One of them offered to conduct us to an old soldier who kept a tavern; there, he thought, we should obtain shelter. He led us to an old, dilapidated house opposite the fort. We kept knocking till the soldier-landlord awoke, and showed himself at the window. At the same moment some one ran past—our sbirro after him without saying a word, and both had vanished in the darkness of the night. What was it?—what did this hot pursuit mean? After some time the sbirro returned; he had imagined the runner was the murderer. "But he," said the gendarme, "is already in the hills, or some fisherman has set him over to Elba or Capraja. A short while ago we shot Arrighi in the mountains, Massoni too, and Serafino. That was a tough fight with Arrighi: he killed five of our people."

The old soldier came to the door, and led us into a large, very dirty apartment. We gladly seated ourselves round the table, and made a hearty supper on excellent Corsican wine, which has somewhat of the fire of the Spanish, good wheaten bread, and fresh ewe-milk cheese. A steaming oil-lamp illuminated this Homeric repast of forlorn travellers; and there was no lack of good humour to it. Many a health was drained to the heroes of Corsica, and our soldier-host brought bottle after bottle from the corner. There were four nations of us together, Corsican, Frenchman, German, and Lombard. I once mentioned the name of Louis Bonaparte, and put a question—the company was struck dumb, and the faces of the lively Frenchmen lengthened perceptibly.

Gradually the day dawned outside. We left the casa of the old Corsican, and, wandering to the shore, feasted our eyes upon the sea, glittering in the mild radiance of the early morning. The sun was rising fast, and lit up the three islands visible from Bastia—Capraja, Elba, and the small Monte Christo. A fourth island in the same direction is Pianosa, the ancient Planasia, on which Agrippa Posthumus, the grandson of Augustus, was strangled by order of Tiberius; as its name indicates, it is flat, and therefore cannot be distinguished from our position. The constant view of these three blue islands, along the edge of the horizon, makes the walks around Bastia doubly beautiful.

I seated myself on the wall of the old fort and looked out upon the sea, and on the little haven of the town, in which hardly half a dozen vessels were lying. The picturesque brown rocks of the shore, the green heights with their dense olive-groves, little chapels on the strand, isolated gray towers of the Genoese, the sea, in all the pomp of southern colouring, the feeling of being lost in a distant island, all this made, that morning, an indelible impression on my soul.

As I left the fort to settle myself in a locanda, now by daylight, a scene presented itself which was strange, wild, and bizarre enough. A crowd of people had collected before the fort, round two mounted carabineers; they were leading by a long cord a man who kept springing about in a very odd manner, imitating all the movements of a horse. I saw that he was a madman, and flattered himself with the belief that he was a noble charger. None of the bystanders laughed, though the caprioles of the unfortunate creature were whimsical enough. All stood grave and silent; and as I saw these men gazing so mutely on the wretched spectacle, for the first time I felt at ease in their island, and said to myself, the Corsicans are not barbarians. The horsemen at length rode away with the poor fellow, who trotted like a horse at the end of his line along the whole street, and seemed perfectly happy. This way of getting him to his destination by taking advantage of his fixed idea, appeared to me at once sly and *naïve*.

CHAPTER II
THE CITY OF BASTIA

The situation of Bastia, though not one of the very finest, takes one by surprise. The town lies like an amphitheatre round the little harbour; the sea here does not form a gulf, but only a landing-place—a *cala*. A huge black rock bars the right side of the harbour, called by the people Leone, from its resemblance to a lion. Above it stands the gloomy Genoese fort, called the Donjon. To the left, the quay runs out in a mole, at the extremity of which is a little lighthouse. The town ascends in terraces above the harbour; its houses are high, crowded together, tower-shaped, and have many balconies: away beyond the town rise the green hills, with some forsaken cloisters, beautiful olive-groves, and numerous fruit-gardens of oranges, lemons, and almonds.

Bastia has its name from the fortifications or bastions, erected there by the Genoese. The city is not ancient; neither Pliny, Strabo, nor Ptolemy, mentions any town as occupying its site. Formerly the little marina of the neighbouring town of Cardo stood here. In the year 1383, the Genoese Governor, Lionello Lomellino, built the Donjon or Castle, round which a new quarter of the town arose, which was called the Terra Nuova, the original lower quarter now receiving the name of Terra Vecchia. Both quarters still form two separate cantons. The Genoese now transferred the seat of their Corsican government to Bastia, and here resided the Fregosos, Spinolas, Dorias—within a space of somewhat more than four hundred years, eleven Dorias ruled in Corsica—the Fiescos, Cibbàs, the Guistiniani, Negri, Vivaldi, Fornari, and many other nobles of celebrated Genoese families. When Corsica, under French supremacy, was divided into two departments in 1797, which were named after the rivers Golo and Liamone, Bastia remained the principal town of the department of the Golo. In the year 1811, the two parts were again united, and the smaller Ajaccio became the capital of the country. Bastia, however, has not yet forgotten that it was once the capital, though it has now sunk to a sub-prefecture; and it is, in fact, still, in point of trade, commerce, and intelligence, the leading city of Corsica. The mutual jealousy of the Bastinese and the citizens of Ajaccio is almost comical, and would appear a mere piece of ridiculous provincialism, did we not know that the division of Corsica into the country this side and beyond the mountains, is historical, and dates from a remote antiquity, while the character of the inhabitants of the two halves is also entirely different. Beyond the mountains which divide Corsica from north to south, the people are much ruder and wilder, and all go armed; this side the mountains there is much more culture, the land is better tilled, and the manners of the population are gentler.

The Terra Vecchia of Bastia has nowadays, properly speaking, become the Terra Nuova, for it contains the best streets. The stateliest of them is the Via Traversa, a street of six and seven-storied houses, bending towards the sea; it is only a few years old, and still continues to receive additions. Its situation reminded me of the finest street I have ever seen, the Strada Balbi and Nuova in Genoa. But the houses, though of palatial magnitude, have nothing to boast of in the way of artistic decoration, or noble material. The very finest kinds of stone exist in Corsica in an abundance scarcely credible—marble, porphyry, serpentine, alabaster, and the costliest granite; and yet they are hardly ever used. Nature is everywhere here abandoned to neglect; she is a beautiful princess under a spell.

They are building a Palace of Justice in the Via Traversa at present, for the porticos of which I saw them cutting pillars in the marble quarries of Corte. Elsewhere, I looked in vain for marble ornament; and yet—who would believe it?—the whole town of Bastia is paved with marble—a reddish sort, quarried in Brando. I do not know whether it is true that Bastia has the best pavement in the world; I have heard it said.

Despite its length and breadth, the Via Traversa is the least lively of all the streets of Bastia. All the bustle and business are concentrated in the Place Favalelli, on the quay, and in the Terra Nuova, round the Fort. In the evening, the fashionable world promenades in the large Place San Nicolao, by the sea, where are the offices of the sub-prefecture, and the highest court of justice.

Not a single building of any architectural pretensions fetters the eye of the stranger here; he must find his entertainment in the beautiful walks along the shore, and on the olive-shaded hills. Some of the churches are large, and richly decorated; but they are clumsy in exterior, and possess no particular artistic attraction. The Cathedral, in which a great many Genoese seigniors lie entombed, stands in the Terra Nuova; in the Terra Vecchia is the large Church of St. John the Baptist. I mention it merely on account of Marbœuf's tomb. Marbœuf governed Corsica for sixteen years; he was the friend of Carlo Bonaparte, once so warm an adherent of Paoli; and it was he who opened the career of Napoleon, for he procured him his place in the military school of Brienne. His tomb in the church referred to bears no inscription; the monument and epitaph, as they originally existed, were destroyed in the Paolistic revolution against France. The Corsican patriots at that time wrote on the tomb of Marbœuf: "The monument which disgraceful falsehood and venal treachery dedicated to the tyrant of groaning Corsica, the true liberty and liberated truth of all rejoicing Corsica have now destroyed." After Napoleon had become Emperor, Madame Letitia wished to procure the widow of Marbœuf a high position among the ladies of honour in the imperial court; but Napoleon luckily avoided such gross want of tact, perceiving how unsuitable it was to offer Mme. Marbœuf a subordinate charge in the very family which owed so much to the patronage of her husband. He granted Marbœuf's son a yearly pension of ten thousand francs; but the young general fell at the head of his regiment in Russia. The little theatre in Bastia is a memorial of Marbœuf; it was built at his expense.

Another Frenchman of note lies buried in the Church of St. John—Count Boissieux, who died in the year 1738. He was a nephew of the celebrated Villars; but as a military man, had no success.

The busy stir in the markets, and the life about the port, were what interested me by far the most in Bastia.

There was the fish-market, for example. I never omitted paying a morning visit to the new arrivals from the sea; and when the fishermen had caught anything unusual, they showed it me in a friendly way, and would say—"This, Signore, is a *murena*, and this is the *razza*, and these are the *pesce spada*, and the *pesce prete*, and the beautiful red *triglia*, and the *capone*, and the *grongo*." Yonder in the corner, as below caste, sit the pond-fishers: along the east coast of Corsica are large ponds, separated from the sea by narrow tongues of land, but connected with it by inlets. The fishermen take large and well-flavoured fish in these, with nets of twisted rushes, eels in abundance—*mugini*, *ragni*, and *soglie*. The prettiest of all these fish is the murena; it is like a snake, and as if formed of the finest porphyry. It pursues the lobster (*legusta*), into which it sucks itself; the legusta devours the scorpena, and the scorpena again the murena. So here we have another version of the clever old riddle of the wolf, the lamb, and the cabbage, and how they were to be carried across a river. I am too little of a diplomatist to settle this intricate cross-war of the three fishes; they are often caught all three in the same net. Tunny and anchovies are caught in great quantities in the gulfs of Corsica, especially about Ajaccio and Bonifazio. The Romans had no liking for Corsican slaves—they were apt to be refractory; but the Corsican fish figured on the tables of the great, and even Juvenal has a word of commendation for them.

The market in the Place Favalelli presents in the morning a fresh, lively, motley picture. There sit the peasant women with their vegetables, and the fruit-girls with their baskets, out of which the beautiful fruits of the south look laughingly. One only needs to visit this market to learn what the soil of Corsica can produce in the matter of fruit; here are pears and apples, peaches and apricots, plums of every sort; there green almonds, oranges and lemons, pomegranates; near them potatoes, then bouquets of flowers, yonder green and blue figs, and the inevitable *pomi d'oro* (*pommes d'amour*); yonder again the most delicious melons, at a soldo or penny each; and in August come the muscatel-grapes of Cape Corso. In the early morning, the women and girls come down from the villages round Bastia, and bring their fruit into the town. Many graceful forms are to be seen among them. I was wandering one evening along the shore towards Pietra Nera, and met a young girl, who, with her empty fruit-basket on her head, was returning to her village. "*Buona sera—Evviva, Siore.*" We were soon in lively conversation. This young Corsican girl related to me the history of her heart with the utmost simplicity;—how her mother was compelling her to marry a young man she did not like. "Why do you not like him?" "Because his *ingegno* does not please me, *ah madonna!*" "Is he jealous?" "*Come un diavolo, ah madonna! I* nearly ran off to Ajaccio already." As we walked along talking, a Corsican came up, who, with a pitcher in his hand, was going to a neighbouring spring. "If you wish a draught of water," said he, "wait a little till I come down, and you, Paolina, come to me by and bye: I have something to say to you about your marriage."

"Look you, sir," said the girl, "that is one of our relations; they are all fond of me, and when they meet me, they do not pass me with a good evening; and none of them will hear of my marrying Antonio." By this time we were approaching her house. Paolina suddenly turned to me, and said with great seriousness—"Siore, you must turn back now; if I go into my village along with you, the people will talk ill of me (*faranne mal grido*). But come to-morrow, if you like, and be my mother's guest, and after that we will send you to our relations, for we have friends enough all over Cape Corso." I returned towards the city, and in presence of the unspeakable beauty of the sea, and the silent calm of the hills, on which the goat-herds had begun to kindle their fires, my mood became quite Homeric, and I could not help thinking of the old hospitable Phæacians and the fair Nausicaa.

The head-dress of the Corsican women is the mandile, a handkerchief of any colour, which covers the forehead, and smoothly enwrapping the head, is wound about the knot of hair behind; so that the hair is thus concealed. The mandile is in use all over Corsica; it looks Moorish and Oriental, and is of high antiquity, for there are female figures on Etrurian vases represented with the mandile. It is very becoming on young girls, less so on elderly women; it makes the latter look like the Jewish females. The men wear the pointed brown or red baretto, the ancient Phrygian cap, which Paris, son of Priam, wore. The marbles representing this Trojan prince give him the baretto; the Persian Mithras also wears it, as I have observed in the common symbolic group where Mithras is seen slaying the bull. Among the Romans, the Phrygian cap was the usual symbol of the barbarians; the well-known Dacian captives of the triumphal arch of Trajan which now stand on the arch of Constantine, wear it; so do other barbarian kings and slaves, Sarmatian and Asiatic, whom we find represented in triumphal processions. The Venetian Doge also wore a Phrygian cap as a symbol of his dignity.

The women in Corsica carry all their burdens on their head, and the weight they will thus carry is hardly credible; laden in this way, they often hold the spindle in their hand, and spin as they walk along. It is a picturesque sight, the women of Bastia carrying their two-handled brazen water-pitchers on their head; these bear a great resemblance to the antique consecrated vases of the temples; I never saw them except in Bastia; beyond the mountains they fetch their water in stone pitchers, of rude but still slightly Etruscan form.

"Do you see yonder woman with the water-pitcher on her head?" "Yes, what is remarkable about her?" "She might perhaps have been this day a princess of Sweden, and the consort of a king." "*Madre di Dio!*" "Do you see yonder village on the hillside? that is Cardo. The common soldier Bernadotte one day fell in love with a peasant girl of Cardo. The parents would not let the poor fellow court her. The *povero diavolo*, however, one day became a king, and if he had married that girl, she would have been a queen; and now her daughter there, with the water on her head, goes about and torments herself that she is not Princess of Sweden." It was on the highway from Bastia to San Fiorenzo that Bernadotte worked as a common soldier on the roads. At Ponte d'Ucciani he was made corporal, and very proud he was of his advancement. He now watched as superintendent over the workmen; afterwards he copied the rolls for Imbrico, clerk of court at Bastia. There is still a great mass of them in his handwriting among the archives at Paris.

It was on the Bridge of Golo, some miles from Bastia, that Massena was made corporal. Yes, Corsica is a wonderful island. Many a one has wandered among the lonely hills here, who never dreamed that he was yet to wear a crown. Pope Formosus made a beginning in the ninth century—he was a native of the Corsican village of Vivario; then a Corsican of Bastia followed him in the sixteenth century, Lazaro, the renegade, and Dey of Algiers; in the time of Napoleon, a Corsican woman was first Sultaness of Morocco; and Napoleon himself was first Emperor of Europe.

CHAPTER III
ENVIRONS OF BASTIA

How beautiful the walks are here in the morning, or at moon-rise! A few steps and you are by the sea, or among the hills, and there or here, you are rid of the world, and deep in the refreshing solitude of nature. Dense olive-groves fringe some parts of the shore. I often lay among these, beside a little retired tomb, with a Moorish cupola, the burial-vault of some family, and looked out upon the sea, and the three islands on its farthest verge. It was a spot of delicious calm; the air was so sunny, so soothingly still, and wherever the eye rested, holiday repose and hermit loneliness, a waste of brown rocks on the strand, covered with prickly cactus, solitary watch-towers, not a human being, not a bird upon the water; and to the right and left, warm and sunny, the high blue hills.

I mounted the heights immediately above Bastia. From these there is a very pleasant view of the town, the sea, and the islands. Vineyards, olive-gardens, orange-trees, little villas of forms the most bizarre; here and there a fan-palm, tombs among cypresses, ruins quite choked in ivy, are scattered on every side. The paths are difficult and toilsome; you wander over loose stones, over low walls, between bramble-hedges, among trailing ivy, and a wild and rank profusion of thistles. The view of the shore to the south of Bastia surprised me. The hills there, like almost all the Corsican hills, of a fine pyramidal form, retire farther from the shore, and slope gently down to a smiling plain. In this level lies the great pond of Biguglia, encircled with reeds, dead and still, hardly a fishing-skiff cutting its smooth waters. The sun was just sinking as I enjoyed this sight. The lake gleamed rosy red, the hills the same, and the sea was full of the evening splendour, with a single ship gliding across. The repose of a grand natural scene calms the soul. To the left I saw the cloister of San Antonio, among olive-trees and cypresses; two priests sat in the porch, and some black-veiled nuns were coming out of the church. I remembered a picture I had once seen of evening in Sicily, and found it here reproduced.

Descending to the highway, I came to a road which leads to Cervione; herdsmen were driving home their goats, riders on little red horses flew past me, wild fellows with bronzed faces, all with the Phrygian cap on their heads, the dark brown Corsican jacket of sheeps'-wool hanging loosely about them, double-barrels slung upon their backs. I often saw them riding double on their little animals: frequently a man with a woman behind him, and if the sun was hot they were always holding a large umbrella above them. The parasol is here indispensable; I frequently saw both men and women—the women clothed, the men naked—sitting at their ease in the shallow water near the shore, and holding the broad parasol above their heads, evidently enjoying themselves mightily. The women here ride like the men, and manage their horses very cleverly. The men have always the zucca or round gourd-bottle slung behind them; often, too, a pouch of goatskin, zaino, and round their middle is girt the carchera—a leathern belt which holds their cartridges.

Before me walked numbers of men returning from labour in the fields; I joined them, and learned that they were not Corsicans, but Italians from the Continent. More than five thousand labourers come every year from Italy, particularly from Leghorn, and the country about Lucca and Piombino, to execute the field labour for the lazy Corsicans. Up to the present day the Corsicans have maintained a well-founded reputation for indolence, and in this they are thoroughly unlike other brave mountaineers, as, for example, the Samnites. All these foreign workmen go under the common appellation of Lucchesi. I have been able personally to convince myself with what utter contempt these poor and industrious men are looked on by the Corsicans, because they have left their home to work in the sweat of their brow, exposed to a pestilential atmosphere, in order to bring their little earnings to their families. I frequently heard the word "Lucchese" used as an opprobrious epithet; and particularly among the mountains of the interior is all field-work held in detestation as unworthy of a freeman; the Corsican is a herdsman, as his forefathers have been from time immemorial; he contents himself with his goats, his repast of chestnuts, a fresh draught from the spring, and what his gun can bring down.

I learned at the same time that there were at present in Corsica great numbers of Italian democrats, who had fled to the island on the failure of the revolution. There were during the summer about one hundred and fifty of them scattered over the island, men of all ranks; most of them lived in Bastia. I had opportunities of becoming acquainted with the most respectable of these refugees, and of accompanying them on their walks. They formed a company as motley as political Italy herself—Lombards, Venetians, Neapolitans, Romans, and Florentines. I experienced the fact that in a country where there is little cultivated society, Italians and Germans immediately exercise a mutual attraction, and have on neutral ground a brotherly feeling for each other. There was a universality in the events and results of the year 1848, which broke down many limitations, and produced certain views of life and certain theories within which individuals, to whatever nationalities they may belong, feel themselves related and at home. I found among these exiles in Corsica men and youths of all classes, such as are to be met with in similar companies at home—enthusiastic and sanguine spirits; others again, men of practical experience, sound principle, and clear intellect.

The world is at present full of the political fugitives of European nations; they are especially scattered over the islands, which have long been, and are in their nature destined to be, used as asylums. There are many exiles in the Ionian Islands and in the islands of Greece, many in Sardinia and Corsica, many in the islands of the English Channel, most of all in Britain. It is a general and European lot which has fallen to these exiles—only the locality is different; and banishment itself, as a result of political crime, or political misfortune, is as old as the history of organized states. I remembered well how in former times the islands of the Mediterranean—Samos, Delos, Ægina, Corcyra, Lesbos, Rhodes—sheltered the political refugees of Greece, as often as revolution drove them from Athens or Thebes, or Corinth or Sparta. I thought of the many exiles whom Rome sent to the islands in the time of the Emperors, as Agrippa Posthumus to Planasia, the philosopher Seneca to Corsica itself. Corsica particularly has been at all times not only a place of refuge, but a place of banishment; in the strictest sense of the word, therefore, an island of *bandits*, and this it still is at the present day. The avengers of blood wander homeless in the mountains, the political fugitives dwell homeless in the towns. The ban of outlawry rests upon both, and if the law could reach them, their fate would be the prison, if not death.

Corsica, in receiving these poor banished Italians, does more than simply practise her cherished religion of hospitality, she discharges a debt of gratitude. For in earlier centuries Corsican refugees found the most hospitable reception in all parts of Italy; and banished Corsicans were to be met with in Rome, in Florence, in Venice, and in Naples. The French government has hitherto treated its guests on the island with liberality and tolerance. The remote seclusion of their position compels these exiles to a life of contemplative quiet; and they are, perhaps precisely on this account, more fortunate than their brethren in misfortune in Jersey or London.

CHAPTER IV
FRANCESCO MARMOCCHI OF FLORENCE—
THE GEOLOGY OF CORSICA

Hic sola hæc duo sunt, exul, et exilium.—Seneca *in Corsica.*

Προσκυνοῦντες τὴν εἱμαρμένην σοφοί.—Æschyl. *Prom.*

I was told in a bookseller's shop into which I had gone in search of
a Geography of the island, that there was one then in the press, and that
its author was Francesco Marmocchi, a banished Florentine. I immediately
sought this gentleman out, and made in him one of the most valuable
of all my Italian acquaintances. I found a man of prepossessing exterior,
considerably above thirty, in a little room, buried among books. Possibly
the rooms of most political exiles do not present such a peaceful aspect. On
the bookshelves were the best classical authors; and my eye lighted with no
small pleasure on Humboldt's *Cosmos*; on the walls were copperplate views
of Florence, and an admirable copy of a Perugino; all this told not only
of the seclusion of a scholar, but of that of a highly cultivated Florentine.
There are perhaps few greater contrasts than that between Florence and
Corsica, and my own feelings were at first certainly peculiar, when, after
six weeks' stay in Florence, I suddenly exchanged the Madonnas of Raphael
for the Corsican banditti; but it is always to be remembered that Corsica is
an island of enchanting beauty; and though banishment to paradise itself
would remain banishment, still the student of nature may at least, as Seneca
did, console himself here with the grandeur and beauty around him, in
undisturbed tranquillity. All that Seneca wrote from his Corsican exile to
his mother on the consolation to be found in contemplating nature, and
in science, Francesco Marmocchi may fully apply to himself. This former
Florentine professor seemed to me, in his dignified retirement and learned
leisure, the happiest of all exiles.

Francesco Marmocchi was minister of Tuscany during the revolution,
along with Guerazzi; he was afterwards secretary to the ministry: more

fortunate than his political friend, he escaped from Florence to Rome, and then from Rome to Corsica, where he had already lived three years. His unwearied activity, and the stoical serenity with which he bears his exile, attest the manly vigour of his character. Francesco Marmocchi is one of the most esteemed and talented Italian geographers. Besides his great work, a Universal Geography in six quarto volumes, a new edition of which is at present publishing, he has written a special Geography of Italy in two volumes; a Historical Geography of the Ancient World, of the Middle Ages, and of Modern Times; a Natural History of Italy, and other works. I found him correcting the proof-sheets of his little Geography of Corsica, an excellent hand-book, which he has unfortunately been obliged to write in French. This book is published in Bastia, by Fabiani; it has afforded me some valuable information about Corsica.

One morning before sunrise we went into the hills round Cardo, and here, amid the fresh bloom of the Corsican landscape, if the reader will suppose himself in our company, we shall take the geographer himself for guide and interpreter, and hear what he has to say upon the island. I give almost the very words of his Geography.

Corsica owes her existence to successive conglobations of upheaved masses; during an extended period she has had three great volcanic processes, to which the bizarre and abrupt contours of her landscape are to be ascribed. These three upheavals may be readily distinguished. The first masses of Corsican land that rose were those that occupy the entire south-western side. This earliest upheaval took place in a direction from north-west to south-east; its marks are the two great ribs of mountain which run parallel, from north-east to south-west, down towards the sea, and form the most important promontories of the west coast. The axis of Corsica at that time must therefore have been different from its later one; and the islands in the channel of Bonifazio, as well as a part of the north-east of Sardinia, then stood in connexion with Corsica. The material of this first upheaval is mostly granite; consequently at the period of this primeval revolution there was no life of any sort on the island.

The direction of the second upheaval was from south-west to north-east, and the material here again consists largely of granitoids. But as we advance to the north-east, we find the granite gradually giving way to the ophiolitic (*ophiolitisch*) earth system. The second upheaval is, however, hardly discernible. It is clear that it destroyed most of the northern ridge of the first; but Corsican geology has preserved very few traces of it.

The undoubted effect of the third and last upheaval was the almost entire destruction of the southern portion of the first; and it was at this time the island received its present form. It occurred in a direction from north to south. So long as the masses of this last eruption have not come in contact with the masses of previous upheavals, their direction remains regular, as is shown by the mountain-chain of Cape Corso. But it had to burst its way through the towering masses of the southern ridge with a fearful shock; it broke them up, altering its direction, and sustaining interruption at many points, as is shown by the openings of the valleys, which lead from the interior to the plain of the east coast, and have become the beds of the streams that flow into the sea on this side—the Bevinco, the Golo, the Tavignano, the Fiumorbo, and others.

The rock strata of this third upheaval are primitive ophiolitic and primitive calcareous, covered at various places by secondary formations.

The primitive masses, which occupy, therefore, the south and west of the island, consist almost entirely of granite. At their extremities they include some layers of gneiss and slate. The granite is almost everywhere covered—a clear proof that it was elevated at a period antecedent to that during which the covering masses were forming in the bosom of the ocean, to be deposited in horizontal strata on the crystalline granite masses. Strata of porphyry and eurite pierce the granite; a decided porphyritic formation crowns Mounts Cinto, Vagliorba, and Perturato, the highest summits of Niolo, overlying the granite. From two to three feet of mighty greenstone penetrate these porphyritic rocks.

The intermediary masses occupy the whole of Cape Corso, and the east of the island. They consist of bluish gray limestone, huge masses of talc, stalactites, serpentine, euphotides, quartz, felspar, and porphyries.

The tertiary formations appear only in isolated strips, as at San Fiorenzo, Volpajola, Aleria, and Bonifazio. They exhibit numerous fossils of marine animals of subordinate species—sea-urchins, polypi, and many other petrifactions in the limestone layers.

In regard to the plains of the east coast of Corsica, as the plains Biguglia, Mariana, and Aleria, they are diluvial deposits of the period when the floods destroyed vast numbers of animal species. Among the diluvial fossils in the neighbourhood of Bastia, the head of a lagomys has been found—a small hare without tail, existing at the present day in Siberia.

There is no volcano in Corsica; but traces of extinct volcanoes may be seen near Porto Vecchio, Aleria, Balistro, San Manza, and at other points.

It seems almost incredible that an island like Corsica, so close to Sardinia and Tuscany, and, above all, so near the iron island of Elba, should be so poor in metals as it really is. Numerous indications of metallic veins are, it is true, to be found everywhere, now of iron or copper, now of lead, antimony, manganese, quicksilver, cobalt, gold and silver, but these, as the engineer Gueymard has shown in his work on the geology and mineralogy of Corsica, are illusory.

The only metal mines of importance that can be wrought, are, at present, the iron mines of Olmeta and Farinole in Cape Corso, an iron mine near Venzolasca, the copper mine of Linguizzetta, the antimony mine of Ersa in Cape Corso, and the manganese mine near Alesani.

On the other hand, Corsica is an inexhaustible treasury of the rarest and most valuable stones, an elysium of the geologist. But they lie unused; no one digs the treasure.

It may not be out of place here to give a detail of these beautiful stones, arranged in the usual geological order.

1. *Granites.*—Red granite, resembling the Oriental granite, between Orto and the lake of Ereno; coral-red granite at Olmiccia; rose-red granite at Cargese; red granite, tending to purple, at Aitone; rosy granite of Carbuccia; rosy granite of Porto; rose-red granite at Algajola; granite with garnets (the bigness of a nut) at Vizzavona.

2. *Porphyries.*—Variegated porphyry in Niolo; black porphyry with rosy spots at Porto Vecchio; pale yellow porphyry, with rosy felspar at Porto Vecchio; grayish green porphyry, with amethyst, on the Restonica.

3. *Serpentines.*—Green, very hard serpentines; also transparent serpentines at Corte, Matra, and Bastia.

4. Eurites, amphibolites, and euphotides; globular eurite at Curso and Girolata, in Niolo, and elsewhere; globular amphibolite, commonly termed orbicular granite (the nodules consist of felspar and amphiboles in concentric layers) in isolated blocks at Sollucaro, on the Taravo, in the valley of Campolaggio and elsewhere; amphibolite, with crystals of black hornblende in white felspar at Olmeto, Levie, and Mela; euphotides, called

also Verde of Corsica, and Verde d'Orezza, in the bed of the Fiumalto, and in the valley of Bevinco.

5. *Jasper* and *Agates.*—Jasper (in granites and porphyries) in Niolo, and the valley of Stagno; agates (also in the granites and porphyries) in the same localities.

6. *Marble* and *Alabaster.*—White statuary marble of dazzling splendour at Ortiporio, Casacconi, Borgo de Cavignano, and elsewhere; bluish gray marble at Corte; yellow alabaster in the valley of S. Lucia, near Bastia; white alabaster, semi-transparent, foliated and fibrous, in a grotto behind Tuara, in the gulf of Girolata.

CHAPTER V
A SECOND LESSON, THE
VEGETATION OF CORSICA

It was an instructive lesson that Francesco Marmocchi, *quondam* professor of natural history, *quondam* minister of Tuscany, now Fuoruscito, and poor solitary student, gave me, that rosiest of all morning hours as we stood high up on the green Mount Cardo, the fair Mediterranean extended at our feet, exactly of such a colour as Dante has described: *color del Oriental zaffiro.*

"See," said Marmocchi, "where the blue outline shows itself, yonder is the beautiful Toscana."

Ah, I see Toscana well; plainly I see fair Florence, and the halls where the statues of the great Tuscans stand, Giotto, Orcagna, Nicola Pisano, Dante, Petrarca, Boccacio, Macchiavelli, Galilei, and the godlike Michael Angelo; three thousand Croats—I can see them—are parading there among the statues; the air is so clear, you can see and hear everything: listen, Francesco, to the verses the marble Michael Angelo is now addressing to Dante:—

"Dear is to me my sleep, and that I am of stone;

While this wo lasts, this ignominy deep,

To see nought, and to hear nought, that alone

Is well; then wake me not, speak low, and weep!"

But do you see how this dry brown rock has decorated himself over and over with flowers? On his head he wears a glorious plume of myrtles, white with blossom, and his breast is wound with a threefold cord of honour; with ivy, bramble, and the white wild vine—the clematis. There are no fairer garlands than those wreaths of clematis with their clusters of white blossom, and delicate leaves; the ancients loved them well, and willingly in lyric hours wore them round their heads.

Within the compass of a few paces, what a profusion of different plants! Here are rosemary and cytisus, there wild asparagus, beside it a tall bush of lilac-blossomed erica; here again the poisonous euphorbia, which sheds a milk-white juice when you break it; and here the sympathetic helianthemum, with its beautiful golden flowers, which one by one all fall off when you have broken a single twig; yonder, outlandish and bizarre, stands the prickly cactus, like a Moorish heathen, near it the wild olive shrub, the cork-oak, the lentiscus, the wild fig, and at their roots bloom the well-known children of our northern homes—the scabiosa, the geranium, and the mallow. How exquisite, pungent, invigorating are the perfumes that all this blooming vegetation breathes forth; the rue there, the lavender, the mint, and all those labiatae. Did not Napoleon say on St. Helena, as his mournful thoughts turned again to his native island: "All was better there, to the very smell of the soil; with shut eyes I should know Corsica from its fragrance alone."

Let us hear something from Marmocchi now, on the botany of Corsica in general.

Corsica is the most central region of the great plant-system of the Mediterranean—a system characterized by a profusion of fragrant Labiatæ and graceful Caryophylleæ. These plants cover all parts of the island, and at all seasons of the year fill the air with their perfume.

On account of the central position of Corsica, its vegetation connects itself with that of all the other provinces of the immense botanic region referred to; through Cape Corso it is connected with the plants of Liguria, through the east coast with those of Tuscany and Rome, through the west and south coasts with the botany of Provence, Spain, Barbary, Sicily, and the East; and finally, through the mountainous and lofty region of the interior, with that of the Alps and Pyrenees. What a wondrous opulence, and astonishing variety, therefore, in the Corsican vegetation!—a variety and opulence that infinitely heightens the beauty of the various regions of this island, already rendered so picturesque by their geological configuration.

Some of the forests, on the slopes of the mountains, are as beautiful as the finest in Europe—particularly those of Aitone and Vizzavona; besides, many provinces of Corsica are covered with boundless groves of chestnuts, the trees in which are as large and fruitful as the finest on the Apennines or Etna. Plantations of olives, from their extent entitled to be called forests, clothe the eminences, and line the valleys that run towards the sea, or lie open to its influences. Even on the rude sides of the higher mountains, the grape-vine twines itself round the orchard-fences, and spreads to the view its green leaves and purple fruit. Fertile plains, golden with rich harvests, stretch along the coasts of the island, and wheat and rye enliven the hillsides, here and there, with their fresh green, which contrasts agreeably with the dark verdure of the copsewoods, and the cold tones of the naked rock.

The maple and walnut, like the chestnut, thrive in the valleys and on the heights of Corsica; the cypress and the sea-pine prefer the less elevated regions; the forests are full of cork oaks and evergreen oaks; the arbutus and the myrtle grow to the size of trees. Pomaceous trees, but particularly the wild olive, cover wide tracts on the heights. The evergreen thorn, and the broom of Spain and Corsica, mingle with heaths in manifold variety, and all equally beautiful; among these may be distinguished the *erica arborea*, which frequently reaches an uncommon height.

On the tracts which are watered by the overflowing of streams and brooks, grow the broom of Etna, with its beautiful golden-yellow blossoms, the cisti, the lentisks, the terebinths, everywhere where the hand of man has not touched the soil. Further down, towards the plains, there is no hollow or valley which is not hung with the rhododendron, whose twigs, towards the sea-coast, entwine with those of the tamarisk.

The fan-palm grows on the rocks by the shore, and the date-palm, probably introduced from Africa, on the most sheltered spots of the coast. The *cactus opuntia* and the American agave grow everywhere in places that are warm, rocky, and dry.

What shall I say of the magnificent cotyledons, of the beautiful papilionaceous plants, of the large verbasceæ, the glorious purple digitalis, that deck the mountains of the island? And of the mallows, the orchises, the liliaceæ, the solanaceæ, the centaurea, and the thistles—plants which so beautifully adorn the sunny and exposed, or cool and shady regions where their natural affinities allow them to grow?

The fig, the pomegranate, the vine, yield good fruit in Corsica, even where the husbandman neglects them, and the climate and soil of the coasts of this beautiful island are so favourable to the lemon and the orange, and the other trees of the same family, that they literally form forests.

The almond, the cherry, the plum, the apple-tree, the pear tree, the peach, and the apricot, and, in general, all the fruit trees of Europe, are here common. In the hottest districts of the island, the fruits of the St. John's bread-tree, the medlar of various kinds, the jujube tree, reach complete ripeness.

The hand of man, if man were willing, might introduce in the proper quarters, and without much trouble, the sugar-cane, the cotton plant, tobacco, the pine-apple, madder, and even indigo, with success. In a word, Corsica might become for France a little Indies in the Mediterranean.

This singularly magnificent vegetation of the island is favoured by the climate. The Corsican climate has three distinct zones of temperature, graduated according to the elevation of the soil. The first climatic zone rises from the level of the sea to the height of five hundred and eighty metres (1903 English feet); the second, from the line of the former, to the height of one thousand nine hundred and fifty metres (6398 feet); the third, to the summit of the mountains.

The first zone or region of the coast is warm, like the parallel tracts of Italy and Spain. Its year has properly only two seasons, spring and summer; seldom does the thermometer fall 1° or 2° below zero of Reaumur (27° or 28° Fah.); and when it does so, it is only for a few hours. All along the coast, the sun is warm even in January, the nights and the shade cool, and this at all seasons of the year. The sky is clouded only during short intervals; the heavy sirocco alone, from the south-east, brings lingering vapours, till the vehement south-west—the libeccio, again dispels them. The moderate cold of January is rapidly followed by a dog-day heat of eight months, and the temperature mounts from 8° to 18° of Reaumur (50° to 72° Fah.), and even to 26° (90° Fah.) in the shade. It is, then, a misfortune for the vegetation, if no rain falls in March or April—and this misfortune occurs often; but the Corsican trees have, in general, hard and tough leaves, which withstand the drought, as the oleander, the myrtle, the cistus, the lentiscus, the wild olive. In Corsica, as in all warm climates, the moist and shady regions are almost pestilential; you cannot walk in these in the evening without contracting long and severe fever, which, unless an entire change of air intervene, will end in dropsy and death.

The second climatic zone resembles the climate of France, more especially that of Burgundy, Morvan, and Bretagne. Here the snow, which generally appears in November, lasts sometimes twenty days; but, singularly enough, up to a height of one thousand one hundred and sixty metres (3706 feet), it does no harm to the olive; but, on the contrary, increases its fruitfulness. The chestnut seems to be the tree proper to this zone, as it ceases at the elevation of one thousand nine hundred and fifty metres (6398 feet), giving place to the evergreen oaks, firs, beeches, box-trees, and junipers. In this climate, too, live most of the Corsicans in scattered villages on mountain slopes and in valleys.

The third climate is cold and stormy, like that of Norway, during eight months of the year. The only inhabited parts are the district of Niolo, and the two forts of Vivario and Vizzavona. Above these inhabited spots no vegetation meets the eye but the firs that hang on the gray rocks. There the vulture and the wild-sheep dwell, and there are the storehouse and cradle of the many streams that pour downwards into the valleys and plains.

Corsica may therefore be considered as a pyramid with three horizontal gradations, the lowermost of which is warm and moist, the uppermost cold and dry, while the intermediate shares the qualities of both.

CHAPTER VI
LEARNED MEN

If we reflect on the number of great men that Corsica has produced within the space of scarcely a hundred years, we cannot but be astonished that an island so small, and so thinly populated, is yet so rich in extraordinary minds. Its statesmen and generals are of European note; and if it has not been so fruitful in scientific talent, this is a consequence of its nature as an island, and of its iron history.

But even scientific talent of no mean grade has of late years been active in Corsica, and names like Pompei, Renucci, Savelli, Rafaelli, Giubeja, Salvatore Viali, Caraffa, Gregori, are an honour to the island. The men of most powerful intellect among these belong to the legal profession. They have distinguished themselves particularly in jurisprudence, and as historians of their own country.

A man the most remarkable and meritorious of them all, and whose memory will not soon die in Corsica, was Giovanni Carlo Gregori. He was born in Bastia in 1797, and belonged to one of the best families in the island. Devoting himself to the study of law, he first became auditor in Bastia, afterwards judge in Ajaccio, councillor at the king's court in Riom, then at the appeal court in Lyons, where he was also active as president of the Academy of Sciences, and where, on the 27th of May 1852, he died. He has written important treatises on Roman jurisprudence; but he had a patriotic passion for the history of his native country, and with this he was unceasingly occupied. He had resolved to write a history of Corsica, had made detailed researches, and collected the necessary materials for it; but death overtook him, and the loss of his work to Corsica cannot be sufficiently lamented. Nevertheless, Gregori has done important service to his native country: he edited the new edition of the national historian Filippini, a continuation of whose work it had been his purpose to write; he also edited the Corsican history of Petrus Cyrnæus; and in the year 1843 he published a highly important work—the Statutes of Corsica. In his earlier years he had written a Corsican tragedy, with Sampiero for a hero, which I have not seen.

Gregori maintained a most lively literary connexion with Italy and Germany. His acquirements were unusually extended, and his activity of the genuine Corsican stubbornness. Among his posthumous manuscripts are a part of his History of Corsica, and rich materials for a history of the commerce of the naval powers. The death of Gregori filled not only Corsica, but the men of science in France and Italy, with deep sorrow.

He and Renucci also rendered good service to the public library of Bastia, which contains sixteen thousand volumes, and occupies a large building formerly belonging to the Jesuits. They may be said, in fact, to have *made* this library, which ranks with that of Ajaccio as second in the island. Science in Corsica is still, on the whole, in its infancy. As the historian Filippini, the contemporary of Sampiero, complains,—indolence, the mainly warlike bent given to the nature of the Corsicans by their perpetual struggles, and the consequent ignorance, entirely prevented the formation of a literature. But it is remarkable, that in the year 1650 the Corsicans founded an Academy of Sciences, the first president of which was Geronimo Biguglia, the poet, advocate, theologian, and historian. It is well known that people in those times were fond of giving such academies the most whimsical names; the Corsicans called theirs the Academy dei Vagabondi (of the Vagabonds), and a more admirable and fitting appellation they could not at that period have selected. The Marquis of Cursay, whose memory is still affectionately cherished by the Corsicans, restored this Academy; and Rousseau, himself entitled to the name of Vagabond from his wandering life, wrote a little treatise for this Corsican institution on the question: "Which is the most necessary virtue for heroes, and what heroes have been deficient in this virtue?"—a genuinely Corsican subject.

The educational establishments—the Academy just referred to has been dissolved—are, in Bastia, as in Corsica in general, extremely inadequate. Bastia has a Lyceum, and some lower schools. I was present at a distribution of prizes in the highest of the girls' schools. It took place in the court of the old college of the Jesuits, which was prettily decorated, and in the evening brilliantly illuminated. The girls, all in white, sat in rows before the principal citizens and magistrates of the town, and received bay-wreaths—those who had won them. The head mistress called the name of the happy victress, who thereupon went up to her desk and received the wreath, which she then brought to one of the leading men of the town, silently conferring on him the favour of crowning her, which ceremony was then gone through in due form. Innumerable such bay-wreaths were distributed; and many a pretty child bore away perhaps ten or twelve of them for her immortal works, receiving them all very gracefully. It seemed to me, however, that wealthy parents, or celebrated old families, were too much flattered; and they never ceased crowning Miss Colonna d'Istria, Miss Abatucci, Miss Saliceti—so that these young ladies carried more bays home with them than would serve to crown the immortal poets of a century. The graceful little festival—in which there was certainly too much French flattering of vanity—was closed by a play, very cleverly acted by the young ladies.

Bastia has a single newspaper—*L'Ere Nouvelle, Journal de la Corse*—which appears only on Fridays. Up till this summer, the advocate Arrighi, a man of talent, was the editor. The new Prefect of Corsica, described to me as a young official without experience, exceedingly anxious to bring himself into notice, like the Roman prefects of old in their provinces, had been constantly finding fault with the Corsican press, the most innocent in the world; and threatening, on the most trifling pretexts, to withdraw the Government permission to publish the paper in question, till at length M. Arrighi was compelled to retire. The paper, entirely Bonapartist in its politics, still exists; the only other journal in Corsica is the Government paper in Ajaccio.

There are three bookselling establishments in Bastia, among which the Libreria Fabiani would do honour even to a German city. This house has published some beautiful works.

CHAPTER VII
CORSICAN STATISTICS—RELATION
OF CORSICA TO FRANCE

In the Bastian Journal for July 16, 1852, I found the statistics of Corsica according to calculations made in 1851, and shall here communicate them. Inhabitants

In 1740,	120,380
1760,	130,000
1790,	150,638
1821,	180,348
1827,	185,079
1831,	197,967
1836,	207,889
1841,	221,463
1846,	230,271
1851,	236,251

The population of the several arrondissements, five in number, was as follows:—In the arrondissement of Ajaccio, 55,008; Bastia, 20,288; Calvi, 24,390; Corte, 56,830; Sartene, 29,735.[B]

Corsica is divided into sixty-one cantons, 355 communes; contains 30,438 houses, and 50,985 households.

Males.

Unmarried,	75,543
Married,	36,715
Widowers,	5,680

117,938

Females.

Unmarried,	68,229
Married,	36,916
Widows,	13,168

118,313

236,187 of the inhabitants are Roman Catholics, fifty-four Reformed Christians. The French born on the island, *i.e.*, the Corsicans included, are 231,653:—Naturalized French, 353; Germans, 41; English, 12; Dutch, 6; Spaniards, 7; Italians, 3806; Poles, 12; Swiss, 85; other foreigners, 285.

Of diseased people, there were in the year 1851, 2554; of these 435 were blind in both eyes, 568 in one eye; 344 deaf and dumb; 183 insane; 176 club-footed.

Occupation—32,364 men and women were owners of land; 34,427 were day-labourers; 6924 domestics; people in trades connected with building— masons, carpenters, painters, blacksmiths, &c., 3194; dealers in wrought goods, and tailors, 4517; victual-dealers, 2981; drivers of vehicles, 1623; dealers in articles of luxury—watchmakers, goldsmiths, engravers, &c., 55; monied people living on their incomes, 13,160; government officials, 1229; communal magistrates, 803; military and marinari, 5627; apothecaries and physicians, 311; clergy, 955; advocates, 200; teachers, 635; artists, 105; *littérateurs*, 51; prostitutes, 91; vagabonds and beggars, 688; sick in hospital, 85.

One class, and that the most original class in the island, has no figure assigned to it in the above list—I mean the herdsmen. The number of bandits is stated to be 200; and there may be as many Corsican bandits in Sardinia.

That the reader may be able to form a clear idea of the general administration of Corsica, I shall here furnish briefly its more important details.

Corsica has been a department since the year 1811. It is governed by a prefect, who resides in Ajaccio. He also discharges the functions of sub-prefect for the arrondissement of Ajaccio. He has four sub-prefects under him in the other four arrondissements. The prefect is assisted by the

Council of the prefecture, consisting of three members, besides the prefect as president, and deciding on claims of exemption, &c., in connexion with taxes, the public works, the communal and national estates. There is an appeal to the Council of State.

The General Council, the members of which are elected by the voters of each canton, assembles yearly in Ajaccio to deliberate on the public affairs of the nation. It is competent to regulate the distribution of the direct taxes over the arrondissements. The General Council can only meet by a decree of the supreme head of the state, who determines the length of the sitting. There is a representative for each canton, in all, therefore, there are sixty-one.

In the chief town of each arrondissement meets a provincial council of as many members as there are cantons in the arrondissement. The citizens who, according to French law, are entitled to vote, are also voters for the Legislative Assembly. There are about 50,000 voters in Corsica.

Mayors, with adjuncts named by the prefect, conduct the affairs of the communes; the people have retained so much of their democratic rights, that they are allowed to elect the municipal council over which the mayor presides.

As regards the administration of justice, the high court of the department is the Appeal Court of Bastia, which consists of one chief president, two *présidents de chambre*, seventeen councillors, one auditor, one procurator-general, two advocates-general, one substitute, five clerks of court.

The Court of Assize holds its sittings in Bastia, and consists of three appeal-councillors, the procurator-general, and a clerk of court. It sits usually once every four months. There is a Tribunal of First Instance in the principal town of each arrondissement. There is also in each canton a justice of the peace. Each commune has a tribunal of simple municipal police, consisting of the mayor and his adjuncts.

The ecclesiastical administration is subject to the diocese of Ajaccio, the bishop of which—the only one in Corsica—is a suffragan of the Archbishop of Aix.

Corsica forms the seventeenth military division of France. Its head-quarters are in Bastia, where the general of the division resides. The gendarmerie, so important for Corsica, forms the seventeenth legion, and is also stationed in Bastia. It is composed of four companies, with four *chefs*, sixteen lieutenancies, and one hundred and two brigades.

I add a few particulars in regard to agriculture and industrial affairs. Agriculture, the foundation of all national wealth, is very low in Corsica. This is very evident from the single fact, that the cultivated lands of the island amount to a trifle more than three-tenths of the surface. The exact area of the island is 874,741 hectars.[C] The progress of agriculture is infinitely retarded by family feuds, bandit-life, the community of land in the parishes, the want of roads, the great distance of the tilled grounds from the dwellings, the unwholesome atmosphere of the plains, and most of all by the Corsican indolence.

Native industry is in a very languishing state. It is confined to the merest necessaries—the articles indispensable to the common handicrafts, and to sustenance; the women almost everywhere wear the coarse brown Corsican cloth (*panno Corso*), called also *pelvue*; the herdsmen prepare cheese, and a sort of cheesecake, called *broccio*; the only saltworks are in the Gulf of Porto Vecchio. There are anchovy, tunny, and coral fisheries on many parts of the coast, but they are not diligently pursued.

The commerce of Corsica is equally trifling. The principle export is oil, which the island yields so abundantly, that with more cultivation it might produce to the value of sixty millions of francs; it also exports pulse, chestnuts, fish, fresh and salted, wood, dyeing plants, hides, corals, marble, a considerable amount of manufactured tobacco, especially cigars, for which the leaf is imported. The main imports are—grain of various kinds, as rye, wheat, and rice; sugar, coffee, cattle, cotton, lint, leather, wrought and unwrought iron, brick, glass, stoneware.

The export and import are grievously disproportionate. The Customs impose ruinous restrictions on all manufacture and all commerce; they hinder foreigners from exchanging their produce for the produce of the country; hence the Corsicans must pay tenfold for their commodities in France, while even wine is imported from Provence free of duty, and thus checks the native cultivation of the vine. For Corsica is, in point of fact, precluded from exporting wine to France; France herself being a productive wine country. Even meal and vegetables are sent to the troops from Provence. The export of tobacco to the Continent is forbidden.[D] The tyrannical customs-regulations press with uncommon severity on the poor island; and though she is compelled to purchase articles from France to the value of three millions yearly, she sends into France herself only a million and a half. And Corsica yields the exchequer yearly 1,150,000 francs.

Bastia, Ajaccio, Isola Rossa, and Bonifazio are the principal trading towns.

But however melancholy the condition of Corsica may be in an industrial and a commercial point of view, its limited population protects it at least from the scourge of pauperism, which, in the opulent and cultivated countries of the Continent, can show mysteries of a much more frightful character than those of bandit-life and the Vendetta.

For five-and-twenty years now, with unimportant interruptions, have the French been in possession of the island of Corsica; and they have neither succeeded in healing the ever open wound of the Corsican people, nor have they, with all the means that advanced culture places at their disposal, done anything for the country, beyond introducing a few very trifling improvements. The island that has twice given France her Emperor, and twice dictated her laws, has gained nothing by it but the satisfaction of her revenge. The Corsican will never forget the disgraceful way in which France appropriated his country; and a high-spirited people never learns to love its conquerors. When I heard the Corsicans, even of the present day, bitterly inveighing against Genoa, I said to them—"Leave the old Republic of Genoa alone; you have had your full Vendetta on her—Napoleon, a Corsican, annihilated her; France betrayed you, and bereft you of your nationality; you have had your full Vendetta on France, for you sent her your Corsican Napoleon, who enslaved her; and even now this great France is a Corsican conquest, and your own province."

Two emperors, two Corsicans, on the throne of France, bowing her down with despotic violence;—well, if an ideal conception can have the worth of reality, then we are compelled to say, never was a brave subjugated people more splendidly avenged on its subduers. The name of Napoleon, it may be confidently affirmed, is the only tie that binds the Corsican nation to France; without this its relation to France would be in no respect different from that of other conquered countries to their foreign masters. I have read, in many authors, the assertion that the Corsican nation is at the core of its heart French. I hold this assertion to be a mistake, or an intentional falsehood. I have never seen the least ground for it. The difference between Corsican and Frenchman in nationality, in the most fundamental elements of character and feeling, puts a deep gulf between the two. The Corsican is decidedly an Italian; his language is acknowledged to be one of the purest dialects of Italian, his nature, his soil, his history, still link the lost son to his old mother-country. The French feel themselves strange in the island, and both soldiers and officials consider their period of service there as a "dreary exile in the isle of goats." The Corsican does not even understand such a temperament as the French—for he is grave, taciturn, chaste, consistent, thoroughly a man, and steadfast as the granite of his country.

Corsican patriotism is not extinct. I saw it now and then burst out. The old grudge still stirs the bosom of the Corsican, when he remembers the battle of Ponte Nuovo. Travelling one day, in a public conveyance, over the battle-field of Ponte Nuovo, a Corsican sitting beside me, a man from the interior, pulled me vehemently by the arm, as we came in sight of the famous bridge, and cried, with a passionate gesture—"This is the spot where the Genoese murdered our freedom—I mean the French." The reader will understand this, when he remembers that the name of Genoese means the same as deadly foe; for hatred of Genoa, the Corsicans themselves say, is with them undying. Another time I asked a Corsican, a man of education, if he was an Italian. "Yes," said he, "for I am a Corsican." I understood him well, and reached him my hand. These are isolated occurrences—accidents, but frequently a living word, caught from the mouth of the people, throws a vivid light on its state of feeling, and suddenly reveals the truth that does not stand in books compiled by officials.

I have heard it said again and again, and in all parts of the country—"We Corsicans would gladly be Italian—for we are in reality Italians, if Italy were only united and strong; as she is at present, we must be French, for we need the support of a great power; by ourselves we are too poor."

The Government does all it can to dislodge the Italian language, and replace it with the French. All educated Corsicans speak French, and, it is said, well; fashion, necessity, the prospect of office, force it upon many. Sorry I was to meet Corsicans (they were always young men) who spoke French with each other evidently out of mere vanity. I could not refrain on such occasions from expressing my astonishment that they so thoughtlessly relinquished their beautiful native tongue for that of the French. In the cities French is much spoken, but the common people speak nothing but Italian, even when they have learned French at school, or by intercourse with Frenchmen. French has not at all penetrated into the mountainous districts of the interior, where the ancient, venerated customs of the elder Corsicans—their primitive innocence, single-heartedness, justice, generosity, and love of liberty—remain unimpaired. Sad were it for the noble Corsican people if they should one day exchange the virtues of their rude but great forefathers for the refined corruption of enervated Parisian society. The moral rottenness of society in France has robbed the French nation of its strength. It has stolen like an infection into society in other countries, deepened their demoralization, and made incapacity for action general. It has disturbed the hallowed foundation of all human society—the family relation. But a people is ripe for despotism that has lost the spirit of family. The whole heroic history of the Corsicans has its source in the natural law of the inviolability and sacredness of the family relation, and in that alone; even their free constitution which they gave themselves in the course of years, and completed under Paoli, is but a development of the family. All the virtues of the Corsicans spring from this spirit; even the frightful night-sides of their present condition, such as the Vendetta, belong to the same root.

We look with shuddering on the avenger of blood, who descends from his mountain haunts, to stab his foe's kindred, man by man; yet this bloody vampire may, in manly vigour, in generosity, and in patriotism, be a very hero compared with such bloodless, sneaking villains, as are to be found contaminating with their insidious presence the great society of our civilisation, and secretly sucking out the souls of their fellow-men.

CHAPTER VIII
BRACCIAMOZZO, THE BANDIT

"Che bello onor s'acquista in far Vendetta." —Dante.

The second day after my arrival in Bastia, I was awakened during the night by an appalling noise in my locanda, in the street of the Jesuits. It was as if the Lapithæ and Centaurs had got together by the ears. I spring to the door, and witness, in the *salle-à-manger*, the following scene: —Mine host infuriated and vociferating at the pitch of his voice—his firelock levelled at a man who lies before him on his knees, other people vociferating, interfering, and trying to calm him down; the man on his knees implores mercy: they put him out of the house. It was a young man who had given himself out in the locanda for a Marseillese, had played the fine gentleman, and, in the end, could not pay his bill.

The second day after this, I happened to cross early in the morning the Place San Nicolao, the public promenade of the Bastinese, on my way to bathe. The executioners were just erecting a guillotine beside the town-house, though not in the centre of the Place, still on the promenade itself. Carabineers and a crowd of people surrounded the shocking scene, to which the laughing sea and the peaceful olive-groves formed a contrast painfully impressive. The atmosphere was close and heavy with the sirocco. Sailors and workmen stood in groups on the quay, silently smoking their little chalk-pipes, and gazing at the red scaffold, and not a few of them, in the pointed barretto, brown jacket, hanging half off, half on; their broad breasts bare, red handkerchiefs carelessly knotted about their necks, looked as if they had more to do with the guillotine than merely to stare at it. And, in fact, there probably was not one among the crowd who was not likely to meet with the same fate, if accident but willed it, that the hallowed custom of the Vendetta should stain his band with murder, and murder should force him to the life of the bandit.

"Who is it they are going to execute?"

"Bracciamozzo (Stump-arm). He is only three-and-twenty. The sbirri caught him in the mountains; but he defended himself like a devil—they shot him in the arm—the arm was taken off, and it healed."

"What has he done?"

"*Dio mio!*—he has killed ten men!"

"Ten men! and for what?"

"Out of *capriccio*."

I hastened into the sea to refresh myself with a bath, and then back into my locanda, in order to see no more of what passed. I was horror-struck at what I had heard and seen, and a shuddering came over me in this wild solitude. I took out my Dante; I felt as if I must read some of his wild phantasies in the *Inferno*, where the pitch-devils thrust the doomed souls down with harpoons as often as they rise for a mouthful of air. My locanda lay in the narrow and gloomy street of the Jesuits. An hour had elapsed, when a confused hum, and the trample of horses' feet brought me to the window—they were leading Bracciamozzo past, accompanied by the monks called the Brothers of Death, in their hooded capotes, that leave nothing of the face free but the eyes, which gleam spectrally out through the openings left for them—veritable demon-shapes, muttering in low hollow tones to themselves, horrible, as if they had sprung from Dante's Hell into reality. The bandit walked with a firm step between two priests, one of whom held a crucifix before him. He was a young man of middle size, with beautiful bronze features and raven-black curly hair, his face pale, and the pallor heightened by a fine moustache. His left arm was bound behind his back, the other was broken off near the shoulder. His eye, fiery no doubt as a tiger's, when the murderous lust for blood tingled through his veins, was still and calm. He seemed to be murmuring prayers. His pace was steady, and his bearing upright. Gendarmes rode at the head of the procession with drawn swords; behind the bandit, the Brothers of Death walked in pairs; the black coffin came last of all—a cross and a death's-head rudely painted on it in white. It was borne by four Brothers of Mercy. Slowly the procession moved along the street of the Jesuits, followed by the murmuring crowd; and thus they led the vampire with the broken wing to the scaffold. My eyes have never lighted on a scene more horrible, seldom on one whose slightest details have so daguerreotyped themselves in my memory.

I was told afterwards that the bandit died without flinching, and that his last words were: "I pray God and the world for forgiveness, for I acknowledge that I have done much evil."

This young man, people said to me, had not become a murderer from personal reasons of revenge, that is, in order to fulfil a Vendetta; he had become a bandit from ambition. His story throws a great deal of light on the frightful state of matters in the island. When Massoni was at the height of his fame [this man had avenged the blood of a relation, and then become bandit], Bracciamozzo, as the people began to call the young Giacomino, after his arm had been mutilated, carried him the means of sustenance: for these bandits have always an understanding with friends and with goat-herds, who bring them food in their lurking-places, and receive payment when the outlaws have money. Giacomino, intoxicated with the renown of the bold bandit Massoni, took it into his head to follow his example, and become the admiration of all Corsica. So he killed a man, took to the bush, and was a bandit. By and bye he had killed ten men, and the people called him Vecchio—the old one, probably because, though still quite young, he had already shed as much blood as an old bandit. One day Vecchio shot the universally esteemed physician Malaspina, uncle of a hospitable entertainer of my own, a gentleman of Balagna; he concealed himself in some brushwood, and fired right into the *diligenza* as it passed along the road from Bastia. The mad devil then sprang back into the mountains, where at length justice overtook him.

A career of this frightful description, then, is possible for a man in Corsica. Nobody there despises the bandit; he is neither thief nor robber, but only fighter, avenger, and free as the eagle on the hills. Hot-headed youths are fired with the thought of winning fame by daring deeds of arms, and of living in the ballads of the people. The inflammable temperament of these men—who have been tamed by no culture, who shun labour as a disgrace, and, thirsting for action, know nothing of the world but the wild mountains among which Nature has cooped them up within their sea-girt island—seems, like a volcano, to insist on vent. On another, wider field, and under other conditions, the same men who house for years in caverns, and fight with sbirri in the bush, would become great soldiers like Sampiero and Gaffori. The nature of the Corsicans is the combative nature; and I can find no more fitting epithet for them than that which Plato applies to the race of men who are born for war, namely, "impassioned."[E] The Corsicans are impassioned natures; passionate in their jealousy and in their pursuit of fame; passionately quick in honour, passionately prone to revenge. Glowing with all this fiery impetuosity, they are the born soldiers that Plato requires.

After Bracciamozzo's execution, I was curious to see whether the *beau monde* of Bastia would promenade as usual on the Place San Nicolao in the evening, and I did not omit walking in that direction. And lo! there they were, moving up and down on the Place Nicolao, where in the morning bandit blood had flowed—the fair dames of Bastia. Nothing now betrayed the scene of the morning; it was as if nothing had happened. I also wandered there; the colouring of the sea was magically beautiful. The fishing-skiffs floated on it with their twinkling lights, and the fishermen sang their beautiful song, *O pescator dell' onda*.

In Corsica they have nerves of granite, and no smelling-bottles.

CHAPTER IX
THE VENDETTA, OR REVENGE TO THE DEATH

"Eterna faremo Vendetta." —*Corsican Ballad.*

The origin of the bandit life is to be sought almost exclusively in the ancient custom of the Vendetta, that is, of exacting blood for blood. Almost all writers on this subject, whom I have read, state that the Vendetta began to be practised in the times when Genoese justice was venal, or favoured murder. Without doubt, the constant wars, and defective administration of justice greatly contributed to the evil, and allowed the barbarous custom to become inveterate, but its root lies elsewhere. For the law of blood for blood does not prevail in Corsica only, it exists also in other countries— in Sardinia, in Calabria, in Sicily, among the Albanians and Montenegrins, among the Circassians, Druses, Bedouins, &c.

Like phenomena must arise under like conditions; and these are not far to seek, for the social condition of all these peoples is similar. They all lead a warlike and primitive life; nature around them is wild and impressive; they are all, with the exception of the Bedouins, poor mountaineers inhabiting regions not easily accessible to culture, and clinging, with the utmost obstinacy, to their primitive condition and ancient barbarous customs; further, they are all equally penetrated with the same intense family sympathies, and these form the sacred basis of such social life as they possess. In a state of nature, and in a society rent asunder by prevailing war and insecurity, the family becomes a state in itself; its members cleave fast to each other; if one is injured, the entire little state is wronged. The family exercises justice only through itself, and the form this exercise of justice takes, is revenge. And thus it appears that the law of blood for blood, though barbarous, still springs from the injured sense of justice, and the natural affection of blood-relations, and that its source is a noble one—the human heart. The Vendetta is barbarian justice. Now the high sense of justice characterizing the Corsicans is acknowledged and eulogized even by the authors of antiquity.

Two noble and great passions have, all along, swayed the the Corsican mind—the love of family and the love of country. In the case of a quite poor people, living in a sequestered island—an island, moreover, mountainous, rugged, and stern—these passions could not but be intense, for to that nation they were all the world. Love of country produced that heroic history of Corsica which we know, and which is in reality nothing but an inveterate Vendetta against Genoa, handed down for ages from father to son; and love of family has produced the no less bloody, and no less heroic history of the Vendetta, the tragedy of which is not yet played to an end. The exhaustless native energy of this little people is really something inconceivable, since, while rending itself to pieces in a manner the most sanguinary, it, at the same time, possessed the strength to maintain so interminable and so glorious a struggle with its external foes.

The love of his friends is still to the Corsican what it was in the old heroic times—a religion; only the love of his country is with him a higher duty. Many examples from Corsican history show this. As among the ancient Hellenes, fraternal love ranked as love's highest and purest form, so it is ranked among the Corsicans. In Corsica, the fraternal relation is viewed as the holiest of all relations, and the names of brother and sister indicate the purest happiness the heart can have—its noblest treasure, or its saddest loss. The eldest brother, as the stay of the family, is revered simply in his character as such. I believe nothing expresses so fully the range of feeling, and the moral nature of a people, as its songs. Now the Corsican song is strictly a dirge, which is at the same time a song of revenge; and most of these songs of revenge are dirges of the sister for her brother who has fallen. I have always found in this poetry that where-ever all love and all laudation are heaped upon the dead, it is said of him, He was my brother. Even the wife, when giving the highest expression to her love, calls her husband, brother. I was astonished to find precisely the same modes of expression and feeling in the Servian popular poetry; with the Servian woman, too, the most endearing name for her husband is brother, and the most sacred oath among the Servians is when a man swears by his brother. Among unsophisticated nations, the natural religion of the heart is preserved in their most ordinary sentiments and relations—for these have their ground in that which alone is lasting in the circumstances of human life; the feeling of a people cleaves to what is simple and enduring. Fraternal love and filial love express the simplest and most enduring relations on earth, for they are relations without passion. And the history of human wo begins with Cain the fratricide.

Wo, therefore, to him who has slain the Corsican's brother or blood-relation! The deed is done; the murderer flees from a double dread—of justice, which punishes murder; and of the kindred of the slain, who avenge murder. For as soon as the deed has become known, the relations of the fallen man take their weapons, and hasten to find the murderer. The murderer has escaped to the woods; he climbs perhaps to the perpetual snow, and lives there with the wild sheep: all trace of him is lost. But the murderer has relatives—brothers, cousins, a father; these relatives know that they must answer for the deed with their lives. They arm themselves, therefore, and are upon their guard. The life of those who are thus involved in a Vendetta is most wretched. He who has to fear the Vendetta instantly shuts himself up in his house, and barricades door and window, in which he leaves only loop-holes. The windows are lined with straw and with mattresses; and this is called *inceppar le fenestre*. The Corsican house among the mountains, in itself high, almost like a tower, narrow, with a high stone stair, is easily turned into a fortress. Intrenched within it, the Corsican keeps close, always on his guard lest a ball reach him through the window. His relatives go armed to their labour in the field, and station sentinels; their lives are in danger at every step. I have been told of instances in which Corsicans did not leave their intrenched dwellings for ten, and even for fifteen years, spending all this period of their lives besieged, and in deadly fear; for Corsican revenge never sleeps, and the Corsican never forgets. Not long ago, in Ajaccio, a man who had lived for ten years in his room, and at last ventured upon the street, fell dead upon the threshold of his house as he re-entered: the ball of him who had watched him for ten years had pierced his heart.

I see, walking about here in the streets of Bastia, a man whom the people call Nasone, from his large nose. He is of gigantic size, and his repulsive features are additionally disfigured by the scar of a frightful wound in his eye. Some years ago he lived in the neighbouring village of Pietra Nera. He insulted another inhabitant of the place; this man swore revenge. Nasone intrenched himself in his house, and closed up the windows, to protect himself from balls. A considerable time passed, and one day he ventured abroad; in a moment his foe sprang upon him, a pruning-knife in his hand. They wrestled fearfully; Nasone was overpowered; and his adversary, who had already given him a blow in the neck, was on the point of hewing off his head on the stump of a tree, when some people came up. Nasone recovered; the other escaped to the macchia. Again a considerable time passed. Once more Nasone ventured into the street: a ball struck him in the eye. They raised the wounded man; and again his giant nature conquered, and healed him. The furious bandit now ravaged his enemy's vineyard during the night, and attempted to fire his house. Nasone removed to the city, and goes about there as a living example of Corsican revenge—an object of horror to the peaceable stranger who inquires his history. I saw the hideous man one day on the shore, but not without his double-barrel. His looks made my flesh creep; he was like the demon of revenge himself.

Not to take revenge is considered by the genuine Corsicans as degrading. Thirst for vengeance is with them an entirely natural sentiment—a passion that has become hallowed. In their songs, revenge has a *cultus*, and is celebrated as a religion of filial piety. Now, a sentiment which the poetry of a people has adopted as an essential characteristic of the nationality is ineradicable; and this in the highest degree, if woman has ennobled it as *her* feeling. Girls and women have composed most of the Corsican songs of revenge, and they are sung from mountain-top to shore. This creates a very atmosphere of revenge, in which the people live and the children grow up, sucking in the wild meaning of the Vendetta with their mother's milk. In one of these songs, it is said that twelve lives are insufficient to avenge the fallen man's—boots! That is Corsican. A man like Hamlet, who struggles to fill himself with the spirit of the Vendetta, and cannot do it, would be pronounced by the Corsicans the most despicable of all poltroons. Nowhere in the world, perhaps, does human blood and human life count for so little as in Corsica. The Corsican is ready to take life, but he is also ready to die.

Any one who shrinks from avenging himself—a milder disposition, perhaps, or a tincture of philosophy, giving him something of Hamlet's hesitancy—is allowed no rest by his relations, and all his acquaintances upbraid him with pusillanimity. To reproach a man for suffering an injury to remain unavenged is called *rimbeccare*. The old Genoese statute punished the *rimbecco* as incitation to murder. The law runs thus, in the nineteenth chapter of these statutes:—

"Of those who upbraid, or say *rimbecco*.—If any one upbraids or says *rimbecco* to another, because that other has not avenged the death of his father, or of his brother, or of any other blood-relation, or because he has not taken vengeance on account of other injuries and insults done upon himself, the person so upbraiding shall be fined in from twenty-five to fifty lire for each time, according to the judgment of the magistrate, and regard being had to the quality of the person, and to other circumstances; and if he does not pay forthwith, or cannot pay within eight days, then shall he be banished from the island for one year, or the corda shall be put upon him once, according to the judgment of the magistrate."

In the year 1581, the severity of the law was so far increased, that the tongue of any one saying *rimbecco* was publicly pierced. Now, it is especially the women who incite the men to revenge, in their dirges over the corpse of the person who has been slain, and by exhibiting the bloody shirt. The mother fastens a bloody rag of the father's shirt to the dress of her son, as a perpetual admonition to him that he has to effect vengeance. The passions of these people have a frightful, a demoniac glow.

In former times the Corsicans practised the chivalrous custom of previously *proclaiming* the war of the Vendetta, and also to what degree of consanguinity the vengeance was to extend. The custom has fallen into disuse. Owing to the close relationship between various families, the Vendetta, of course, crosses and recrosses from one to another, and the Vendetta that thus arises is called in Corsica, *Vendetta transversale*.

In intimate and perfectly natural connexion with this custom, stand the Corsican family feuds, still at the present day the scourge of the unhappy island. The families in a state of Vendetta, immediately draw into it all their relatives, and even friends; and in Corsica, as in other countries where the social condition of the population is similar, the tie of clan is very strong. Thus wars between families arise within one and the same village, or between village and village, glen and glen; and the war continues, and blood is shed for years. Vendetta, or lesser injuries—frequently the merest accidents—afford occasion, and with temperaments so passionate as those of the Corsicans, the slightest dispute may easily terminate in blood, as they all go armed. The feud extends even to the children; instances have been known in which children belonging to families at feud have stabbed and shot each other. There are in Corsica certain relations of clientship— remains of the ancient feudal system of the time of the seigniors, and this clientship prevails more especially in the country beyond the mountains, where the descendants of the old seigniors live on their estates. They have no vassals now, but dependants, friends, people in various ways bound to them. These readily band together as the adherents of the house, and are then, according to the Corsican expression, the *geniali*, their protectors being the *patrocinatori*. Thus, as in the cities of mediæval Italy, we have still in Corsica wars of families, as a last remnant of the feuds of the seigniors. The granite island has maintained an obstinate grasp on her antiquity; her warlike history and constant internal dissensions, caused by the ambition and overbearing arrogance of the seigniors, have stamped the spirit of party on the country, and till the present day it remains rampant.

In Corsica, the frightful word "enemy" has still its full old meaning. The enemy is there the deadly enemy; he who is at enmity with another, goes out to take his enemy's life, and in so doing risks his own. We, too, have brought the old expression "deadly enemy" with us from a more primitive state, but the meaning we attach to it is more abstract. *Our* deadly enemies have no wish to murder us—they do us harm behind our backs, they calumniate us, they injure us secretly in all possible ways, and often we do not so much as know who they are. The hatreds of civilisation have usually something mean in them; and hence, in our modern society, a man of noble feeling can no longer be an enemy—he can only despise. But deadly foes in Corsica attack the life; they have loudly and publicly sworn revenge to the death, and wherever they find each other, they stab and shoot. There is a frightful manliness in this; it shows an imposing, though savage and primitive force of character. Barbarous as such a state of society is, it nevertheless compels us to admire the natural force which it develops, especially as the Corsican avenger is frequently a really tragic individual, urged by fate, because by venerated custom, to murder. For even a noble nature can here become a Cain, and they who wander as bandits on the hills of this island, are often bearers of the curse of barbarous custom, and not of their own vileness, and may be men of virtues that would honour and signalize them in the peaceable life of a civil community.

A single passion, sprung from noble source — revenge, and nothing but revenge! it is wonderful with what irresistible might it seizes on a man. Revenge is, for the poor Corsicans, the dread goddess of Fate, who makes their history. And thus through a single passion man becomes the most frightful demon, and more merciless than the Avenging Angel himself, for he does not content himself with the first-born. Yet dark and sinister as the human form here appears, the dreadful passion, nevertheless, produces its bright contrast. Where foes are foes for life and death, friends are friends for life and death; where revenge lacerates the heart with tiger blood-thirstiness, there love is capable of resolutions the most sublime; there we find heroic forgetfulness of self, and the Divine clemency of forgiveness; and nowhere else is it possible to see the Christian precept, Love thine enemy, realized in a more Christian way than in the land of the Vendetta.

Often, too, mediators, called *parolanti*, interfere between the parties at feud, who swear before them an oath of reconciliation. This oath is religiously sacred; he who breaks it is an outlaw, and dishonoured before God and man. It is seldom broken, but it is broken, for the demon has made his lair in human hearts.

CHAPTER X
BANDIT LIFE

"On! on! These are his footsteps plainly;
Trust the dumb lead of the betraying track!
For as the bloodhounds trace the wounded deer,
So we, by his sweat and blood, do scent him out."

Æschyl *Eumen.*

How the Corsican may be compelled to live as bandit, may be suddenly hurled from his peaceable home, and the quiet of civic life, into the mountain fastnesses, to wander henceforth with the ban of outlawry on him, will be clear from what we have seen of the Vendetta.

The Corsican bandit is not, like the Italian, a thief and robber, but strictly what his name implies—a man whom the law has *banned*. According to the old statute, all those are *banditti* on whom sentence of banishment from the island has been passed, because justice has not been able to lay hands on them. They were declared outlaws, and any one was free to slay a bandit if he came in his way. The idea of banishment has quite naturally been extended to all whom the law proscribes.

The isolation of Corsica, want of means, and love of their native soil, prevent the outlawed Corsicans from leaving their island. In former times, Corsican bandits occasionally escaped to Greece, where they fought bravely; at present, many seek refuge in Italy, and still more in Sardinia, if they prefer to leave their country. Flight from the law is nowhere in the world a simpler matter than in Corsica. The blood has scarcely been shed before the doer of the deed is in the hills, which are everywhere close at hand, and where he easily conceals himself in the impenetrable macchia. From the moment that he has entered the macchia, he is termed bandit. His relatives and friends alone are acquainted with his traces; as long as it is possible, they furnish him with necessaries; many a dark night they secretly receive him into their houses; and however hard pressed, the bandit always finds some goat-herd who will supply his wants.

The main haunts of the bandits are between Tor and Mount Santo Appiano, in the wildernesses of Monte Cinto and Monte Rotondo, and in the inaccessible regions of Niolo. There the deep shades of natural forests that have never seen an axe, and densest brushwood of dwarf-oak, albatro, myrtles, and heath, clothe the declivities of the mountains; wild torrents roar unseen through gloomy ravines, where every path is lost; and caves, grottos, and shattered rocks, afford concealment. There the bandit lives, with the falcon, the fox, and the wild sheep, a life more romantic and more comfortless than that of the American savage. Justice takes her course. She has condemned the bandit *in contumaciam*. The bandit laughs at her; he says in his strange way, "I have got the *sonetto!*" meaning the sentence *in contumaciam*. The sbirri are out upon his track—the avengers of blood the same—he is in constant flight—he is the Wandering Jew of the desolate hills. Now come the conflicts with the gendarmes, heroic, fearful conflicts; his hands grow bloodier; but not with the blood of sbirri only, for the bandit is avenger too; it is not for love to his wretched life—it is far rather for revenge that he lives. He has sworn death to his enemy's kindred. One can imagine what a wild and fierce intensity his vengeful feelings must acquire in the frightful savageness of nature round him, and in its yet more frightful solitude, under constant thoughts of death, and dreams of the scaffold. Sometimes the bandit issues from the mountains to slay his enemy; when he has accomplished his vengeance, he vanishes again in the hills. Not seldom the Corsican bandit rises into a Carl Moor[F]—into an avenger upon society of real or supposed injuries it has done him. The history of the bandit Capracinta of Prunelli is still well known in Corsica. The authorities had unjustly condemned his father to the galleys; the son forthwith took to the macchia with some of his relations, and these avengers from time to time descended from the mountains, and stabbed and shot personal enemies, soldiers, and spies; they one day captured the public executioner, and executed the man himself.

It frequently happens, as we might naturally expect, that the bandits allow themselves to become the tools of others who have a Vendetta to accomplish, and who have recourse to them for the obligation of a dagger or a bullet. In a country of such limited extent, and where the families are so intricately and so widely connected, the bandits cannot but become formidable. They are the sanguinary scourges of the country; agriculture is neglected, the vineyards lie waste—for who will venture into the field if he is menaced by Massoni or Serafino? There are, moreover, among the bandits, men who were previously accustomed to exercise influence upon others, and to take part in public life. Banished to the wilderness, their inactivity becomes intolerable to them; and I was assured that some, in their caverns and hiding-places, continue even to read newspapers which they contrive to procure. They frequently exert an influence of terror on the communal elections, and even on the elections for the General Council. It is no unusual thing for them to threaten judges and witnesses, and to effect a bloody revenge for the sentence pronounced. This, and the great mildness of the verdicts usually brought in by Corsican juries, have been the ground of a wish, already frequently expressed, for the abolition of the jury in Corsica. It is not to be denied that a Corsican jury-box may be influenced by the fear of the vengeance of the bandits; but if we accuse them indiscriminately of excessive leniency, we shall in many cases do these jurymen wrong; for the bandit life and its causes must be viewed under the conditions of Corsican society. I was present at the sitting of a jury in Bastia, an hour after the execution of Bracciamozzo, and in the same building in front of which he had been guillotined; the impression of the public execution seemed to me perceptible in the appearance of the jury and the spectators, but not in that of the prisoner at the bar. He was a young man who had shot some one—he had a stolid hardened face, and his skull looked like a negro's, as if you might use it for an anvil. Neither what had lately occurred, nor the solemnity of the proceedings of the assize, made the slightest impression on the fellow; he showed no trace of embarrassment or fear, but answered the interrogatories of the examining judge with the greatest *sang-froid*, expressing himself briefly and concisely as to the circumstances of his murderous act. I have forgotten to how many years' confinement he was sentenced.

Although the Corsican bandit never lowers himself to common robbery, he holds it not inconsistent with his knightly honour to extort money. The bandits levy black-mail, they tax individuals, frequently whole villages, according to their means, and call in their tribute with great strictness. They impose these taxes as kings of the bush; and I was told their subjects paid them more promptly and conscientiously than they do their taxes to the imperial government of France. It often happens, that the bandit sends a written order into the house of some wealthy individual, summoning him to deposit so many thousand francs in a spot specified; and informing him that if he refuses, himself, his house, and his vineyards, will be destroyed. The usual formula of the threat is—*Si preparasse*—let him prepare. Others, again, fall into the hands of the bandits, and have to pay a ransom for their release. All intercourse becomes thus more and more insecure; agriculture impossible. With the extorted money, the bandits enrich their relatives and friends, and procure themselves many a favour; they cannot put the money to any immediate personal use—for though they had it in heaps, they must nevertheless continue to live in the caverns of the mountain wilds, and in constant flight.

Many bandits have led their outlaw life for fifteen or twenty years, and, small as is the range allowed them by their hills, have maintained themselves successfully against the armed power of the State, victorious in every struggle, till the bandit's fate at length overtook them. The Corsican banditti do not live in troops, as in this way the country could not support them; and, moreover, the Corsican is by nature indisposed to submit to the commands of a leader. They generally live in twos, contracting a sort of brotherhood. They have their deadly enmities among themselves too, and their deadly revenge; this is astonishing, but so powerful is the personal feel of revenge with the Corsican, that the similarity of their unhappy lot never reconciles bandit with bandit, if a Vendetta has existed between them. Many stories are told of one bandit's hunting another among the hills, till he had slain him, on account of a Vendetta. Massoni and Serafino, the two latest bandit heroes of Corsica, were at feud, and shot at each other when opportunity offered. A shot of Massoni's had deprived Serafino of one of his fingers.

The history of the Corsican bandits is rich in extraordinary, heroic, chivalrous, traits of character. Throughout the whole country they sing the bandit dirges; and naturally enough, for it is their own fate, their own sorrow, that they thus sing. Numbers of the bandits have become immortal; but the bold deeds of one especially are still famous. His name was Teodoro, and he called himself king of the mountains. Corsica has thus had two kings of the name of Theodore. Teodoro Poli was enrolled on the list of conscripts, one day in the beginning of the present century. He had begged to be allowed time to raise money for a substitute. He was seized, however, and compelled to join the ranks. Teodoro's high spirit and love of freedom revolted at this. He threw himself into the mountains, and began to live as bandit. He astonished all Corsica by his deeds of audacious hardihood, and became the terror of the island. But no meanness stained his fame; on the contrary, his generosity was the theme of universal praise, and he forgave even relatives of his enemies. His personal appearance was remarkably handsome, and, like his namesake, the king, he was fond of rich and fantastic dress. His lot was shared by his mistress, who lived in affluence on the contributions (*taglia*) which Teodoro imposed upon the villages. Another bandit, called Brusco, to whom he had vowed inviolable friendship, also lived with him, and his uncle Augellone. Augellone means *bird of ill omen* — it is customary for the bandits to give themselves surnames as soon as they begin to play a part in the macchia. The Bird of Ill Omen became envious of Brusco, because Teodoro was so fond of him, and one day he put the cold iron a little too deep into his breast. He thereupon made off into the rocks. When Teodoro heard of the fall of Brusco, he cried aloud for grief, not otherwise than Achilles at the fall of Patroclus, and, according to the old custom of the avengers, began to let his beard grow, swearing never to cut it till he had bathed in the blood of Augellone. A short time passed, and Teodoro was once more seen with his beard cut. These are the little tragedies of which the mountain fastnesses are the scene, and the bandits the players—for the passions of the human heart are everywhere the same. Teodoro at length fell ill. A spy gave information of the hiding-place of the sick lion, and the wild wolf-hounds, the sbirri, were immediately among the hills—they killed Teodoro in a goat-herd's shieling. Two of them, however, learned how dangerously he could still handle his weapons. The popular ballad sings of him, that he fell with the pistol in his hand and the firelock by his side, *come un fiero paladino*—like a proud paladin. Such was the respect which this king of the mountains had inspired, that the people continued to pay his tribute, even after his fall. For at his death there was still some due, and those who owed the arrears came and dropped their money respectfully into the cradle of the little child, the offspring of Teodoro and his queen. Teodoro met his death in the year 1827.

Gallocchio is another celebrated outlaw. He had conceived an attachment for a girl who became faithless to him, and he had forbidden any other to seek her hand. Cesario Negroni wooed and won her. The young Gallocchio gave one of his friends a hint to wound the father-in-law. The wedding guests are dancing merrily, merrily twang the fiddles and the mandolines—a shot! The ball had missed its way, and pierced the father-in-law's heart. Gallocchio now becomes bandit. Cesario intrenches himself. But Gallocchio forces him to leave the building, hunts him through the mountains, finds him, kills him. Gallocchio now fled to Greece, and fought there against the Turks. One day the news reached him that his own brother had fallen in the Vendetta war which had continued to rage between the families involved in it by the death of the father-in-law, and that of Cesario. Gallocchio came back, and killed two brothers of Cesario; then more of his relatives, till at length he had extirpated his whole family. The red Gambini was his comrade; with his aid he constantly repulsed the gendarmes; and on one occasion they bound one of them to a horse's tail, and dragged him so over the rocks. Gambini fled to Greece, where the Turks cut off his head; but Gallocchio died in his sleep, for a traitor shot him.

Santa Lucia Giammarchi is also famous; he held the bush for sixteen years; Camillo Ornano ranged the mountains for fourteen years; and Joseph Antommarchi was seventeen years a bandit.

The celebrated bandit Serafino was shot shortly before my arrival in Corsica; he had been betrayed, and was slain while asleep. Arrighi, too, and the terrible Massoni, had met their death a short time previously—a death as wild and romantic as their lives had been.

Massoni was a man of the most daring spirit, and unheard of energy; he belonged to a wealthy family in Balagna. The Vendetta had driven him into the mountains, where he lived many years, supported by his relations, and favoured by the herdsmen, killing, in frequent struggles, a great number of sbirri. His companions were his brother and the brave Arrighi. One day, a man of the province of Balagna, who had to avenge the blood of a kinsman on a powerful family, sought him out, and asked his assistance. The bandit received him hospitably, and as his provisions happened to be exhausted at the time, went to a shepherd of Monte Rotondo, and demanded a lamb; the herdsman gave him one from his flock. Massoni, however, refused it, saying—"You give me a lean lamb, and yet to-day I wish to do honour to a guest; see, yonder is a fat one, I must have it;" and instantly he shot the fat lamb down, and carried it off to his cave.

The shepherd was provoked by the unscrupulous act. Meditating revenge, he descended from the hills, and offered to show the sbirri Massoni's lurking-place. The shepherd was resolved to avenge the blood of his lamb. The sbirri came up the hills, in force. These Corsican gendarmes, well acquainted with the nature of their country, and practised in banditti warfare, are no less brave and daring than the game they hunt. Their lives are in constant danger when they venture into the mountains; for the bandits are watchful—they keep a look-out with their telescopes, with which they are always provided, and when danger is discovered they are up and away more swiftly than the muffro, the wild sheep; or they let their pursuers come within ball-range, and they never miss their mark.

The sbirri, then, ascended the hills, the shepherd at their head; they crept up the rocks by paths which he alone knew. The bandits were lying in a cave. It was almost inaccessible, and concealed by bushes. Arrighi and the brother of Massoni lay within, Massoni himself sat behind the bushes on the watch.

Some of the sbirri had reached a point above the cave, others guarded its mouth. Those above looked down into the bush to see if they could make out anything. One sbirro took a stone and pitched it into the bush, in which he thought he saw some black object; in a moment a man sprang out, and fired a pistol to awake those in the cavern. But the same instant were heard the muskets of the sbirri, and Massoni fell dead on the spot.

At the report of the fire-arms a man leapt out of the cave, Massoni's brother. He bounded like a wild-goat in daring leaps from crag to crag, the balls whizzing about his head. One hit him fatally, and he fell among the rocks. Arrighi, who saw everything that passed, kept close within the cave. The gendarmes pressed cautiously forward, but for a while no one dared to enter the grotto, till at length some of the hardiest ventured in. There was nobody to be seen; the sbirri, however, were not to be cheated, and confident that the cavern concealed their man, camped about its mouth.

Night came. They lighted torches and fires. It was resolved to starve Arrighi into surrender; in the morning some of them went to a spring near the cave to fetch water—the crack of a musket once, twice, and two sbirri fell. Their companions, infuriated, fired into the cavern—all was still.

The next thing to be done was to bring in the two dead or dying men. After much hesitation a party made the attempt, and again it cost one of them his life. Another day passed. At last it occurred to one of them to smoke the bandit out like a badger—a plan already adopted with success in Algiers. They accordingly heaped dry wood at the entrance of the cave, and set fire to it; but the smoke found egress through chinks in the rock. Arrighi heard every word that was said, and kept up actual dialogues with the gendarmes, who could not see, much less hit him. He refused to surrender, although pardon was promised him. At length the procurator, who had been brought from Ajaccio, sent to the city of Corte for military and an engineer. The engineer was to give his opinion as to whether the cave might be blown up with gunpowder. The engineer came, and said it was possible to throw petards into it. Arrighi heard what was proposed, and found the thought of being blown to atoms with the rocks of his hiding-place so shocking, that he resolved on flight.

He waited till nightfall, then rolling some stones down in a false direction, he sprang away from rock to rock, to reach another mountain. The uncertain shots of the sbirri echoed through the darkness. One ball struck him on the thigh. He lost blood, and his strength was failing; when the day dawned, his bloody track betrayed him, as its bloody sweat the stricken deer. The sbirri took up the scent. Arrighi, wearied to death, had lain down under a block. On this block a sbirro mounted, his piece ready. Arrighi stretched out his head to look around him—a report, and the ball was in his brain.

So died these three outlawed avengers, fortunate that they did not end on the scaffold. Such was their reputation, however, with the people, that none of the inhabitants of Monte Rotondo or its neighbourhood would lend his mule to convey away the bodies of the fallen men. For, said these people, we will have no part in the blood that you have shed. When at length mules had been procured, the dead men, bandits and sbirri, were put upon their backs, and the troop of gendarmes descended the hills, six corpses hanging across the mule-saddles, six men killed in the banditti warfare.

If this island of Corsica could again give forth all the blood which in the course of centuries has been shed upon it—the blood of those who have fallen in battle, and the blood of those who have fallen in the Vendetta—the red deluge would inundate its cities and villages, and drown its people, and crimson the sea from the Corsican shore to Genoa. Verily, violent death has here his peculiar realm.

It is difficult to believe what the historian Filippini tells us, that, in thirty years of his own time, 28,000 Corsicans had been murdered out of revenge. According to the calculation of another Corsican historian, I find that in the thirty-two years previous to 1715, 28,715 murders had been committed in Corsica. The same historian calculates that, according to this proportion, the number of the victims of the Vendetta, from 1359 to 1729, was 333,000. An equal number, he is of opinion, must be allowed for the wounded. We have, therefore, within the time specified, 666,000 Corsicans struck by the hand of the assassin. This people resembles the hydra, whose heads, though cut off, constantly grow on anew.

According to the speech of the Corsican Prefect before the General Council of the Departments, in August 1852, 4300 murders (*assassinats*) have been committed since 1821; during the four years ending with 1851, 833; during the last two of these 319, and during the first seven months of 1852, 99.

The population of the island is 250,000.

The Government proposes to eradicate the Vendetta and the bandit life by a general disarming of the people. How this is to be effected, and whether it is at all practicable, I cannot tell. It will occasion mischief enough, for the bandits cannot be disarmed along with the citizens, and their enemies will be exposed defenceless to their balls. The bandit life, the family feuds, and the Vendetta, which the law has been powerless to prevent, have hitherto made it necessary to permit the carrying of arms. For, since the law cannot protect the individual, it must leave him at liberty to protect himself; and thus it happens that Corsican society finds itself, in a sense, without the pale of the state, in the condition of natural law, and armed self-defence. This is a strange and startling phenomenon in Europe in our present century. It is long since the wearing of pistols and daggers was forbidden, but every one here carries his double-barreled gun, and I have found half villages in arms, as if in a struggle against invading barbarians—a wild, fantastic spectacle, these reckless men all about one in some lonely and dreary region of the hills, in their shaggy pelone, and Phrygian cap, the leathern cartridge-belt about their waist, and gun upon their shoulder.

Nothing is likely to eradicate the Vendetta, murder, and the bandit life, but advanced culture. Culture, however, advances very slowly in Corsica. Colonization, the making of roads through the interior, such an increase of general intercourse and industry as would infuse life into the ports—this might amount to a complete disarming of the population. The French Government, utterly powerless against the defiant Corsican spirit, most justly deserves reproach for allowing an island which possesses the finest climate; districts of great fertility; a position commanding the entire Mediterranean between Spain, France, Italy, and Africa; and the most magnificent gulfs and harbours; which is rich in forests, in minerals, in healing springs, and in fruits, and is inhabited by a brave, spirited, highly capable people—for allowing Corsica to become a Montenegro or Italian Ireland.

BOOK IV
WANDERINGS IN CORSICA

CHAPTER I
SOUTHERN PART OF CAPE CORSO

Cape Corso is the long narrow peninsula which Corsica throws out to the north.

It is traversed by a rugged mountain range, called the Serra, the highest summits of which, Monte Alticcione and Monte Stello, reach an altitude of more than 5000 feet. Rich and beautiful valleys run down on both sides to the sea.

I had heard a great deal of the beauty of the valleys of this region, of their fertility in wine and oranges, and of the gentle manners of their inhabitants, so that I began my wanderings in it with true pleasure. A cheerful and festive impression is produced at the very first by the olive-groves that line the excellent road along the shore, through the canton San Martino. Chapels appearing through the green foliage; the cupolas of family tombs; solitary cottages on the strand; here and there a forsaken tower, in the rents of which the wild fig-tree clings, while the cactus grows profusely at its base,—make the country picturesque. The coast of Corsica is set round and round with these towers, which the Pisans and Genoese built to ward off the piratical attacks of the Saracens. They are round or square, built of brown granite, and stand isolated. Their height is from thirty to fifty feet. A company of watchers lay within, and alarmed the surrounding country when the Corsairs approached. All these towers are now forsaken, and gradually falling to ruin. They impart a strangely romantic character to the Corsican shores.

It was pleasant to wander through this region in the radiant morning; the eye embraced the prospect seawards, with the fine forms of the islands of Elba, Capraja, and Monte Cisto, and was again relieved by the mountains and valleys descending close to the shore. The heights here enclose, like sides of an amphitheatre, little, blooming, shady dales, watered by noisy brooks. Scattered round, in a rude circle, stand the black villages, with their tall church-towers and old cloisters. On the meadows are herdsmen with their herds, and where the valley opens to the sea, always a tower and a solitary hamlet by the shore, with a boat or two in its little haven.

Every morning at sunrise, troops of women and girls may be seen coming from Cape Corso to Bastia, with produce for the market. They have a pretty blue or brown dress for the town, and a clean handkerchief wound as mandile round the hair. These forms moving along the shore through the bright morning, with their neat baskets, full of laughing, golden fruit, enliven the way very agreeably; and perhaps it would be difficult to find anything more graceful than one of those slender, handsome girls pacing towards you, light-footed and elastic as a Hebe, with her basket of grapes on her head. They are all in lively talk with their neighbours as they pass, and all give you the same beautiful, light-hearted *Evviva*. Nothing better certainly can one mortal wish another than that he should *live*.

But now forward, for the sun is in Leo, and in two hours he will be fierce. And behind the Tower of Miomo, towards the second pieve of Brando, the road ceases, and we must climb like the goat, for there are few districts in Cape Corso supplied with anything but footpaths. From the shore, at the lonely little Marina di Basina, I began to ascend the hills, on which lie the three communes that form the pieve of Brando. The way was rough and steep, but cheered by gushing brooks and luxuriant gardens. The slopes are quite covered with these, and they are full of grapes, oranges, and olives— fruits in which Brando specially abounds. The fig-tree bends low its laden branches, and holds its ripe fruit steadily to the parched mouth, unlike the tree of Tantalus.

On a declivity towards the sea, is the beautiful stalactite cavern of Brando, not long since discovered. It lies in the gardens of a retired officer. An emigrant of Modena had given me a letter for this gentleman, and I called on him at his mansion. The grounds are magnificent. The Colonel has transformed the whole shore into a garden, which hangs above the sea, dreamy and cool with silent olives, myrtles, and laurels; there are cypresses and pines, too, isolated or in groups, flowers everywhere, ivy on the walls, vine-trellises heavy with grapes, oranges tree on tree, a little summer-house hiding among the greenery, a cool grotto deep under ground, loneliness, repose, a glimpse of emerald sky, and the sea with its hermit islands, a glimpse into your own happy human heart;—it were hard to tell when it might be best to live here, when you are still young, or when you have grown old.

An elderly gentleman, who was looking out of the villa, heard me ask the gardener for the Colonel, and beckoned me to come to him. His garden had already shown me what kind of a man he was, and the little room into which I now entered told his character more and more plainly. The walls were covered with symbolic paintings; the different professions were fraternizing in a group, in which a husbandman, a soldier, a priest, and a scholar, were shaking hands; the five races were doing the same in another picture, where a European, an Asiatic, a Moor, an Australian, and a Redskin, sat sociably drinking round a table, encircled by a gay profusion of curling vine-wreaths. I immediately perceived that I was in the beautiful land of Icaria, and that I had happened on no other personage than the excellent uncle of Goethe's Wanderjahre. And so it was. He was the uncle—a bachelor, a humanistic socialist, who, as country gentleman and land-owner, diffused widely around him the beneficial influences of his own great though noiseless activity.

He came towards me with a cheerful, quiet smile, the *Journal des Débats* in his hand, pleased apparently with what he had been reading in it.

"I have read in your garden and in your room, signore, the *Contrat Social* of Rousseau, and some of the *Republic* of Plato. You show me that you are the countryman of the great Pasquale."

We talked long on a great variety of subjects—on civilisation and on barbarism, and how impotent theory was proving itself. But these are old affairs, that every reflecting man has thought of and talked about.

Much musing on this interview, I went down to the grotto after taking leave of the singular man, who had realized for me so unexpectedly the creation of the poet. After all, this is a strange island. Yesterday a bandit who has murdered ten men out of *capriccio*, and is being led to the scaffold; to-day a practical philosopher, and philanthropic advocate of universal brotherhood—both equally genuine Corsicans, their history and character the result of the history of their nation. As I passed under the fair trees of the garden, however, I said to myself that it was not difficult to be a philanthropist in paradise. I believe that the wonderful power of early Christianity arose from the circumstance that its teachers were poor, probably unfortunate men.

There is a Corsican tradition that St. Paul landed on Cape Corso—the Promontorium Sacrum, as it was called in ancient times—and there preached the gospel. It is certain that Cape Corso was the district of the island into which Christianity was first introduced. The little region, therefore, has long been sacred to the cause of philanthropy and human progress.

The daughter of one of the gardeners led me to the grotto. It is neither very high nor very deep, and consists of a series of chambers, easily traversed. Lamps hung from the roof. The girl lighted them, and left me alone. And now a pale twilight illuminated this beautiful crypt, of such bizarre stalactite formations as only a Gothic architect could imagine—in pointed arches, pillar-capitals, domed niches, and rosettes. The grottos of Corsica are her oldest Gothic churches, for Nature built them in a mood of the most playful fantasy. As the lamps glimmered, and shone on, and shone through, the clear yellow stalactite, the cave was completely like the crypt of some cathedral. Left in this twilight, I had the following little fantasy in stalactite—

A wondrous maiden sat wrapped in a white veil on a throne of the clearest alabaster. She never moved. She wore on her head a lotos-flower, and on her breast a carbuncle. The eye could not cease to gaze on the veiled maiden, for she stirred a longing in the bosom. Before her kneeled many little gnomes; the poor fellows were all of dropstone, all stalactites, and they wore little yellow crowns of the fairest alabaster. They never moved; but they all held their hands stretched out towards the white maiden, as if they wished to lift her veil, and bitter drops were falling from their eyes. It seemed to me as if I knew some of them, and as if I must call them by their names. "This is the goddess Isis," said the toad sneeringly; she was sitting on a stone, and, I think, threw a spell on them all with her eyes. "He who does not know the right word, and cannot raise the veil of the beautiful maiden, must weep himself to stone like these. Stranger, wilt thou say the word?"

I was just falling asleep—for I was very tired, and the grotto was so dim and cool, and the drops tinkled so slowly and mournfully from the roof—when the gardener's daughter entered, and said: "It is time!" "Time!

to raise the veil of Isis?—O ye eternal gods!" "Yes, Signore, to come out to the garden and the bright sun." I thought she said well, and I immediately followed her.

"Do you see this firelock, Signore? We found it in the grotto, quite coated with the dropstone, and beside it were human bones; likely they were the bones and gun of a bandit; the poor wretch had crept into this cave, and died in it like a wounded deer." Nothing was now left of the piece but the rusty barrel. It may have sped the avenging bullet into more than one heart. Now I hold it in my hand like some fossil of horrid history, and it opens its mouth and tells me stories of the Vendetta.

CHAPTER II
FROM BRANDO TO LURI

"Say, whither rov'st thou lonely through the hills,

A stranger in the region?" — *Odyssey*.

I now descended to Erba Lunga, an animated little coast village, which sends fishing-boats daily to Bastia. The oppressive heat compelled me to rest here for some hours.

This was once the seat of the most powerful seigniors of Cape Corso, and above Erba Lunga stands the old castle of the Signori dei Gentili. The Gentili, with the Seigniors da Mare, were masters of the Cape. The neighbouring island of Capraja also belonged to the latter family. Oppressively treated by its violent and unscrupulous owners, the inhabitants rebelled in 1507, and placed themselves under the Bank of Genoa. Cape Corso was always, from its position, considered as inclining to Genoa, and its people were held to be unwarlike. Even at the present day the men of the Corsican highlands look down on the gentle and industrious people of the peninsula with contempt. The historian Filippini says of the Cape Corsicans: "The inhabitants of Cape Corso clothe themselves well, and are, on account of their trade and their vicinity to the Continent, much more domestic than the other Corsicans. Great justice, truth, and honour, prevail among them. All their industry is in wine, which they export to the Continent." Even in Filippini's time, therefore, the wine of Cape Corso was in reputation. It is mostly white; the vintage of Luri and Rogliano is said to be the best; this wine is among the finest that Southern Europe produces, and resembles the Spanish, the Syracusan, and the Cyprian. But Cape Corso is also rich in oranges and lemons.

If you leave the sea and go higher up the hills, you lose all the beauty of this interesting little wine-country, for it nestles low in the valleys. The whole of Cape Corso is a system of such valleys on both its coasts; but the dividing ranges are rugged and destitute of shade; their low wood gives no shelter from the sun. Limestone, serpentine, talc, and porphyry, show themselves. After a toilsome journey, I at length arrived late in the evening in the valley of Sisco. A paesane had promised me hospitality there, and

I descended into the valley rejoicing in the prospect. But which was the commune of Sisco? All around at the foot of the hills, and higher up, stood little black villages, the whole of them comprehended under the name Sisco. Such is the Corsican custom, to give all the hamlets of a valley the name of the pieve, although each has its own particular appellation. I directed my course to the nearest village, whither an old cloister among pines attracted me, and seemed to say: Pilgrim, come, have a draught of good wine. But I was deceived, and I had to continue climbing for an hour, before I discovered my host of Sisco. The little village lay picturesquely among wild black rocks, a furious stream foaming through its midst, and Monte Stello towering above it.

I was kindly received by my friend and his wife, a newly married couple, and found their house comfortable. A number of Corsicans came in with their guns from the hills, and a little company of country-people was thus formed. The women did not mingle with us; they prepared the meal, served, and disappeared. We conversed agreeably till bedtime. The people of Sisco are poor, but hospitable and friendly. On the morrow, my entertainer awoke me with the sun; he took me out before his house, and then gave me in charge to an old man, who was to guide me through the labyrinthine hill-paths to the right road for Crosciano. I had several letters with me for other villages of the Cape, given me by a Corsican the evening before. Such is the beautiful and praiseworthy custom in Corsica; the hospitable entertainer gives his departing guest a letter, commending him to his relations or friends, who in their turn receive him hospitably, and send him away with another letter. For days thus you travel as guest, and are everywhere made much of; as inns in these districts are almost unknown, travelling would otherwise be an impossibility.

Sisco has a church sacred to Saint Catherine, which is of great antiquity, and much resorted to by pilgrims. It lies high up on the shore. Once a foreign ship had been driven upon these coasts, and had vowed relics to the church for its rescue; which relics the mariners really did consecrate to the holy Saint Catherine. They are highly singular relics, and the folk of Sisco may justly be proud of possessing such remarkable articles, as, for example, a piece of the clod of earth from which Adam was modelled, a few almonds from the garden of Eden, Aaron's rod that blossomed, a piece of manna, a piece of the hairy garment of John the Baptist, a piece of Christ's cradle, a piece of the rod on which the sponge dipped in vinegar was raised to Christ's lips, and the celebrated rod with which Moses smote the Red Sea.

Picturesque views abound in the hills of Sisco, and the country becomes more and more beautiful as we advance northwards. I passed through a great number of villages—Crosciano, Pietra, Corbara, Cagnano—on the slopes of

Monte Alticcione, but I found some of them utterly poverty-stricken; even their wine was exhausted. As I had refused breakfast in the house of my late entertainer, in order not to send the good people into the kitchen by sunrise, and as it was now mid-day, I began to feel unpleasantly hungry. There were neither figs nor walnuts by the wayside, and I determined that, happen what might, I would satisfy my craving in the next paese. In three houses they had nothing—not wine, not bread—all their stores were expended. In the fourth, I heard the sound of a guitar. I entered. Two gray-haired men in ragged *blouses* were sitting, the one on the bed, the other on a stool. He who sat on the bed held his *cetera*, or cithern, in his arm, and played, while he seemed lost in thought. Perhaps he was dreaming of his vanished youth. He rose, and opening a wooden chest, brought out a half-loaf carefully wrapped in a cloth, and handed me the bread that I might cut some of it for myself. Then he sat down again on the bed, played his cithern, and sang a *vocero*, or dirge. As he sang, I ate the bread of the bitterest poverty, and it seemed to me as if I had found the old harper of *Wilhelm Meister*, and that he sung to me the song—

> "Who ne'er his bread with tears did eat,
>
> Who ne'er the weary midnight hours
>
> Weeping upon his bed hath sate,
>
> He knows you not, ye heavenly powers!"

Heaven knows how Goethe has got to Corsica, but this is the second of his characters I have fallen in with on this wild cape.

Having here had my hunger stilled, and something more, I wandered onwards. As I descended into the vale of Luri, the region around me, I found, had become a paradise. Luri is the loveliest valley in Cape Corso, and also the largest, though it is only ten kilometres long, and five broad. [G] Inland it is terminated by beautiful hills, on the highest of which stands a black tower. This is the tower of Seneca, so called because, according to the popular tradition, it was here that Seneca spent his eight years of Corsican exile. Towards the sea, the valley slopes gently down to the marina of Luri. A copious stream waters the whole dale, and is led in canals through the gardens. Here lie the communes which form the pieve of Luri, rich, and comfortable-looking, with their tall churches, cloisters, and towers, in the midst of a vegetation of tropical luxuriance. I have seen many a beautiful valley in Italy, but I remember none that wore a look so laughing and winsome as that fair vale of Luri. It is full of vineyards, covered with oranges and lemons, rich in fruit-trees of every kind, in melons, and all sorts of garden produce, and the higher you ascend, the denser become the groves of chestnuts, walnuts, figs, almonds, and olives.

CHAPTER III
PINO

A good road leads upwards from the marina of Luri. You move in one continual garden—in an atmosphere of balsamic fragrance. Cottages approaching the elegant style of Italian villas indicate wealth. How happy must the people be here, if their own passions deal as gently with them as the elements. A man who was dressing his vineyard saw me passing along, and beckoned me to come in, and I needed no second bidding. Here is the place for swinging the thyrsus-staff; no grape disease here—everywhere luscious maturity and joyous plenty. The wine of Luri is beautiful, and the citrons of this valley are said to be the finest produced in the countries of the Mediterranean. It is the thick-skinned species of citrons called *cedri* which is here cultivated; they are also produced in abundance all along the west coast, but more especially in Centuri. The tree, which is extremely tender, demands the utmost attention. It thrives only in the warmest exposures, and in the valleys which are sheltered from the Libeccio. Cape Corso is the very Elysium of this precious tree of the Hesperides.

I now began to cross the Serra towards Pino, which lies at its base on the western side. My path lay for a long time through woods of walnut-trees, the fruit of which was already ripe; and I must here confirm what I had heard, that the nut-trees of Corsica will not readily find their equals. Fig-trees, olives, chestnuts, afford variety at intervals. It is pleasant to wander through the deep shades of a northern forest of beeches, oaks, or firs, but the forests of the south are no less glorious; walking beneath these trees one feels himself in noble company. I ascended towards the Tower of Fondali, which lies near the little village of the same name, quite overshadowed with trees, and finely relieving their rich deep green. From its battlements you look down over the beautiful valley to the blue sea, and above you rise the green hills, summit over summit, with forsaken black cloisters on them; on the highest rock of the Serra is seen the Tower of Seneca, which, like a stoic standing wrapt in deep thought, looks darkly down over land and sea. The many towers that stand here—for I counted numbers of them—indicate that this valley of Luri was richly cultivated, even in earlier times; they were doubtless built for its protection. Even Ptolemy is acquainted with the Vale of Luri, and in his Geography calls it Lurinon.

I climbed through a shady wood and blooming wilderness of trailing plants to the ridge of the Serra, close beneath the foot of the cone on which the Tower of Seneca stands. From this point both seas are visible, to the right and to the left. I now descended towards Pino, where I was expected by some Carrarese statuaries. The view of the western coast with its red reefs and little rocky zig-zag coves, and of the richly wooded pieve of Pino, came upon me with a most agreeable surprise. Pino has some large turreted mansions lying in beautiful parks; they might well serve for the residence of any Roman Duca:—for Corsica has its *millionnaires*. On the Cape live about two hundred families of large means—some of these possessed of quite enormous wealth, gained either by themselves or by relations, in the Antilles, Mexico, and Brazil.

One fortunate Crœsus of Pino inherited from an uncle of his in St. Thomas a fortune of ten millions of francs. Uncles are most excellent individuals. To have an uncle is to have a constant stake in the lottery. Uncles can make anything of their nephews—*millionnaires*, immortal historical personages. The nephew of Pino has rewarded his meritorious relative with a mausoleum of Corsican marble—a pretty Moorish family tomb on a hill by the sea. It was on this building my Carrarese friends were engaged.

In the evening we paid a visit to the Curato. We found him walking before his beautifully-situated parsonage, in the common brown Corsican jacket, and with the Phrygian cap of liberty on his head. The hospitable gentleman led us into his parlour. He seated himself in his arm-chair, ordered the Donna to bring wine, and, when the glasses came in, reached his cithern from the wall. Then he began with all the heartiness in the world to play and sing the Paoli march. The Corsican clergy were always patriotic men, and in many battles fought in the ranks with their parishioners. The parson of Pino now put his Mithras-cap to rights, and began a serenade to the beautiful Marie. I shook him heartily by the hand, thanked him for wine and song, and went away to the paese where I was to lodge for the night. Next morning we proposed wandering a while longer in Pino, and then to visit Seneca in his tower.

On this western coast of Cape Corso, below Pino, lies the fifth and last pieve of the Cape, called Nonza. Near Nonza stands the tower which I mentioned in the History of the Corsicans, when recording an act of heroic patriotism. There is another intrepid deed connected with it. In the year 1768 it was garrisoned by a handful of militia, under the command of an old captain, named Casella. The French were already in possession of the Cape, all the other captains having capitulated. Casella refused to follow their example. The tower mounted one cannon; they had plenty of ammunition, and the militia had their muskets. This was sufficient, said the old captain, to defend the place against a whole army; and if matters came to the worst, then you could blow yourself up. The militia knew their man, and that he was in the habit of doing what he said. They accordingly took themselves off during the night, leaving their muskets, and the old captain found himself alone. He concluded, therefore, to defend the tower himself. The cannon was already loaded; he charged all the pieces, distributed them over the various shot-holes, and awaited the French. They came, under the command of General Grand-Maison. As soon as they were within range, Casella first discharged the cannon at them, and then made a diabolical din with the muskets. The French sent a flag of truce to the tower, with the information that the entire Cape had surrendered, and summoning the commandant to do the same with all his garrison, and save needless bloodshed. Hereupon Casella replied that he would hold a council of war, and retired. After some time he reappeared and announced that the garrison of Nonza would capitulate under condition that it should be allowed to retire with the honours of war, and with all its baggage and artillery, for which the French were to furnish conveyances. The conditions were agreed to. The French had drawn up before the tower, and were now ready to receive the garrison, when old Casella issued, with his firelock, his pistols, and his sabre. The French waited for the garrison, and, surprised that the men did not make their appearance, the officer in command asked why they were so long in coming out. "They *have* come out," answered the Corsican; "for I am the garrison of the Tower of Nonza." The duped officer became furious, and rushed upon Casella. The old man drew his sword, and stood on the defensive. In the meantime, Grand-Maison himself hastened up, and, having heard the story, was sufficiently astonished. He instantly put his officer under strict arrest, and not only fulfilled every stipulation of Casella's to the letter, but sent him with a guard of honour, and a letter expressive of his admiration, to Paoli's head-quarters.

Above Pino extends the canton of Rogliano, with Ersa and Centuri—a district of remarkable fertility in wine, oil, and lemons, and rivalling Luri in cultivation. The five pievi of the entire Cape—Brando, Martino, Luri, Rogliano, and Nonza—contain twenty-one communes, and about 19,000 inhabitants; almost as many, therefore, as the island of Elba. Going northwards, from Rogliano over Ersa, you reach the extreme northern point of Corsica, opposite to which, with a lighthouse on it, lies the little island of Girolata.

CHAPTER IV
THE TOWER OF SENECA

"Melius latebam procul ab invidiæ malis
Remotus inter Corsici rupes maris."

Roman Tragedy of Octavia.

The Tower of Seneca can be seen at sea, and from a distance of many miles. It stands on a gigantic, quite naked mass of granite, which rises isolated from the mountain-ridge, and bears on its summit the black weather-beaten pile. The ruin consists of a single round tower—lonely and melancholy it stands there, hung with hovering mists, all around bleak heath-covered hills, the sea on both sides deep below.

If, as imaginative tradition affirms, the banished stoic spent eight years of exile here, throning among the clouds, in the silent rocky wilds—then he had found a place not ill adapted for a philosopher disposed to make wise reflections on the world and fate; and to contemplate with wonder and reverence the workings of the eternal elements of nature. The genius of Solitude is the wise man's best instructor; in still night hours he may have given Seneca insight into the world's transitoriness, and shown him the vanity of great Rome, when the exile was inclined to bewail his lot. After Seneca returned from his banishment to Rome, he sometimes, perhaps, among the abominations of the court of Nero, longed for the solitary days of Corsica. There is an old Roman tragedy called *Octavia*, the subject of which is the tragic fate of Nero's first empress.[H] In this tragedy Seneca appears as the moralizing figure, and on one occasion delivers himself as follows:—

"O Lady Fortune, with the flattering smile
On thy deceitful face, why hast thou raised
One so contented with his humble lot
To height so giddy? Wheresoe'er I look,
Terrors around me threaten, and at last
The deeper fall is sure. Ah, happier far—
Safe from the ills of envy once I hid—

Among the rocks of sea-girt Corsica.
I was my own; my soul was free from care,
In studious leisure lightly sped the hours.
Oh, it was joy,—for in the mighty round
Of Nature's works is nothing more divine,—
To look upon the heavens, the sacred sun,
With all the motions of the universe,
The seasonable change of morn and eve,
The orb of Phœbe and the attendant stars,
Filling the night with splendour far and wide.
All this, when it grows old, shall rush again
Back to blind chaos; yea, even now the day,
The last dread day is near, and the world's wreck
Shall crush this impious race."

A rude sheep-track led us up the mountain over shattered rocks. Half-way up to the tower, completely hidden among crags and bushes, lies a forsaken Franciscan cloister. The shepherds and the wild fig-tree now dwell in its halls, and the raven croaks the *de profundis*. But the morning and the evening still come there to hold their silent devotions, and kindle incense of myrtle, mint, and cytisus. What a fragrant breath of herbs is about us! what morning stillness on the mountains and the sea!

We stood on the Tower of Seneca. We had clambered on hands and feet to reach its walls. By holding fast to projecting ledges and hanging perilously over the abyss, you can gain a window. There is no other entrance into the tower; its outer works are destroyed, but the remains show that a castle, either of the seigniors of Cape Corso or of the Genoese, stood here. The tower is built of astonishingly firm material; its battlements, however, are rent and dilapidated. It is unlikely that Seneca lived on this Aornos, this height forsaken by the very birds, and certainly too lofty a flight for moral philosophers—a race that love the levels. Seneca probably lived in one of the Roman colonies, Aleria or Mariana, where the stoic, accustomed to the conveniences of Roman city life, may have established himself comfortably in some house near the sea; so that the favourite mullet and tunny had not far to travel from the strand to his table.

A picture from the fearfully beautiful world of imperial Rome passed before me as I sat on Seneca's tower. Who can say he rightly and altogether comprehends this world? It often seems to me as if it were Hades, and as if the whole human race of the period were holding in its obscure twilight a great diabolic carnival of fools, dancing a gigantic, universal ballet before the Emperor's throne, while the Emperor sits there gloomy as Pluto, only breaking out now and then into insane laughter; for it is the maddest carnival this; old Seneca plays in it too, among the Pulcinellos, and appears in character with his bathing-tub.

Even a Seneca may have something tragi-comic about him, if we think of him, for example, in the pitiably ludicrous shape in which he is represented in the old statue that bears his name. He stands there naked, a cloth about his loins, in the bath in which he means to die, a sight heart-rending to behold, with his meagre form so tremulous about the knees, and his face so unutterably wo-begone. He resembles one of the old pictures of St. Jerome, or some starveling devotee attenuated by penance; he is tragi-comic, provocative of laughter no less than pity, as many of the representations of the old martyrs are, the form of their suffering being usually so whimsical.

Seneca was born, B.C. 3, at Cordova, in Spain, of equestrian family. His mother, Helvia, was a woman of unusual ability; his father, Lucius Annæus, a rhetorician of note, who removed with his family to Rome. In the time of Caligula, Seneca the younger distinguished himself as an orator, and Stoic philosopher of extraordinary learning. A remarkably good memory had been of service to him. He himself relates that after hearing two thousand names once repeated, he could repeat them again in the same order, and that he had no difficulty in doing the same with two hundred verses.

In favour at the court of Claudius, he owed his fall to Messalina. She accused him of an intrigue with the notorious Julia, the daughter of Germanicus, and the most profligate woman in Rome. The imputation is doubly comical, as coming from a Messalina, and because it makes us think of Seneca the moralist as a Don Juan. It is hard to say how much truth there is in the scandalous story, but Rome was a strange place, and nothing can be more bizarre than some of the characters it produced. Julia was got out of the way, and Don Juan Seneca sent into banishment among the barbarians of Corsica. The philosopher now therefore became, without straining the word, a Corsican bandit.

There was in those days no more terrible punishment than that of exile, because expulsion from Rome was banishment from the world. Eight long years Seneca lived on the wild island. I cannot forgive my old friend, therefore, for recording nothing about its nature, about the history and condition of its inhabitants, at that period. A single chapter from the pen of Seneca on these subjects, would now be of great value to us. But to have said nothing about the barbarous country of his exile, was very consistent with his character as Roman. Haughty, limited, void of sympathetic feeling for his kind, was the man of those times. How different is the relation in which we now stand to nature and history!

For the banished Seneca the island was merely a prison that he detested. The little that he says about it in his book *De Consolatione ad Matrem Helviam*, shows how little he knew of it. For though it was no doubt still more rude and uncultivated than at present, its natural grandeur was the same. He composed the following epigrams on Corsica, which are to be found in his poetical works:—

> "Corsican isle, where his town the Phocæan colonist planted,
>
> Corsica, called by the Greeks Cyrnus in earlier days,
>
> Corsica, less than thy sister Sardinia, longer than Elba,
>
> Corsica, traversed by streams—streams that the fisherman loves,
>
> Corsica, dreadful land! when thy summer's suns are returning,
>
> Scorch'd more cruelly still, when the fierce Sirius shines;
>
> Spare the sad exile—spare, I mean, the hopelessly buried—
>
> Over his living remains, Corsica, light lie thy dust."

The second has been said to be spurious, but I do not see why our heart-broken exile should not have been its author, as well as any of his contemporaries or successors in Corsican banishment.

> "Rugged the steeps that enclose the barbarous Corsican island,
>
> Savage on every side stretches the solitude vast;
>
> Autumn ripens no fruits, nor summer prepares here a harvest.
>
> Winter, hoary and chill, wants the Palladian gift;[I]
>
> Never rejoices the spring in the coolness of shadowy verdure,
>
> Here not a blade of grass pierces the desolate plain,
>
> Water is none, nor bread, nor a funeral-pile for the stranger—
>
> Two are there here, and no more—the Exile alone with his Wo."[J]

The Corsicans have not failed to take revenge on Seneca. Since he gives them and their country such a disgraceful character, they have connected a scandalous story with his name. Popular tradition has preserved only a single incident from the period of his residence in Corsica, and it is as follows:—As Seneca sat in his tower and looked down into the frightful island, he saw the Corsican virgins, that they were fair. Thereupon the philosopher descended, and he dallied with the daughters of the land. One comely shepherdess did he honour with his embrace; but the kinsfolk of the maiden came upon him suddenly, and took him, and scourged the philosopher with nettles.

Ever since, the nettle grows profusely and ineradicably round the Tower of Seneca, as a warning to moral philosophers. The Corsicans call it *Ortica de Seneca*.

Unhappy Seneca! He is always getting into tragi-comic situations. A Corsican said to me: "You have read what Seneca says of us? *ma era un birbone*—but he was a great rascal." *Seneca morale*, says Dante,—*Seneca birbone*, says the Corsican—another instance of his love for his country.

Other sighs of exile did the unfortunate philosopher breathe out in verse—some epigrams to his friends, one on his native city of Cordova. If Seneca wrote any of the tragedies which bear his name in Corsica, it must certainly have been the Medea. Where could he have found a locality more likely to have inspired him to write on a subject connected with the Argonauts, than this sea-girt island? Here he might well make his chorus sing those remarkable verses which predict Columbus:—

"A time shall come
In the late ages,
When Ocean shall loosen
The bonds of things;
Open and vast
Then lies the earth;
Then shall Tiphys
New worlds disclose.
And Thule no more
Be the farthest land."

Now the great navigator Columbus was born in the Genoese territory, not far from Corsica. The Corsicans will have it that he was born in Calvi, in Corsica itself, and they maintain this till the present day.

CHAPTER V
SENECA MORALE

— —"e vidi Orfeo

Tullio, e Livio, e Seneca morale." —Dante.

Fair fruits grew for Seneca in his exile; and perhaps he owed some of his exalted philosophy rather to his Corsican solitude than to the teachings of an Attalus or a Socio. In the Letter of Consolation to his mother, he writes thus at the close:—You must believe me happy and cheerful, as when in prosperity. That is true prosperity when the mind devotes itself to its pursuits without disturbing thoughts, and, now pleasing itself with lighter studies, now thirsting after truth, elevates itself to the contemplation of its own nature and of that of the universe. First, it investigates the countries and their situations, then the nature of the circumfluent sea, and its changes of ebb and flow; then it contemplates the terrible powers that lie between heaven and earth—the thunder, lightnings, winds, rain, snow and hail, that disquiet this space; at last, when it has wandered through the lower regions, it takes its flight to the highest, and enjoys the beautiful spectacle of celestial things, and, mindful of its own eternity, enters into all which has been and shall be to all eternity.

When I took up Seneca's Letter of Consolation to his mother, I was not a little curious to see how he would console her. How would one of the thousand cultivated exiles scattered over the world at the present time console *his* mother? Seneca's letter is a quite methodically arranged treatise, consisting of seventeen chapters. It is a more than usually instructive contribution to the psychology of these old Stoics. The son is not so particularly anxious to console his mother as to write an excellent and elegant treatise, the logic and style of which shall procure him admiration. He is quite proud that his treatise will be a species of composition hitherto unknown in the world of letters. The vain man writes to his mother like an author to a critic with whom he is coolly discussing the *pros* and *cons* of his subject. I have, says he, consulted all the works of the great geniuses who have written upon the methods of moderating grief, but I have found no example of any one's consoling his friends when it was himself they were lamenting. In this new case, therefore, in which I found myself, I was embarrassed, and feared lest

I might open the wounds instead of healing them. Must not a man who raises his head from the funeral-pile itself to comfort his relatives, need new words, such as the common language of daily life does not supply him with? Every great and unusual sorrow must make its own selection of words, if it does not refuse itself language altogether. I shall venture to write to you, therefore, not in confidence on my talent, but because I myself, the consoler, am here to serve as the most effectual consolation. For your son's sake, to whom you can deny nothing, you will not, as I trust (though all grief is stubborn), refuse to permit bounds to be set to your grief.

He now begins to console after his new fashion, reckoning up to his mother all that she has already suffered, and drawing the conclusion that she must by this time have become callous. Throughout the whole treatise you hear the skeleton of the arrangement rattling. Firstly, his mother is not to grieve on his account; secondly, his mother is not to grieve on her own account. The letter is full of the most beautiful stoical contempt of the world.

"Yet it is a terrible thing to be deprived of one's country." What is to be said to this?—Mother, consider the vast multitude of people in Rome; the greater number of them have congregated there from all parts of the world. One is driven from home by ambition, another by business of state, by an embassy, by the quest of luxury, by vice, by the wish to study, by the desire of seeing the spectacles, by friendship, by speculation, by eloquence, by beauty. Then, leaving Rome out of view, which indeed is to be considered the mother-city of them all, go to other cities, go to islands, come here to Corsica—everywhere are more strangers than natives. "For to man is given a desire of movement and of change, because he is moved by the celestial Spirit; consider the heavenly luminaries that give light to the world—none of them remains fixed—they wander ceaselessly on their path, and change perpetually their place." His poetic vein gave Seneca this fine thought. Our well-known wanderer's song has the words—

"Fix'd in the heavens the sun does not stand,

He travels o'er sea, he travels o'er land."[K]

"Varro, the most learned of the Romans," continues Seneca, "considers it the best compensation for the change of dwelling-place, that the nature of things is everywhere the same. Marcus Brutus finds sufficient consolation in the fact that he who goes into exile can take all that he has of truly good with him. Is not what we lose a mere trifle? Wherever we turn, two glorious things go with us—Nature that is everywhere, and Virtue that is our own. Let us travel through all possible countries, and we shall find no part of the earth which man cannot make his home. Everywhere the eye can rise to heaven, and all the divine worlds are at an equal distance from all the earthly. So long, therefore, as my eyes are not debarred that spectacle, with seeing which they are never satisfied; so long as I can behold moon and sun; so long as my gaze can rest on the other celestial luminaries; so long as I can inquire into their rising and setting, their courses, and the causes of their moving faster or slower; so long as I can contemplate the countless stars of night, and mark how some are immoveable—how others, not hastening through large spaces, circle in their own path, how many beam forth with a sudden brightness, many blind the eye with a stream of fire as if they fell, others pass along the sky in a long train of light; so long as I am with these, and dwell, as much as it is allowed to mortals, in heaven; so long as I can maintain my soul, which strives after the contemplation of natures related to it, in the pure ether, of what importance to me is the soil on which my foot treads? This island bears no fruitful nor pleasant trees; it is not watered by broad and navigable streams; it produces nothing that other nations can desire; it is hardly fertile enough to supply the necessities of the inhabitants; no precious stone is here hewn (*non pretiosus lapis hic cæditur*); no veins of gold or silver are here brought to light; but the soul is narrow that delights itself with what is earthly. It must be guided to that which is everywhere the same, and nowhere loses its splendour."

Had I Humboldt's *Cosmos* at hand, I should look whether the great natural philosopher has taken notice of these lofty periods of Seneca, where he treats of the sense of the ancients for natural beauty.

This, too, is a spirited passage:—"The longer they build their colonnades, the higher they raise their towers, the broader they stretch their streets, the deeper they dig their summer grottos, the more massively they pile their banqueting-halls—all the more effectually they cover themselves from the sky.—Brutus relates in his book on virtue, that he saw Marcellus in exile in Mitylene, and that he lived, as far as it was possible for human nature, in the enjoyment of the greatest happiness, and never was more devoted to literature than then. Hence, adds he, as he was to return without him, it seemed to him that he was rather himself going into exile than leaving the other in banishment behind him."

Now follows a panegyric on poverty and moderation, as contrasted with the luxurious gluttony of the rich, who ransack heaven and earth to tickle their palates, bring game from Phasis, and fowls from Parthia, who vomit in order to eat, and eat in order to vomit. "The Emperor Caligula," says Seneca, "whom Nature seems to me to have produced to show what the most degrading vice could do in the highest station, ate a dinner one day, that cost ten million sesterces; and although I have had the aid of the most ingenious men, still I have hardly been able to make out how the tribute of three provinces could be transformed into a single meal." Like Rousseau,

Seneca preaches the return of men to the state of nature. The times of the two moralists were alike; they themselves resemble each other in weakness of character, though Seneca, as compared with Rousseau, was a Roman and a hero.

Scipio's daughters received their dowries from the public treasury, because their father left nothing behind him. "O happy husbands of such maidens," cries Seneca; "husbands to whom the Roman people was father-in-law! Are they to be held happier whose ballet-dancers bring with them a million sesterces as dowry?"

After Seneca has comforted his mother in regard to his own sufferings, he proceeds to comfort her with reference to herself. "You must not imitate the example," he writes to her, "of women whose grief, when it had once mastered them, ended only with death. You know many, who, after the loss of their sons, never more laid off the robe of mourning that they had put on. But your nature has ever been stronger than this, and imposes upon you a nobler course. The excuse of the weakness of the sex cannot avail for her who is far removed from all female frailties. The most prevailing evil of the present time—unchastity, has not ranked you with the common crowd; neither precious stones nor pearls have had power over you, and wealth, accounted the highest of human blessings, has not dazzled you. The example of the bad, which is dangerous even to the virtuous, has not contaminated you—the strictly educated daughter of an ancient and severe house. You were never ashamed of the number of your children, as if they made you old before your time; you never—like some whose beautiful form is their only recommendation—concealed your fruitfulness, as if the burden were unseemly; nor did you ever destroy the hope of children that had been conceived in your bosom. You never disfigured your face with spangles or with paint; and never did a garment please you, that had been made only to show nakedness. Modesty appeared to you the alone ornament—the highest and never-fading beauty!" So writes the son to his mother, and it seems to me there is a most philosophical want of affectation in his style.

He alludes to Cornelia, the mother of the Gracchi; but he does not conceal from himself that grief is a disobedient thing. Traitorous tears, he knows, will appear on the face of assumed serenity. "Sometimes," says Seneca, "we entangle the soul in games and gladiator-shows; but even in the midst of such spectacles, the remembrance of its loss steals softly upon it. Therefore is it better to overcome than to deceive. For when the heart has either been cheated by pleasure, or diverted by business, it rebels again, and derives from repose itself the force for new disquiet; but it is lastingly still if it has yielded to reason." A wise man's voice enunciates here simply and beautifully the alone right, but the bitterly difficult rules for the art of life. Seneca, accordingly, counsels his mother not to use the ordinary means for overcoming her grief—a picturesque tour, or employment in household affairs; he advises mental occupation, lamenting, at the same time, that his father—an excellent man, but too much attached to the customs of the ancients—never could prevail upon himself to give her philosophical cultivation. Here we have an amusing glimpse of the old Seneca, I mean of the father. We know now how he looked. When the fashionable literary ladies and gentlemen in Cordova, who had picked up ideas about the rights of woman, and the elevation of her social position, from the *Republic* of Plato, represented to the old gentleman, that it were well if his young wife attended the lectures of some philosophers, he growled out: "Absurd nonsense; my wife shall not have her head turned with your high-flying notions, nor be one of your silly blue-stockings; cook shall she, bear children, and bring up children!" So said the worthy gentleman, and added, in excellent Spanish, "Basta!"

Seneca now speaks at considerable length of the magnanimity of which woman is capable, having no idea then that he was yet, when dying, to experience the truth of what he said, in the case of his own wife, Paulina. A noble man, therefore, a stoic of exalted virtue, has addressed this Letter of Consolation to Helvia. Is it possible that precisely the same man can think and write like a crawling parasite—like the basest flatterer?

CHAPTER VI
SENECA BIRBONE

"Magni pectoris est inter secunda moderatio." — Seneca.

Here is a second Letter of Consolation, which Seneca wrote in the second or third year of his Corsican exile, to Polybius, the freedman of Claudius, a courtier of the ordinary stamp. Polybius served the over-learned Claudius as literary adviser, and tormented himself with a Latin translation of Homer and a Greek one of Virgil. The loss of his talented brother occasioned Seneca's consolatory epistle to the courtier. He wrote the treatise with the full consciousness that Polybius would read it to the Emperor, and, not to miss the opportunity of appeasing the wrath of Claudius, he made it a model of low flattery of princes and their influential favourites. When we read it, we must not forget what sort of men Claudius and Polybius were.

"O destiny," cries the flatterer, "how cunningly hast thou sought out the vulnerable spot! What was there to rob such a man of? Money? He has always despised it. Life? His genius makes him immortal. He has himself provided that his better part shall endure, for his glorious rhetorical works cannot fail to rescue him from the ordinary lot of mortals. So long as literature is held in honour, so long as the Latin language retains its vigour, or the Greek its grace, so long shall he live with the greatest men, whose genius his own equals, or, if his modesty would object to that, at least approaches. — Unworthy outrage! Polybius mourns, Polybius has an affliction, and the Emperor is gracious to him! By this, inexorable destiny, thou wouldst, without doubt, show that none can be shielded from thee, no, not even by the Emperor! Yet, why does Polybius weep? Has he not his beloved Emperor, who is dearer to him than life? So long as it is well with him, then is it well with all who are yours, then have you lost nothing, then must your eyes be not only dry, but bright with joy. The Emperor is everything to you, in him you have all that you can desire. To him, your divinity, you must therefore raise your glance, and grief will have no power over your soul.

"Destiny, withhold thy hand from the Emperor, and show thy power only in blessing, letting him remain as a physician to mankind, who have suffered now so long, that he may again order and adjust what the madness of his predecessor destroyed. May this star, which has arisen in its brightness on a world plunged into abysses of darkness, shine evermore! May he subdue Germany, open up Britain, and celebrate ancestral victories and new triumphs, of which his clemency, which takes the first place among his virtues, makes me hope that I too shall be a witness. For he did not so cast me down, that he shall not again raise me up: no, it was not even he who overthrew me; but when destiny gave me the thrust, and I was falling, he broke my fall, and, gently intervening with godlike hand, bore me to a place of safety. He raised his voice for me in the senate, and not only gave me, but petitioned for, my life. He will himself see how he has to judge my cause; either his justice will recognise it as good, or his clemency will make it so. The benefit will still be the same, whether he perceives, or whether he wills, that I am innocent. Meanwhile, it is a great consolation to me, in my wretchedness, to see how his compassion travels through the whole world; and as he has again brought back to the light, from this corner in which I am buried, many who lay sunk in the oblivion of a long banishment, I do not fear that he will forget me. But he himself knows best the time for helping each. Nothing shall be wanting on my part that he may not blush to come at length to me. All hail to thy clemency, Cæsar! thanks to which, exiles live more peacefully under thee than the noblest of the people under Caius. They do not tremble, they do not hourly expect the sword, they do not shudder to see a ship coming. Through thee they have at once a goal to their cruel fate, and the hope of a better future, and a peaceful present. Surely the thunderbolts are altogether righteous which even those worship whom they strike."

O nettles, more nettles, noble Corsicans, — *era un birbone!*

The epistle concludes in these terms: "I have written this to you as well as I could, with a mind grown languid and dull through long inactivity; if it appears to you not worthy of your genius, or to supply medicine too slight for your sorrow, consider that the Latin word flows but reluctantly to his pen, in whose ear the barbarians have long been dinning their confused and clumsy jargon."

His flattery did not avail the sorrow-laden exile, but changes in the Roman court ended his banishment. The head of Polybius had fallen. Messalina had been executed. So stupid was Claudius, that he forgot the execution of his wife, and some days after asked at supper why Messalina did not come to table. Thus, all these horrors are dashed with the tragi-comic. The best of comforters, the Corsican bandit, returns. Agrippina, the new empress of Claudius, wishes him to educate her son Nero, now eleven years old. Can there be anything more tragi-comic than Seneca as tutor to Nero? He came, thanking the gods that they had laid upon him such a task as that of educating a boy to be Emperor of the world. He expected now to fill the whole earth with his own philosophy by infusing it into the young Nero. What an undertaking—at once tragical and ridiculous—to bring up a young tiger-cub on the principles of the Stoics! For the rest, Seneca found in his hopeful pupil the materials of the future man totally unspoiled by bungling scholastic methods; for he had grown up in a most divine ignorance, and, till his twelfth year, had enjoyed the tender friendship of a barber, a coachman, and a rope-dancer. From such hands did Seneca receive the boy who was destined to rule over gods and men.

As Seneca was banished to Corsica in the first year of the reign of Claudius, and returned in the eighth, he was privileged to enjoy this "divinity and celestial star" for more than five years. One day, however, Claudius died, for Agrippina gave him poison in a pumpkin which served as drinking-cup. The notorious Locusta had mixed the potion. The death of Claudius furnished Seneca with the ardently longed for opportunity of venting his revenge. Terribly did the philosopher make the Emperor's memory suffer for that eight years' banishment; he wrote on the dead man the satire, called the Apokolokyntosis—a pasquil of astonishing wit and almost incredible coarseness, equalling the writings of Lucian in sparkle and cleverness. The title is happy. The word, invented for the nonce, parodies the notion of the apotheosis of the Emperors, or their reception among the gods; and would be literally translated Pumpkinification, or reception of Claudius among the pumpkins. This satire should be read. It is highly characteristic of the period of Roman history in which it was written—a period when an utterly limitless despotism nevertheless allowed of a man's using such daring freedom of speech, and when an Emperor just dead could be publicly ridiculed by his successor, his own family, and the people, as a jack-pudding, without compromising the imperial dignity. In this Roman world, all is ironic accident, fools' carnival, tragi-comic, and bizarre.

Seneca speaks with all the freedom of a mask and as Roman Pasquino, and thus commences—"What happened on the 13th of October, in the consulship of Asinius Marcellus and Acilius Aviola, in the first year of the new Emperor, at the beginning of the period of blessing from heaven, I shall now deliver to memory. And in what I have to say, neither my vengeance nor my gratitude shall speak a word. If any one asks me where I got such accurate information about everything, I shall in the meantime not answer, if I don't choose. Who shall compel me? Do I not know that I have become a free man, since a certain person took his leave, who verified the proverb— One must either be born a king or a fool? And if I choose to answer, I shall say the first thing that comes into my head." Seneca now affirms, sneeringly, that he heard what he is about to relate from the senator who saw Drusilla [sister and mistress of Caligula] ascend to heaven from the Appian Way.[L] The same man had now, according to the philosopher, been a witness of all that had happened to Claudius on occasion of *his* ascension.

I shall be better understood, continued Seneca, if I say it was on the 13th of October; the hour I am unable exactly to fix, for there is still greater variance between the clocks than between the philosophers. It was, however, between the sixth and the seventh hour—Claudius was just gasping for a little breath, and couldn't find any. Hereupon Mercury, who had always been delighted with the genius of the man, took one of the three Parcæ aside, and said—"Cruel woman, why do you let the poor mortal torment himself so long, since he has not deserved it? He has been gasping for breath for sixty-four years now. What ails you at him? Allow the mathematicians to be right at last, who, ever since he became Emperor, have been assuring us of his death every year, nay, every month. And yet it is no wonder if they make mistakes. Nobody knows the man's hour—for nobody has ever looked on him as born. Do your duty,

> Give him to death,
>
> And let a better fill his empty throne."

Atropos now cuts Claudius's thread of life; but Lachesis spins another—a glittering thread, that of Nero; while Phœbus plays upon his lyre. In well-turned, unprincipled verses, Seneca flatters his young pupil, his new sun—

> "Phœbus the god hath said it; he shall pass
>
> Victoriously his mortal life, like me
>
> In countenance, and like me in my beauty;
>
> In song my rival, and in suasive speech.
>
> A happier age he bringeth to the weary,
>
> For he will break the silence of the laws.
>
> Like Phosphor when he scares the flying stars,
>
> Like Hesper rising, when the stars return;
>
> Or as, when rosy night-dissolving dawn
>
> Leads in the day, the bright sun looks abroad,
>
> And bids the barriers of the darkness yield
>
> Before the beaming chariot of the morn,—
>
> So Cæsar shines, and thus shall Rome behold
>
> Her Nero; mild the lustre of his face,
>
> And neck so fair with loosely-flowing curls."

Claudius meanwhile pumped out the air-bubble of his soul, and thereafter, as a phantasma, ceased to be visible. "He expired while he was listening to the comedians; so that, you perceive, I have good reason for dreading these people." His last words were—"*Vae me, puto concavi me.*"

Claudius is dead, then. It is announced to Jupiter, that a tall personage, rather gray, has arrived; that he threatens nobody knows what, shakes his head perpetually, and limps with his right leg; that the language he speaks is unintelligible, being neither that of the Greeks nor that of the Romans, nor the tongue of any known race. Jupiter now orders Hercules, since he has vagabondized through all the nations of the world, and is likely to know, to see what kind of mortal this may be. When Hercules, who had seen too many monsters to be easily frightened, set eyes on this portentous face, and strange gait, and heard a voice, not like the voice of any terrestial creature, but like some sea-monster's—hoarse, bellowing, confused, he was at first somewhat discomposed, and thought that a thirteenth labour had arrived for him. On closer examination, however, he thought the portent had some resemblance to a man. He therefore asked, in Homer's Greek—

"Who art thou, of what race, and where thy city?"

Claudius was mightily rejoiced to meet with philologers in heaven, and hoped he might find occasion of referring to his own histories. [He had written twenty books of Tyrrhenian, and eight of Carthaginian history, in Greek.] He immediately answers from Homer also, sillily quoting the line—

"From Troy the wind has brought me to the Cicons."

Fever, who alone of all the Roman gods has accompanied Claudius to heaven, gives him the lie, and affirms him to be a Gaul. "And therefore, since as Gaul he could not omit it, he took Rome." [While I write down this sentence of the old Roman's here in Rome, and hear at the same moment Gallic trumpets blowing, its correctness becomes very plain to me.] Claudius immediately gives orders to cut off Fever's head. He prevails on Hercules to bring him into the assembly of the gods. But the god Janus proposes, that from this time forward none of those who "eat the fruits of the field" shall be deified; and Augustus reads his opinion from a written paper, recommending that Claudius should be made to quit Olympus within three days. The gods assent, and Mercury hereupon drags off the Emperor to the infernal regions. On the Via Sacra they fall in with the funeral procession of Claudius, which is thus described: "It was a magnificent funeral, and such expense had been lavished on it, that you could very well see a god was being buried. There were flute-players, horn-blowers, and such crowds of players on brazen instruments, and such a din, that even Claudius could hear it. Everybody was merry and pleased; the Populus Romanus was walking about as if it were a free people. Agatho only, and a few pleaders, wept, and that evidently with all their heart. The jurisconsults were emerging from their obscure retreats—pale, emaciated, gasping for breath, like persons newly recalled to life. One of these noticing how the pleaders laid their heads together and bewailed their misfortunes, came up to them and said: 'I told you your Saturnalia would not last always!'" When Claudius saw his own funeral, he perceived that he was dead; for, with great sound and fury, they were singing the anapæstic nænia:—

Floods of tears pouring,
Beating the bosom,
Sorrow's mask wearing,
Wail till the forum
Echo your dirge.
Ah! he has fallen,
Wisest and noblest,
Bravest of mortals!
He in the race could
Vanquish the swiftest;
He the rebellious
Parthians routed;
With his light arrows
Follow'd the Persian;
Stoutly his right hand
Stretching the bowstring,
Small wound but deadly
Dealt to the headlong
Fugitive foe,
Piercing the painted
Back of the Mede.
He the wild Britons,
Far on the unknown
Shores of the ocean,
And the blue-shielded,
Restless Brigantes,
Forced to surrender

Their necks to the slavish
Chains of the Romans.
Even old Ocean
Trembled, and owned the new
Sway of the axes
And Fasces of Rome.
Weep, weep for the man
Who, with such speed as
Never another
Causes decided,
Heard he but one side,
Heard he e'en no side.
Who now will judge us?
All the year over
List to our lawsuits?
Now shall give way to thee,
Quit his tribunal,
He who gives law in the
Empire of silence,
Prince of Cretan
Cities a hundred.
Beat, beat your breasts now,
Wound them in sorrow,
All ye pleaders
Crooked and venal;
Newly-fledged poets
Swell the lament;
More than all others,
Lift your sad voices,
Ye who made fortunes,
Rattling the dice-box.

When Claudius arrives in the nether regions, a choir of singers hasten towards him, crying: "He is found!—joy! joy!" [This was the cry of the Egyptians when they found the ox Apis.] He is now surrounded by those whom he had caused to be put to death, Polybius and his other freedmen appearing among the rest. Æacus, as judge, examines into the actions of his life, and finds that he has murdered thirty senators, three hundred and fifteen knights, and citizens as the sands of the sea. He thereupon pronounces sentence on Claudius, and dooms him to cast dice eternally from a box with holes in it. Suddenly Caligula appears, and claims him as his slave. He produces witnesses, who prove that he had frequently beat, boxed, and horsewhipped his uncle Claudius; and as nobody seems able to dispute this, Claudius is handed over to Caligula. Caligula presents him to his freedman Menander, whom he is now to help in drawing out law-papers.

Such is a sketch of this remarkable "Apokolokyntosis of Claudius." Seneca, who had basely flattered the Emperor while alive, was also mean enough to drag him through the mire after he was dead. A noble soul does not take revenge on the corpse of its foe, even though that foe may have been but the parody of a man, and as detestable as he was ridiculous. The insults of the coward alone are here in place. The Apokolokyntosis faithfully reflects the degenerate baseness of Imperial Rome.

CHAPTER VII
SENECA EROE

"Alto morire ogni misfatto amenda." —Alfieri.

Pasquino Seneca now transforms himself in a twinkling into the dignified moralist; he writes his treatise "Concerning Clemency, to the Emperor Nero"—a pleasantly contradictory title, Nero and clemency. It is well enough known, however, that the young Emperor, like all his predecessors, governed without cruelty during the first years of his reign. This work of Seneca's is of high merit, wise, and full of noble sentiment.

Nero loaded his teacher with riches; and the author of the panegyric on poverty possessed a princely fortune, gardens, lands, palaces, villas outside the Porta Nomentana, in Baiæ, on the Alban Mount, upwards of six millions in value. He lent money at usurious rates of interest in Italy and in the provinces, greedily scraped and hoarded, fawned like a hound upon Agrippina and her son—till times changed with him.

In four years Nero had thrown off every restraint. The murder of his mother had met with no resistance from the timid Seneca. The high-minded Tacitus makes reproachful allusion to him. At length Nero began to find the philosopher inconvenient. He had already put his prefect Burrhus to death, and Seneca had hastened to put all his wealth at the disposal of the furious monarch; he now lived in complete retirement. But his enemies accused him of being privy to the conspiracy of Calpurnius Piso; and his nephew, the well-known poet Lucan, was, not without ground, affirmed to be similarly implicated. The conduct of Lucan in the matter was incredibly base. He made a pusillanimous confession; condescended to the most unmanly entreaties; and, sheltering himself behind the illustrious example set by Nero in his matricide, he denounced his innocent mother as a participant in the conspiracy. This abominable proceeding did not save him; he was condemned to voluntary death, went home, wrote to his father Annæus Mela Seneca about some emendations of his poems, dined luxuriously, and with the greatest equanimity opened his veins. So self-contradictory are these Roman characters.

Seneca is noble, great, and dignified in his end; he dies with an almost Socratic cheerfulness, with a tranquillity worthy of Cato. He chose bleeding as the means of his death, and consented that his heroic wife Paulina should die in the same way. The two were at that time in a country-house four miles from Rome. Nero kept restlessly despatching tribunes to the villa to see how matters were going on. Word was brought him in haste that Paulina, too, had had her veins opened. Nero instantly sent off an order to prevent her death. The slaves bind the lady's wounds, staunch the bleeding, and Paulina is rescued against her will. She lived some years longer. Meanwhile, the blood flowed from the aged Seneca but sparingly, and with an agonizing slowness. He asked Statius Annæus for poison, and took it, but without success; he then had himself put in a warm bath. He sprinkled the surrounding slaves with water, saying; "I make this libation to Zeus the Liberator." As he still could not die here, he was carried into a vapour bath, and there was suffocated. He was in his sixty-eighth year.

Reader, let us not be too hard on this philosopher, who, after all, was a man of his degenerate time, and whose nature is a combination of splendid talent, love of truth, and love of wisdom, with the most despicable weaknesses. His writings exercised great influence throughout the whole of the Middle Ages, and have purified many a soul from vicious passion, and guided it in nobler paths. Seneca, let us part friends.

CHAPTER VIII
THOUGHTS OF A BRIDE

"The wedding-day is near, when thou must wear
Fair garments, and fair gifts present to all
The youths that lead thee home; for of such things
The rumour travels far, and brings us honour,
Cheering thy father's heart, and loving mother's." —
Odyssey.

Every valley or pieve of Cape Corso has its marina, its little port, and anything more lonely and sequestered than these hamlets on the quiet shore, it would be difficult to find. It was sultry noon when I reached the strand of Luri, the hour when Pan is wont to sleep. The people in the house where I was to wait for the little coasting-vessel, which was to convey me to Bastia, sat all as if in slumber. A lovely girl, seated at the open window, was sewing as if in dream upon a fazoletto, with a mysterious faint smile on her face, and absorbed, plainly, in all sorts of secret, pretty thoughts of her own. She was embroidering something on the handkerchief; and this something, I could see, was a little poem which her happy heart was making on her near marriage. The blue sea laughed through the window behind her back; it knew the story, for the fisher-maiden had made it full confession. The girl had on a sea-green dress, a flowered vest, and the mandile neatly wound about her hair; the mandile was snow-white, checked with triple rows of fine red stripes. To me, too, did Maria Benvenuta make confession of her open mystery, with copious prattle about winds and waves, and the beautiful music and dancing there would be at the wedding, up in the vale of Luri. For after some months will come the marriage festival, and as fine a one it will be as ever was held in Corsica.

On the morning of the day on which Benvenuta is to leave her mother's house, a splendid *trovata* will stand at the entrance of her village, a green triumphal arch with many-coloured ribbons. The friends, the neighbours, the kinsfolk, will assemble on the Piazzetta to form the *corteo*—the bridal procession. Then a youth will go up to the gaily-dressed bride, and complain that she is leaving the place where she was so well cared for in her childhood, and where she never wanted for corals, nor flowers, nor friends. But since now she is resolved to go, he, with all his heart, in the name of her friends, wishes her happiness and prosperity, and bids her farewell. Then Maria Benvenuta bursts into tears, and she gives the youth a present, as a keepsake for the commune. A horse, finely decorated, is brought before the house, the bride mounts it, young men fully armed ride beside her, their hats wreathed with flowers and ribbons, and so the *corteo* moves onwards through the triumphal arch. One youth bears the *freno*—the symbol of fruitfulness, a distaff encircled at its top with spindles, and decked with ribbons. A handkerchief waves from it as flag. This freno in his hand, the *freniere* rides proudly at the head of the procession.

The *cortège* approaches Campo, where the bridegroom lives, and into his house the bride is now to be conducted. At the entrance of Campo stands another magnificent trovata. A youth steps forward, holding high in his hand an olive-twig streaming with ribbons. This, with wise old-fashioned sayings, he puts into the hand of the bride. Here two of the young men of the bride's *corteo* gallop off in furious haste towards the bridegroom's house; they are riding for the *vanto*, that is, the honour of being the first to bring the bride the key of the bridegroom's house. A flower is the symbol of the key. The fastest rider has won it, and exultingly holding it in his hand, he gallops back to the bride, to present to her the symbol. The procession is now moving towards the house. Women and girls crowd the balconies, and strew upon the bride, flowers, rice, grains of wheat, and throw the fruits that are in season among the procession with merry shoutings, and wishes of joy. This is called *Le Grazie*. Ceaseless is the din of muskets, mandolines, and the cornamusa, or bagpipe. Such jubilation as there is in Campo, such shooting, and huzzaing, and twanging, and fiddling! Such a joyous stir as there is in the air of spring-swallows, lark-songs, flying flowers, wheat-grains, ribbons—and all about this little Maria Benvenuta, who sits here at the window, and embroiders the whole story on the fazoletto.

But now the old father-in-law issues from the house, and thus gravely addresses the Corteo of strangers:—"Who are you, men thus armed?—friends or foes? Are you conductors of this *donna gentile*, or have you carried her off, although to appearance you are noble and valiant men?" The bridesman answers, "We are your friends and guests, and we escort this fair and worthy maiden, the pledge of our new friendship. We plucked the fairest flower of the strand of Luri, to bring it as a gift to Campo."

"Welcome, then, my friends and guests, enter my house, and refresh you at the feast;" thus replies again the bridegroom's father, lifts the maiden from her horse, embraces her, and leads her into the house. There the happy bridegroom folds her in his arms, and this is done to quite a reckless amount of merriment on the sixteen-stringed cithern, and the cornamusa.

Now we go into the church, where the tapers are already lit, and the myrtles profusely strewn. And when the pair have been joined, and again enter the bridegroom's house, they see, standing in the guest-chamber, two stools; on these the happy couple seat themselves, and now comes a woman, roguishly smiling, with a little child in swaddling clothes in her arms. She lays the child in the arm of the bride. The little Maria Benvenuta does not blush by any means, but takes the baby and kisses and fondles it right heartily. Then she puts on his head a little Phrygian cap, richly decked with particoloured ribbons. When this part of the ceremony has been gone through, the kinsfolk embrace the pair, and each wishes the good old wish:—

"Dio vi dia buona fortuna,

Tre di maschi e femmin' una:"

—that is, God give you good luck, three sons and a daughter. The bride now distributes little gifts to her husband's relatives; the nearest relation receives a small coin. Then follow the feast and the balls, at which they will dance the *cerca*, and the *marsiliana*, and the *tarantella*.

Whether they will observe the rest of the old usages, as they are given in the chronicle, I do not know. But in former times it was the custom that a young relation of the bride should precede her into the nuptial chamber. Here he jumped and rolled several times over the bridal-bed, then, the bride sitting down on it, he untied the ribbons on her shoes, as respectfully as we see upon the old sculptures Anchises unloosing the sandals of Venus, as she sits upon her couch. The bride now moved her little feet prettily till the shoes slipped to the ground; and to the youth who had untied them, she gave a present of money. To make a long story short, they will have a merry time of it at Benvenuta's wedding, and when long years have gone by, they will still remember it in the Valley of Campo.

All this we gossiped over very gravely in the boatman's little house at Luri; and I know the cradle-song too with which Maria Benvenuta will hush her little son to sleep—

"Ninniná, my darling, my doated-on!!

Ninniná, my one only good!

Thou art a little ship dancing along,

Dancing along on an azure flood,

Fearing not the waves' rough glee,
Nor the winds that sweep the sea
Sweet sleep now get—sleep, mother's pet,
I'll sing thee ninni nani.

"Little ship laden with pearls, my precious one,
Laden with silks and with damasks so gay,
With sails of brocade that have wafted it on
From an Indian port, far, far away;
And a rudder all of gold,
Wrought with skill to worth untold.
Sound sleep now get—sleep, mother's pet,
I'll sing thee ninni nani.

"When thou wast born, thou darling one,
To the holy font they bore thee soon.
God-papa to thee the sun,
And thy god-mamma the moon;
And the baby stars that shine on high,
Rock'd their gold cradles joyfully.
Soft sleep now get—sleep, mother's pet,
I'll sing thee ninni nani.

"Darling of darlings—brighter the heaven,
Deeper its blue as it smiled on thee;
Even the stately planets seven,
Brought thee presents rich and free;
And the mountain shepherds all,
Kept an eight-days' festival!
Sweet sleep now get—sleep, mother's pet,
I'll sing thee ninni nani.

"Nothing was heard but the cithern, my beauty,
Nothing but dancing on every side,
In the sweet vale of Cuscioni
Through the country far and wide
Boccanera and Falconi

Echoed with their wonted glee.
Sound sleep now get—sleep, mother's pet,
I'll sing thee ninni nani.

"Darling, when thou art taller grown,
Free thou shalt wander through meadows fair,
Every flower shall be newly-blown,
Oil shall shine 'stead of dewdrops there,
And the water in the sea
Changed to rarest balsam be.
Soft sleep now get—sleep, mother's pet,
I'll sing thee ninni nani.

"Then the mountains shall rise before baby's eyes,
All cover'd with lambs as white as snow;
And the Chamois wild shall bound after the child,
And the playful fawn and gentle doe;
But the hawk so fierce and the fox so sly,
Away from this valley far must hie.
Sweet sleep now get—sleep, mother's pet,
I'll sing thee ninni nani.

"Darling—earliest blossom mine,
Beauteous thou, beyond compare;
In Bavella born to shine,
And in Cuscioni fair,
Fourfold trefoil leaf so bright,
Kids would nibble—if they might!
Sweet sleep now get—sleep, mother's pet,
I'll sing thee ninni nani."

Should, perhaps, the child be too much excited by such a fanciful song, the mother will sing him this little nanna, whereupon he will immediately fall asleep—

"Ninni, ninni, ninni nanna,
Ninni, ninni, ninni nolu,
Allegrezza di la mamma
Addormentati, O figliuolu."

CHAPTER IX
CORSICAN SUPERSTITIONS

In the meantime, voices from the shore had announced the arrival of the boatmen; I therefore took my leave of the pretty Benvenuta, wished her all sorts of pleasant things, and stepped into the boat. We kept always as close as possible in shore. At Porticcioli, a little town with a Dogana, we ran in to have the names of our four passengers registered. A few sailing vessels were anchored here. The ripe figs on the trees, and the beautiful grapes in the gardens, tempted us; we had half a vineyard of the finest muscatel grapes, with the most delicious figs, brought us for a few pence.

Continuing our voyage in the evening, the beauty of the moonlit sea, and the singular forms of the rocky coast, served to beguile the way pleasantly. I saw a great many towers on the rocks, here and there a ruin, a church, or cloister. As we sailed past the old Church of St. Catherine of Sicco, which stands high and stately on the shore, the weather seemed going "to desolate itself," as they say in Italian, and threatened a storm. The old steersman, as we came opposite St. Catherine, doffed his baretto, and prayed aloud: "Holy Mother of God, Maria, we are sailing to Bastia; grant that we get safely into port!" The boatmen all took off their baretti, and devoutly made the sign of the cross. The moonlight breaking on the water from heavy black clouds; the fear of a storm; the grim, spectrally-lighted shore; and finally, St. Catherine,—suddenly brought over our entire company one of those moods which seek relief in ghost-stories. The boatmen began to tell them, in all varieties of the horrible and incredible. One of the passengers, meanwhile, anxious that at least not all Corsicans should seem, in the strangers' eyes, to be superstitious, kept incessantly shrugging his shoulders, indignant, as a person of enlightenment, that I should hear such nonsense; while another constantly supported his own and the boatmen's opinion, by the asseveration: "I have never seen witches with my own eyes, but that there is such a thing as the black art is undoubted." I, for my part, affirmed that I confidently believed in witches and sorceresses, and that I had had the honour of knowing some very fine specimens. The partisan of the black art, an inhabitant of Luri, had, I may mention, allowed me an interesting glimpse into his mysterious studies, when, in the course of a conversation about London, he very naïvely threw out the question, whether that great city was French or not.

The Corsicans call the witch *strega*. Her *penchant* is to suck, as vampire, the blood of children. One of the boatmen described to me how she looked, when he surprised her once in his father's house; she is black as pitch on the breast, and can transform herself from a cat into a beautiful girl, and from a beautiful girl into a cat. These sorceresses torment the children, make frightful faces at them, and all sorts of *fattura*. They can bewitch muskets, too, and make them miss fire. In this case, you must make a cross over the trigger, and, in general, you may be sure the cross is the best protection against sorcery. It is a very safe thing, too, to carry relics and amulets. Some of these will turn off a bullet, and are good against the bite of the venomous spider—the *malmignatto*.

Among these amulets they had formerly in Corsica a "travelling-stone," such as is frequently mentioned in the Scandinavian legends. It was found at the Tower of Seneca only—was four-cornered, and contained iron. Whoever tied such a stone over his knee made a safe and easy journey.

Many of the pagan usages of ancient Corsica have been lost, many still exist, particularly in the highland pasture-country of Niolo. Among these, the practice of soothsaying by bones is remarkable. The fortune-teller takes the shoulder-blade (*scapula*) of a goat or sheep, gives its surface a polish as of a mirror, and reads from it the history of the person concerned. But it must be the left shoulder-blade, for, according to the old proverb—*la destra spalla sfalla*—the right one deceives. Many famous Corsicans are said to have had their fortunes predicted by soothsayers. It is told that, as Sampiero sat with his friends at table, the evening before his death, an owl was heard to scream upon the house-top, where it sat hooting the whole night; and that, when a soothsayer hereupon read the scapula, to the horror of all, he found Sampiero's death written in it.

Napoleon's fortunes, too, were foretold from a *spalla*. An old herdsman of Ghidazzo, renowned for reading shoulder-blades, inspected the scapula one day, when Napoleon was still a child, and saw thereon, plainly represented, a tree rising with many branches high into the heavens, but having few and feeble roots. From this the herdsman saw that a Corsican would become ruler of the world, but only for a short time. The story of this prediction is very common in Corsica; it has a remarkable affinity with the dream of Mandane, in which she saw the tree interpreted to mean her son Cyrus.

Many superstitious beliefs of the Corsicans, with a great deal of poetic fancy in them, relate to death—the true genius of the Corsican popular poetry; since on this island of the Vendetta, death has so peculiarly his mythic abode; Corsica might be called the Island of Death, as other islands were called of Apollo, of Venus, or of Jupiter. When any one is about to die, a pale light upon the house-top frequently announces what is to happen. The owl screeches the whole night, the dog howls, and often a little drum is heard, which a ghost beats. If any one's death is near, sometimes the dead people come at night to his house, and make it known. They are dressed exactly like the Brothers of Death, in the long white mantles, with the pointed hoods in which are the spectral eye-holes; and they imitate all the gestures of the Brothers of Death, who place themselves round the bier, lift it, bear it, and go before it. This is their dismal pastime all night till the cock crows. When the cock crows, they slip away, some to the churchyard, some into their graves in the church.

The dead people are fond of each other's company; you will see them coming out of the graves if you go to the churchyard at night; then make quickly the sign of the cross over the trigger of your gun, that the ghost-shot may go off well. For a full shot has power over the spectres; and when you shoot among them, they disperse, and not till ten years after such a shot can they meet again.

Sometimes the dead come to the bedside of those who have survived, and say, "Now lament for me no more, and cease weeping, for I have the certainty that I shall yet be among the blessed."

In the silent night-hours, when you sit upon your bed, and your sad heart will not let you sleep, often the dead call you by name: "O Marì!—O Josè!" For your life do not answer, though they cry ever so mournfully, and your heart be like to break. Answer not! if you answer, you must die.

"Andate! andate! the storm is coming! Look at the tromba there, as it drives past Elba!" And vast and dark swept the mighty storm-spectre over the sea, a sight of terrific beauty; the moon was hid, and sea and shore lay wan in the glare of lightning.—God be praised! we are at the Tower of Bastia. The holy Mother of God *had* helped us, and as we stepped on land, the storm began in furious earnest. We, however, were in port.

BOOK V
WANDERINGS IN CORSICA

CHAPTER I
VESCOVATO AND THE CORSICAN HISTORIANS

Some miles to the southwards of Bastia, on the heights of the east coast, lies Vescovato, a spot celebrated in Corsican history. Leaving the coast-road at the tower of Buttafuoco, you turn upwards into the hills, the way leading through magnificent forests of chestnuts, which cover the heights on every side. The general name for this beautiful little district is Casinca; and the region round Vescovato is honoured with the special appellation of Castagniccia, or the land of chestnuts.

I was curious to see this Corsican paese, in which Count Matteo Buttafuoco once offered Rousseau an asylum; I expected to find a village such as I had already seen frequently enough among the mountains. I was astonished, therefore, when I saw Vescovato before me, lost in the green hills among magnificent groves of chestnuts, oranges, vines, fruit-trees of every kind, a mountain brook gushing down through it, the houses of primitive Corsican cast, yet here and there not without indications of architectural taste. I now could not but own to myself that of all the retreats that a misanthropic philosopher might select, the worst was by no means Vescovato. It is a mountain hermitage, in the greenest, shadiest solitude, with the loveliest walks, where you can dream undisturbed, now among the rocks by the wild stream, now under a blossom-laden bush of erica beside an ivy-hung cloister, or you are on the brow of a hill from which the eye looks down upon the plain of the Golo, rich and beautiful as a nook of paradise, and upon the sea.

A bishop built the place; and the bishops of the old town of Mariana, which lay below in the plain, latterly lived here.

Historic names and associations cluster thickly round Vescovato; especially is it honoured by its connexion with three Corsican historians of the sixteenth century—Ceccaldi, Monteggiani, and Filippini. Their memory is still as fresh as their houses are well preserved. The Curato of the place conducted me to Filippini's house, a mean peasant's cottage. I could not repress a smile when I was shown a stone taken from the wall, on which the most celebrated of the Corsican historians had in the fulness of his heart engraved the following inscription:—*Has Ædes ad suum et amicorum usum in commodiorem Formam redegit anno* MDLXXV., *cal. Decemb. A. Petrus Philippinus Archid. Marian.* In sooth, the pretensions of these worthy men were extremely humble. Another stone exhibits Filippini's coat of arms— his house, with a horse tied to a tree. It was the custom of the archdeacon to write his history in his vineyard, which they still show in Vescovato. After riding up from Mariana, he fastened his horse under a pine, and sat down to meditate or to write, protected by the high walls of his garden—for his life was in constant danger from the balls of his enemies. He thus wrote the history of the Corsicans under impressions highly exciting and dramatic.

Filippini's book is the leading work on Corsican history, and is of a thoroughly national character. The Corsicans may well be proud of it. It is an organic growth from the popular mind of the country; songs, traditions, chronicles, and, latterly, professed and conscious historical writing, go to constitute the work as it now lies before us. The first who wrought upon it was Giovanni della Grossa, lieutenant and secretary of the brave Vincentello d'Istria. He collected the old legends and traditions, and proceeded as Paul Diaconus did in his history. He brought down the history of Corsica to the year 1464. His scholar, Monteggiani, continued it to the year 1525,—but this part of the history is meagre; then came Ceccaldi, who continued it to the year 1559; and Filippini, who brought it as far as 1594. Of the thirteen books composing the whole, he has, therefore, written only the last four; but he edited and gave form to the entire work, so that it now bears his name. The *editio princeps* appeared in Tournon in France, in 1594, in Italian, under the following title:—

"The History of Corsica, in which all things are recorded that have happened from the time that it began to be inhabited up till the year 1594. With a general description of the entire Island; divided into thirteen books, and commenced by Giovanni della Grossa, who wrote the first nine thereof, which were continued by Pier Antonio Monteggiani, and afterwards by Marc' Antonio Ceccaldi, and were collected and enlarged by the Very

Reverend Antonpietro Filippini, Archidiaconus of Mariana, the last four being composed by himself. Diligently revised and given to the light by the same Archidiaconus. In Tournon. In the printing-house of Claudio Michael, Printer to the University, 1594."

Although an opponent of Sampiero, and though, from timidity, or from deliberate intent to falsify, frequently guilty of suppressing or perverting facts, he, nevertheless, told the Genoese so many bitter truths in his book, that the Republic did everything in its power to prevent its circulation. It had become extremely scarce when Pozzo di Borgo did his country the signal service of having it edited anew. The learned Corsican, Gregori, was the new editor, and he furnished the work with an excellent introduction; it appeared, as edited by Gregori, at Pisa, in the year 1827, in five volumes. The Corsicans are certainly worthy to have the documentary monuments of their history well attended to. Their modern historians blame Filippini severely for incorporating in his history all the traditions and fables of Grossa. For my part, I have nothing but praise to give him for this; his history must not be judged according to strict scientific rules; it possesses, as we have it, the high value of bearing the undisguised impress of the popular mind. I have equally little sympathy with the fault-finders in their depreciation of Filippini's talent. He is somewhat prolix, but his vein is rich; and a sound philosophic morality, based on accurate observation of life, pervades his writings. The man is to be held in honour; he has done his people justice, though no adherent of the popular cause, but a partisan of Genoa. Without Filippini, a great part of Corsican history would by this time have been buried in obscurity. He dedicated his work to Alfonso d'Ornano, Sampiero's son, in token of his satisfaction at the young hero's reconciling himself to Genoa, and even visiting that city.

"When I undertook to write the History," he says, "I trusted more to the gifts which I enjoy from nature, than to that acquired skill and polish which is expected in those who make similar attempts. I thought to myself that I should stand excused in the eyes of those who should read me, if they considered how great the want of all provision for such an undertaking is in this island (in which I must live, since it has pleased God to cast my lot here); so that scientific pursuits, of whatever kind, are totally impossible, not to speak of writing a pure and quite faultless style." There are other passages in Filippini, in which he complains with equal bitterness of the ignorance of the Corsicans, and their total want of cultivation in any shape. He does not even except the clergy, "among whom," says he, "there are hardly a dozen who have learned grammar; while among the Franciscans, although they have five-and-twenty convents, there are scarcely so many as eight lettered men; and thus the whole nation grows up in ignorance."

He never conceals the faults of his countrymen. "Besides their ignorance," he remarks, "one can find no words to express the laziness of the islanders where the tilling of the ground is concerned. Even the fairest plain in the world—the plain that extends from Aleria to Mariana—lies desolate; and they will not so much as drive away the fowls. But when it chances that they have become masters of a single carlino, they imagine that it is impossible now that they can ever want, and so sink into complete idleness."—This is a strikingly apt characterization of the Corsicans of the present day. "Why does no one prop the numberless wild oleasters?" asks Filippini; "why not the chestnuts? But they do nothing, and therefore are they all poor. Poverty leads to crime; and daily we hear of robberies. They also swear false oaths. Their feuds and their hatred, their little love and their little faithfulness, are quite endless; hence that proverb is true which we are wont to hear: 'The Corsican never forgives.' And hence arises all that calumniating, and all that backbiting, that we see perpetually. The people of Corsica (as Braccellio has written) are, beyond other nations, rebellious, and given to change; many are addicted to a certain superstition which they call Magonie, and thereto they use the men as women. There prevails here also a kind of soothsaying, which they practise with the shoulder-bones of dead animals."

Such is the dark side of the picture which the Corsican historian draws of his countrymen; and he here spares them so little, that, in fact, he merely reproduces what Seneca is said to have written of them in the lines—

"Prima est ulcisi lex, altera vivere raptu,

Tertia mentiri, quarta negare Deos."

On the other hand, in the dedication to Alfonso, he defends most zealously the virtues of his people against Tomaso Porcacchi Aretino da Castiglione, who had attacked them in his "Description of the most famous Islands of the World." "This man," says Filippini, "speaks of the Corsicans as assassins, which makes me wonder at him with no small astonishment, for there will be found, I may well venture to say, no people in the world among whom strangers are more lovingly handled, and among whom they can travel with more safety; for throughout all Corsica they meet with the utmost hospitality and courteousness, without having ever to expend the smallest coin for their maintenance." This is true; a stranger here corroborates the Corsican historian, after a lapse of three hundred years.

As in Vescovato we are standing on the sacred ground of Corsican historiography, I may mention a few more of the Corsican historians. An insular people, with a past so rich in striking events, heroic struggles, and great men, and characterized by a patriotism so unparalleled, might also be expected to be rich in writers of the class referred to; and certainly their numbers, as compared with the small population, are astonishing. I give only the more prominent names.

Next to Filippini, the most note-worthy of the Corsican historiographers is Petrus Cyrnæus, Archdeacon of Aleria, the other ancient Roman colony. He lived in the fifteenth century, and wrote, besides his *Commentarium de Bello Ferrariensi*, a History of Corsica extending down to the year 1482, in Latin, with the title, *Petri Cyrnæi de rebus Corsicis libri quatuor*. His Latin is as classical as that of the best authors of his time; breadth and vigour characterize his style, which has a resemblance to that of Sallust or Tacitus; but his treatment of his materials is thoroughly unartistic. He dwells longest on the siege of Bonifazio by Alfonso of Arragon, and on the incidents of his own life. Filippini did not know, and therefore could not use the work of Cyrnæus; it existed only in manuscript till brought to light from the library of Louis XV., and incorporated in Muratori's large work in the year 1738. The excellent edition (Paris, 1834) which we now possess we owe to the munificence of Pozzo di Borgo, and the literary ability of Gregori, who has added an Italian translation of the Latin text.

This author's estimate of the Corsicans is still more characteristic and intelligent than that of Filippini. Let us hear what he has to say, that we may see whether the present Corsicans have retained much or little of the nature of their forefathers who lived in those early times:—

"They are eager to avenge an injury, and it is reckoned disgraceful not to take vengeance. When they cannot reach him who has done the murder, then they punish one of his relations. On this account, as soon as a murder has taken place, all the relatives of the murderer instantly arm themselves in their own defence. Only children and women are spared." He describes the arms of the Corsicans of his time as follows: "They wear pointed helms, called cerbelleras; others also round ones; further daggers, spears four ells long, of which each man has two. On the left side rests the sword, on the right the dagger.

"In their own country, they are at discord; out of it, they hold fast to each other. Their souls are ready for death (*animi ad mortem parati*). They are universally poor, and despise trade. They are greedy of renown; gold and silver they scarcely use at all. Drunkenness they think a great disgrace. They seldom learn to read and write; few of them hear the orators or the poets; but in disputation they exercise themselves so continually, that when a cause has to be decided, you would think them all very admirable pleaders. Among the Corsicans, I never saw a head that was bald. The Corsicans are of all men the most hospitable. Their own wives cook their victuals for the highest men in the land. They are by nature inclined to silence—made rather for acting than for speaking. They are also the most religious of mortals.

"It is the custom to separate the men from the women, more especially at table. The wives and daughters fetch the water from the well; for the Corsicans have almost no menials. The Corsican women are industrious: you may see them, as they go to the fountain, bearing the pitcher on their head, leading the horse, if they have one, by a halter over their arm, and at the same time turning the spindle. They are also very chaste, and are not long sleepers.

"The Corsicans inter their dead expensively; for they bury them not without exequies, without laments, without panegyric, without dirges, without prayer. For their funeral solemnities are very similar to those of the Romans. One of the neighbours raises the cry, and calls to the nearest village: 'Ho there! cry to the other village, for such a one is just dead.' Then they assemble according to their villages, their towns, and their communities, walking one by one in a long line—first the men and then the women. When these arrive, all raise a great wailing, and the wife and brothers tear the clothes upon their breast. The women, disfigured with weeping, smite themselves on the bosom, lacerate the face, and tear out the hair.—All Corsicans are free."

The reader will have found that this picture of the Corsicans resembles in many points the description Tacitus gives us of the ancient Germans.

Corsican historiography has at no time flourished more than during the heroic fifteenth and sixteenth centuries; it was silent during the seventeenth, because at that period the entire people lay in a state of death-like exhaustion; in the eighteenth, participating in the renewed vitality of the age, it again became active, and we have Natali's treatise *Disinganno sulla guerra di Corsica,* and Salvini's *Giustificazione dell' Insurrezione*—useful books, but of no great literary merit.

Dr. Limperani wrote a History of Corsica to the end of the seventeenth century, a work full of valuable materials, but prosy and long-winded. Very serviceable—in fact, from the documents it contains, indispensable—is the History of the Corsicans, by Cambiaggi, in four quarto volumes. Cambiaggi dedicated his work to Frederick the Great, the admirer of Pasquale Paoli and Corsican heroism.

Now that the Corsican people have lost their freedom, the learned patriots of Corsica—and Filippini would no longer have to complain of the dearth of literary cultivation among his countrymen—have devoted themselves with praiseworthy zeal to the history of their country. These men are generally advocates. We have, for example, Pompei's book, *L'Etat actuel de la Corse*; Gregori edited Filippini and Peter Cyrnæus, and made a collection of the Corsican Statutes—a highly meritorious work. These laws originated in the old traditional jurisprudence of the Corsicans, which the democracy of Sampiero adopted, giving it a more definite and comprehensive form. They underwent further additions and improvements during the supremacy of the Genoese, who finally, in the sixteenth century, collected them into a code. They had become extremely scarce. The new edition is a splendid monument of Corsican history, and the codex itself does the Genoese much credit. Renucci, another talented Corsican, has written a *Storia di Corsica*, in two volumes, published at Bastia in 1833, which gives an abridgment of the earlier history, and a detailed account of events during the eighteenth and nineteenth centuries, up to 1830. The work is rich in material, but as a historical composition feeble. Arrighi wrote biographies of Sampiero and Pasquale Paoli. Jacobi's work in two volumes is the History of Corsica in most general use. It extends down to the end of the war of independence under Paoli, and is to be completed in a third volume. Jacobi's merit consists in having written a systematically developed history of the Corsicans, using all the available sources; his book is indispensable, but defective in critical acumen, and far from sufficiently objective. The latest book on Corsican history, is an excellent little compendium by Camillo Friess, keeper of the Archives in Ajaccio, who told me he proposed writing at greater length on the same subject. He has my best wishes for the success of such an undertaking, for he is a man of original and vigorous intellect. It is to be hoped he will not, like Jacobi, write his work in French, but, as he is bound in duty to his people, in Italian.

CHAPTER II
ROUSSEAU AND THE CORSICANS

I did not neglect to visit the house of Count Matteo Buttafuoco, which was at one time to have been the domicile of Rousseau. It is a structure of considerable pretensions, the stateliest in Vescovato. Part of it is at present occupied by Marshal Sebastiani, whose family belongs to the neighbouring village of Porta.

This Count Buttafuoco is the same man against whom Napoleon wrote an energetic pamphlet, when a fiery young democrat in Ajaccio. The Count was an officer in the French army when he invited Jean Jacques Rousseau to Vescovato. The philosopher of Geneva had, in his *Contrat Social*, written and prophesied as follows with regard to Corsica: "There is still one country in Europe susceptible of legislation—the island of Corsica. The vigour and perseverance displayed by the Corsicans, in gaining and defending their freedom, are such as entitle them to claim the aid of some wise man to teach them how to preserve it. I have an idea that this little island will one day astonish Europe." When the French were sending out their last and decisive expedition against Corsica, Rousseau wrote: "It must be confessed that your French are a very servile race, a people easily bought by despotism, and shamefully cruel to the unfortunate; if they knew of a free man at the other end of the world, I believe they would march all the way thither, for the mere pleasure of exterminating him."

I shall not affirm that this was a second prophecy of Rousseau's, but the first has certainly been fulfilled, for the day has come in which the Corsicans *have* astonished Europe.

The favourable opinion of the Corsican people, thus expressed by Rousseau, induced Paoli to invite him to Corsica in 1764, that he might escape from the persecution of his enemies in Switzerland. Voltaire, always enviously and derisively inclined towards Rousseau, had spread the malicious report that this offer of an asylum in Corsica was merely a ridiculous trick some one was playing on him. Upon this, Paoli had himself written the invitation. Buttafuoco had gone further; he had called upon the philosopher—of whom the Poles also begged a constitution—to compose a code of laws for the Corsicans. Paoli does not seem to have opposed the scheme, perhaps because he considered such a work, though useless for its intended purpose, still as, in one point of view, likely to increase the reputation of the Corsicans. The vain misanthrope thus saw himself in the flattering position of a Pythagoras, and joyfully wrote, in answer, that the simple idea of occupying himself with such a task elevated and inspired his soul; and that he should consider the remainder of his unhappy days nobly and virtuously spent, if he could spend them to the advantage of the brave Corsicans. He now, with all seriousness, asked for materials. The endless petty annoyances in which he was involved, prevented him ever producing the work. But what would have been its value if he had? What were the Corsicans to do with a theory, when they had already given themselves a constitution of practical efficiency, thoroughly popular, because formed on the material basis of their traditions and necessities?

Circumstances prevented Rousseau's going to Corsica—pity! He might have made trial of his theories there—for the island seems the realized Utopia of his views of that normal condition of society which he so lauds in his treatise on the question—Whether or not the arts and sciences have been beneficial to the human race? In Corsica, he would have had what he wanted, in plenty—primitive mortals in woollen blouses, living on goat's-milk and a few chestnuts, neither science nor art—equality, bravery, hospitality—and revenge to the death! I believe the warlike Corsicans would have laughed heartily to have seen Rousseau wandering about under the chestnuts, with his cat on his arm, or plaiting his basket-work. But Vendetta! vendetta! bawled once or twice, with a few shots of the fusil, would very soon have frightened poor Jacques away again. Nevertheless Rousseau's connexion with Corsica is memorable, and stands in intimate relation with the most characteristic features of his history.

In the letter in which he notifies to Count Buttafuoco his inability to accept his invitation, Rousseau writes: "I have not lost the sincere desire of living in your country; but the complete exhaustion of my energies, the anxieties I should incur, and the fatigues I should undergo, with other hindrances arising from my position, compel me, at least for the present, to relinquish my resolution; though, notwithstanding these difficulties, I find I cannot reconcile myself to the thought of utterly abandoning it. I am growing old; I am growing frail; my powers are leaving me; my wishes tempt me on, and yet my hopes grow dim. Whatever the issue may be, receive, and render to Signor Paoli, my liveliest, my heartfelt thanks, for the asylum which he has done me the honour to offer me. Brave and hospitable people! I shall never forget it so long as I live, that your hearts, your arms, were opened to me, at a time when there was hardly another asylum left for me in Europe. If it should not be my good fortune to leave my ashes in your island, I shall at least endeavour to leave there a monument of my gratitude; and I shall do myself honour, in the eyes of the whole world, when I call you my hosts and protectors. What I hereby promise to you, and what you may henceforth rely on, is this, that I shall occupy the rest of my life only with myself or with Corsica; all other interests are completely banished from my soul."

The concluding words promise largely; but they are in Rousseau's usual glowing and rhetorical vein. How singularly such a style, and the entire Rousseau nature, contrast with the austere taciturnity, the manly vigour, the wild and impetuous energy of the Corsican! Rousseau and Corsican seem ideas standing at an infinite distance apart—natures the very antipodes of each other, and yet they touch each other like corporeal and incorporeal, united in time and thought. It is strange to hear, amid the prophetic dreams of a universal democracy predicted by Rousseau, the wild clanging of that Corybantian war-dance of the Corsicans under Paoli, proclaiming the new era which their heroic struggle began. It is as if they would deafen, with the clangour of their arms, the old despotic gods, while the new divinity is being born upon their island, Jupiter—Napoleon, the revolutionary god of the iron age.

CHAPTER III
THE MORESCA—ARMED DANCE
OF THE CORSICANS

The Corsicans, like other brave peoples of fiery and imaginative temperament, have a war-dance, called the Moresca. Its origin is matter of dispute—some asserting it to be Moorish and others Greek. The Greeks called these dances of warlike youths, armed with sword and shield, Pyrrhic dances; and ascribed their invention to Minerva, and Pyrrhus, the son of Achilles. It is uncertain how they spread themselves over the more western countries; but, ever since the struggles of the Christians and Moors, they have been called Moresca; and it appears that they are everywhere practised where the people are rich in traditions of that old gigantic, world-historical contest between Christian and Pagan, Europe and Asia,—as among the Albanians in Greece, among the Servians, the Montenegrins, the Spaniards, and other nations.

I do not know what significance is elsewhere attached to the Moresca, as I have only once, in Genoa, witnessed this magnificent dance; but in Corsica it has all along preserved peculiarities attaching to the period of the Crusades, the Moresca there always representing a conflict between Saracens and Christians; the deliverance of Jerusalem, perhaps, or the conquest of Granada, or the taking of the Corsican cities Aleria and Mariana, by Hugo Count Colonna. The Moresca has thus assumed a half religious, half profane character, and has received from its historical relations a distinctive and national impress.

The Corsicans have at all times produced the spectacle of this dance, particularly in times of popular excitement and struggle, when a national armed sport of this kind was likely of itself to inflame the beholders, while at the same time it reminded them of the great deeds of their forefathers. I know of no nobler pleasure for a free and manly people, than the spectacle of the Moresca, the flower and poetry of the mood that prompts to and exults in fight. It is the only national drama the Corsicans have; as they were without other amusement, they had the heroic deeds of their ancestors represented to them in dance, on the same soil that they had steeped in their blood. It might frequently happen that they rose from the Moresca to rush into battle.

Vescovato, as Filippini mentions, was often the theatre of the Moresca. The people still remember that it was danced there in honour of Sampiero; it was also produced in Vescovato in the time of Paoli. The most recent performance is that of the year 1817.

The representation of the conquest of Mariana, by Hugo Colonna, was that most in favour. A village was supposed to represent the town. The stage was a piece of open ground, the green hills served as amphitheatre, and on their sides lay thousands and thousands, gathered from all parts of the island. Let the reader picture to himself such a public as this—rude, fierce men, all in arms, grouped under the chestnuts, with look, voice, and gesture accompanying the clanging hero-dance. The actors, sometimes two hundred in number, are in two separate troops; all wear the Roman toga. Each dancer holds in his right hand a sword, in his left a dagger; the colour of the plume and the breastplate alone distinguish Moors from Christians. The fiddle-bow of a single violin-player rules the Moresca.

It begins. A Moorish astrologer issues from Mariana dressed in the caftan, and with a long white beard; he looks to the sky and consults the heavenly luminaries, and in dismay he predicts misfortune. With gestures of alarm he hastens back within the gate. And see! yonder comes a Moorish messenger, headlong terror in look and movement, rushing towards Mariana with the news that the Christians have already taken Aleria and Corte, and are marching on Mariana. Just as the messenger vanishes within the city, horns blow, and enter Hugo Colonna with the Christian army. Exulting shouts greet him from the hills.

Hugo, Hugo, Count Colonna,
  O how gloriously he dances!
  Dances like the kingly tiger
  Leaping o'er the desert rocks.

High his sword lifts Count Colonna,
  On its hilt the cross he kisses,
  Then unto his valiant warriors
  Thus he speaks, the Christian knight:

On in storm for Christ and country!
  Up the walls of Mariana
  Dancing, lead to-day the Moorish

Infidels a dance of death!

Know that all who fall in battle,
For the good cause fighting bravely,
Shall to-day in heaven mingle
With the blessed angel-choirs.

The Christians take their position. Flourish of horns. The Moorish king,
Nugalone, and his host issue from Mariana.

Nugalone, O how lightly,
O how gloriously he dances!
Like the tawny spotted panther,
When he dances from his lair.

With his left hand, Nugalone
Curls his moustache, dark and glossy:
Then unto his Paynim warriors
Thus he speaks, the haughty Moor:

Forward! in the name of Allah!
Dance them down, the dogs of Christians!
Show them, as we dance to victory,
Allah is the only God!

Know that all who fall in battle,
Shall to-day in Eden's garden
With the fair immortal maidens
Dance the rapturous houri-dance.

The two armies now file off—the Moorish king gives the signal for
battle, and the figures of the dance begin; there are twelve of them.

Louder music, sharper, clearer!
Nugalone and Colonna
Onward to the charge are springing,
Onward dance their charging hosts.

Lightly to the ruling music
Youthful limbs are rising, falling,
Swaying, bending, like the flower-stalks,

To the music of the breeze.

Now they meet, now gleam the weapons,
  Lightly swung, and lightly parried;
  Are they swords, or are they sunbeams—
  Sunbeams glittering in their hands?

Tones of viol, bolder, fuller!—
  Clash and clang of crossing weapons,
  Varied tramp of changing movement,
  Backward, forward, fast and slow.

Now they dance in circle wheeling,
  Moor and Christian intermingled;—
  See, the chain of swords is broken,
  And in crescents they retire!

Wilder, wilder, the Moresca—
  Furious now the sounding onset,
  Like the rush of mad sea-billows,
  To the music of the storm.

Quit thee bravely, stout Colonna,
  Drive the Paynim crew before thee;
  We must win our country's freedom
  In the battle-dance to-day.

Thus we'll dance down all our tyrants—
  Thus we'll dance thy routed armies
  Down the hills of Vescovato,
  Heaven-accurséd Genoa!

—still new evolutions, till at length they dance the last figure, called the
resa, and the Saracen yields.

When I saw the Moresca in Genoa, it was being performed in honour
of the Sardinian constitution, on its anniversary day, May the 9th; for the
beautiful dance has in Italy a revolutionary significance, and is everywhere
forbidden except where the government is liberal. The people in their
picturesque costumes, particularly the women in their long white veils,
covering the esplanade at the quay, presented a magnificent spectacle.

About thirty young men, all in a white dress fitting tightly to the body; one party with green, the other with red scarfs round the waist, danced the Moresca to an accompaniment of horns and trumpets. They all had rapiers in each hand; and as they danced the various movements, they struck the weapons against each other. This Moresca appeared to have no historical reference.

The Corsicans, like the Spaniards, have also preserved the old theatrical representations of the sufferings of our Saviour; they are now, however, seldom given. In the year 1808, a spectacle of this kind was produced in Orezza, before ten thousand people. Tents represented the houses of Pilate, Herod, and Caiaphas. There were angels, and there were devils who ascended through a trap-door. Pilate's wife was a young fellow of twenty-three, with a coal-black beard. The commander of the Roman soldiery wore the uniform of the French national guards, with a colonel's epaulettes of gold and silver; the officer second in command wore an infantry uniform, and both had the cross of the Legion of Honour on their breast. A priest, the curato of Carcheto, played the part of Judas. As the piece was commencing, a disturbance arose from some unknown cause among the spectators, who bombarded each other with pieces of rock, with which they supplied themselves from the natural amphitheatre.

CHAPTER IV
JOACHIM MURAT

"Espada nunca vencida!
Esfuerço de esfuerço estava." —*Romanza Durandarte.*

There is still a third very remarkable house in Vescovato—the house of the Ceccaldi family, from which two illustrious Corsicans have sprung; the historian already mentioned, and the brave General Andrew Colonna Ceccaldi, in his day one of the leading patriots of Corsica, and Triumvir along with Giafferi and Hyacinth Paoli.

But the house has other associations of still greater interest. It is the house of General Franceschetti, or rather of his wife Catharina Ceccaldi, and it was here that the unfortunate King Joachim Murat was hospitably received when he landed in Corsica on his flight from Provence; and here that he formed the plan for re-conquering his beautiful realm of Naples, by a chivalrous *coup de main.*

Once more, therefore, the history of a bold caballero passes in review before us on this strange enchanted island, where kings' crowns hang upon the trees, like golden apples in the Gardens of the Hesperides.

Murat's end is more touching than that of almost any other of those men who have careered for a while with meteoric splendour through the world, and then had a sudden and lamentable fall.

After his last rash and ill-conducted war in Italy, Murat had sought refuge in France. In peril of his life, wandering about in the vineyards and woods, he concealed himself for some time in the vicinity of Toulon; to an old grenadier he owed his rescue from death by hunger. The same Marquis of Rivière who had so generously protected Murat after the conspiracy of George Cadoudal and Pichegru, sent out soldiers after the fugitive, with orders to take him, alive or dead. In this frightful extremity, Joachim resolved to claim hospitality in the neighbouring island of Corsica. He hoped to find protection among a noble people, in whose eyes the person of a guest is sacred.

He accordingly left his lurking-place, reached the shore in safety, and obtained a vessel which, braving a fearful storm and imminent danger of wreck, brought him safely to Corsica. He landed at Bastia on the 25th of August 1815, and hearing that General Franceschetti, who had formerly served in his guard at Naples, was at that time in Vescovato, he immediately proceeded thither. He knocked at the door of the house of the Maire Colonna Ceccaldi, father-in-law of the general, and asked to see the latter. In the *Mémoires* he has written on Murat's residence in Corsica, and his attempt on Naples, Franceschetti says:—"A man presents himself to me muffled in a cloak, his head buried in a cap of black silk, with a bushy beard, in pantaloons, in the gaiters and shoes of a common soldier, haggard with privation and anxiety. What was my amazement to detect under this coarse and common disguise King Joachim—a prince but lately the centre of such a brilliant court! A cry of astonishment escapes me, and I fall at his knees."

The news that the King of Naples had landed occasioned some excitement in Bastia, and many Corsican officers hastened to Vescovato to offer him their services. The commandant of Bastia, Colonel Verrière, became alarmed. He sent an officer with a detachment of gendarmes to Vescovato, with orders to make themselves masters of Joachim's person. But the people of Vescovato instantly ran to arms, and prepared to defend the sacred laws of hospitality and their guest. The troop of gendarmes returned without accomplishing their object. When the report spread that King Murat had appealed to the hospitality of the Corsicans, and that his person was threatened, the people flocked in arms from all the villages in the neighbourhood, and formed a camp at Vescovato for the protection of their guest, so that on the following day Murat saw himself at the head of a small army. Poor Joachim was enchanted with the *evvivas* of the Corsicans. It rested entirely with himself whether he should assume the crown of Corsica, but he thought only of his beautiful Naples. The sight of a huzzaing crowd made him once more feel like a king. "And if these Corsicans," said he, "who owe me nothing in the world, exhibit such generous kindness, how will my Neapolitans receive me, on whom I have conferred so many benefits?"

His determination to regain Naples became immoveably firm; the fate of Napoleon, after leaving the neighbouring Elba, and landing as adventurer on the coast of France, did not deter him. The son of fortune was resolved to try his last throw, and play for a kingdom or death.

Great numbers of officers and gentlemen meanwhile visited the house of the Ceccaldi from far and near, desirous of seeing and serving Murat. He had formed his plan. He summoned from Elba the Baron Barbarà, one of his old officers of Marine, a Maltese who had fled to Porto Longone, in order to take definite measures with the advice of one who was intimately acquainted with the Calabrian coast. He secretly despatched a Corsican to Naples, to form connexions and procure money there. He purchased three sailing-vessels in Bastia, which were to take him and his followers on board at Mariana, but it came to the ears of the French, and they laid an embargo on them. In vain did men of prudence and insight warn Murat to desist from the foolhardy undertaking. He had conceived the idea—and nothing could convince him of his mistake—that the Neapolitans were warmly attached to him, that he only needed to set foot on the Calabrian coast, in order to be conducted in triumph to his castle; and he was encouraged in this belief by men who came to him from Naples, and told him that King Ferdinand was hated there, and that people longed for nothing so ardently as to have Murat again for their king.

Two English officers appeared in Bastia, from Genoa; they came to Vescovato, and made offer to King Joachim of a safe conduct to England. But Murat indignantly refused the offer, remembering how England had treated Napoleon.

Meanwhile his position in Vescovato became more and more dangerous, and his generous hosts Ceccaldi and Franceschetti were now also seriously menaced, as the Bourbonist commandant had issued a proclamation which declared all those who attached themselves to Joachim Murat, or received him into their houses, enemies and traitors to their country.

Murat, therefore, concluded to leave Vescovato as soon as possible. He still negotiated for the restoration of his sequestrated vessels; he had recourse to Antonio Galloni, commandant of Balagna, whose brother he had formerly loaded with kindnesses. Galloni sent him back the answer, that he could do nothing in the matter; that, on the contrary, he had received orders from Verrière to march on the following day with six hundred men to Vescovato, and take him prisoner; that, however, out of consideration for his misfortunes, he would wait four days, pledging himself not to molest him, provided he left Vescovato within that time.

When Captain Moretti returned to Vescovato with this reply, and unable to hold out any prospect of the recovery of the vessels, Murat shed tears. "Is it possible," he cried, "that I am so unfortunate! I purchase ships in order to leave Corsica, and the Government seizes them; I burn with impatience to quit the island, and find every path blocked up. Be it so! I will send away those brave men who so generously guard me—I will stay here alone—I will bare my breast to Galloni, or I will find means to release myself from the bitter and cruel fate that persecutes me"—and here he looked at the pistols lying on the table. Franceschetti had entered the room; with emotion he said to Murat that the Corsicans would never suffer him to be harmed. "And I," replied Joachim, "cannot suffer Corsica to be endangered or embarrassed on my account; I must be gone!"

The four days had elapsed, and Galloni showed himself with his troops before Vescovato. But the people stood ready to give him battle; they opened fire. Galloni withdrew; for Murat had just left the village.

It was on the 17th of September that he left Vescovato, accompanied by Franceschetti, and some officers and veterans, and escorted by more than five hundred armed Corsicans. He had resolved to go to Ajaccio and embark there. Wherever he showed himself—in the Casinca, in Tavagna, in Moriani, in Campoloro, and beyond the mountains, the people crowded round him and received him with *evvivas*. The inhabitants of each commune accompanied him to the boundaries of the next. In San Pietro di Venaco, the priest Muracciole met him with a numerous body of followers, and presented to him a beautiful Corsican horse. In a moment Murat had leapt upon its back, and was galloping along the road, proud and fiery, as when, in former days of more splendid fortune, he galloped through the streets of Milan, of Vienna, of Berlin, of Paris, of Naples, and over so many battle-fields.

In Vivario he was entertained by the old parish priest Pentalacci, who had already, during a period of forty years, extended his hospitality to so many fugitives—had received, in these eventful times, Englishmen, Frenchmen, and Corsicans, and had once even sheltered the young Napoleon, when his life was threatened by the Paolists. As they sat at breakfast, Joachim asked the old man what he thought of his design on Naples. "I am a poor parish priest," said Pentalacci, "and understand neither war nor diplomacy; but I am inclined to doubt whether your Majesty is likely to win a crown *now*, which you could not keep formerly when you were at the head of an army." Murat replied with animation: "I am as certain of again winning my kingdom, as I am of holding this handkerchief in my hand."

Joachim sent Franceschetti on before, to ascertain how people were likely to receive him in Ajaccio,—for the relatives of Napoleon, in that town, had taken no notice of him since his arrival in the island; and he had, therefore, already made up his mind to stay in Bocognano till all was ready for the embarkation. Franceschetti, however, wrote to him, that the citizens of Ajaccio would be overjoyed to see him within their walls, and that they pressingly invited him to come.

On the 23d of September, at four o'clock in the afternoon, Murat entered Ajaccio for the second time in his life; he had entered it the first time covered with glory—an acknowledged hero in the eyes of all the world—for it was when he landed with Napoleon, as the latter returned from Egypt. At his entry now the bells were rung, the people saluted him with *vivats*, bonfires burned in the streets, and the houses were illuminated. But the authorities of the city instantly quitted it, and Napoleon's relations—the Ramolino family—also withdrew; the Signora Paravisini alone had courage and affection enough to remain, to embrace her relative, and to offer him hospitality in her own house. Murat thought fit to live in a public locanda.

The garrison of the citadel of Ajaccio was Corsican, and therefore friendly to Joachim. The commandant shut it up within the fortress, and declared the town in a state of siege. Murat now made the necessary preparations for his departure; previously to which he drew up a proclamation addressed to the Neapolitan people, consisting of thirty-six articles; it was printed in Ajaccio.

On the 28th of September, an English officer named Maceroni,[M] made his appearance, and requested an audience of Joachim. He had brought passes for him from Metternich, signed by the latter, by Charles Stuart, and by Schwarzenberg. They were made out in the name of Count Lipona, under which name—an anagram of Napoli—security to his person and an asylum in German Austria or Bohemia were guaranteed him. Murat entertained Maceroni at table; the conversation turned upon Napoleon's last campaign, and the battle of Waterloo, of which Maceroni gave a circumstantial account, praising the cool bravery of the English infantry, whose squares the French cavalry had been unable to break. Murat said: "Had I been there, I am certain I should have broken them;" to which Maceroni replied: "Your Majesty would have broken the squares of the Prussians and Austrians, but never those of the English." Full of fire Murat cried—"And I should have broken those of the English too: for Europe knows that I never yet found a square, of whatever description, that I did not break!"

Murat accepted Metternich's passes, and at first pretended to agree to the proposal; then he said that he must go to Naples to conquer his kingdom. Maceroni begged of him with tears to desist while it was yet time. But the king dismissed him.

On the same day, towards midnight, the unhappy Murat embarked, and, as his little squadron left the harbour of Ajaccio, several cannon-shots were fired at it from the citadel, by order of the commandant; it was said the cannons had only been loaded with powder. The expedition consisted of five small vessels besides a fast-sailing felucca called the Scorridora, under the command of Barbarà, and in these there were in all two hundred men, inclusive of subaltern officers, twenty-two officers, and a few sailors.

The voyage was full of disasters. Fortune—that once more favoured Napoleon when, seven months previously, he sailed from Elba with his six ships and eight hundred men to regain his crown—had no smiles for Murat. It is touching to see how the poor ex-king, his heart tossed with anxieties and doubts, hovers hesitatingly on the Calabrian coast; how he is forsaken by his ships, and repelled as if by the warning hand of fate from the unfriendly shore; how he is even at one time on the point of making sail for Trieste, and saving himself in Austria, and yet how at last the chivalrous dreamer, his mental vision haunted unceasingly by the deceptive semblance of a crown, adopts the fantastic and fatal resolution of landing in Pizzo.

"Murat," said the man who told me so much of Murat's days in Ajaccio, and who had been an eye-witness of what passed then, "was a brilliant cavalier with very little brains." It is true enough. He was the hero of a historical romance, and you cannot read the story of his life without being profoundly stirred. He sat his horse better than a throne. He had never learnt to govern; he had only, what born kings frequently have not, a kingly bearing, and the courage to be a king; and he was most a king when he had ceased to be acknowledged as such: this *ci-devant* waiter in his father's tavern, Abbé, and cashiered subaltern, fronted his executioners more regally than Louis XVI., of the house of Capet, and died not less proudly than Charles of England, of the house of Stuart.

A servant showed me the rooms in Franceschetti's in which Murat had lived. The walls were hung with pictures of the battles in which he had signalized himself, such as Marengo, Eylau, the military engagement at Aboukir, and Borodino. His portrait caught my eye instantly. The impassioned and dreamy eye, the brown curling hair falling down over the forehead, the soft romantic features, the fantastic white dress, the red scarf, were plainly Joachim's. Under the portrait I read these words—"1815. *Tradito!!! abbandonato!!! li 13 Octobre assassinato!!!*" (betrayed, forsaken; on the 13th of October, murdered);—groanings of Franceschetti's, who had accompanied him to Pizzo. The portrait of the General hangs beside that of Murat, a high warlike form, with a physiognomy of iron firmness, contrasting forcibly with the troubadour face of Joachim. Franceschetti sacrificed his all for Murat—he left wife and child to follow him; and although he disapproved of the undertaking of his former king, kept by his side to the last. An incident which was related to me, and which I also saw mentioned in the General's *Mémoires*, indicates great nobility of character, and does honour to his memory. When the rude soldiery of Pizzo were pressing in upon Murat, threatening him with the most brutal maltreatment, Franceschetti sprang forward and cried, "I—I am Murat!" The stroke of a sabre stretched him on the earth, just as Murat rushed to intercept it by declaring who he was. All the officers and soldiers who were taken prisoners with Murat at Pizzo were thrown into prison, wounded or not, as it might happen. After Joachim's execution, they and Franceschetti were taken to the citadel of Capri, where they remained for a considerable time, in constant expectation of death, till at length the king sent the unhoped-for order for their release. Franceschetti returned to Corsica; but he had scarcely landed, when he was seized by the French as guilty of high treason, and carried away to the citadel of Marseilles. The unfortunate man remained a prisoner in Provence for several years, but was at length set at liberty, and allowed to return to his family in Vescovato. His fortune had been ruined by Murat; and this general, who had risked his life for his king, saw himself compelled to send his wife to Vienna to obtain from the wife of Joachim a partial re-imbursement of his outlay, and, as the journey proved fruitless, to enter into a protracted law-process with Caroline Murat, in which he was nonsuited at every stage. Franceschetti died in 1836. His two sons, retired officers, are among the most highly respected men in Corsica, and have earned the gratitude of their countrymen by the improvements they have introduced in agriculture.

His wife, Catharina Ceccaldi, now far advanced in years, still lives in the same house in which she once entertained Murat as her guest. I found the noble old lady in one of the upper rooms, engaged in a very homely employment, and surrounded with pigeons, which fluttered out of the window as I entered; a scene which made me feel instantly that the healthy and simple nature of the Corsicans has been preserved not only in the cottages of the peasantry, but also among the upper classes. I thought of her brilliant youth, which she had spent in the beautiful Naples, and at the court of Joachim; and in the course of the conversation she herself referred to the time when General Franceschetti, and Coletta, who has also published a special memoir on the last days of Murat, were in the service of the Neapolitan soldier-king. It is pleasant to see a strong nature that has victoriously weathered the many storms of an eventful life, and has remained true to itself when fortune became false; and I contemplated this venerable matron with reverence, as, talking of the great things of the past, she carefully split the beans for the mid-day meal of her children and grandchildren. She spoke of the time, too, when Murat lived in the house. "Franceschetti," she said, "made the most forcible representations to him, and told him unreservedly that he was undertaking an impossibility. Then Murat would say sorrowfully, 'You, too, want to leave me! Ah! my Corsicans are going to leave me in the lurch!' We could not resist him."

Leaving Vescovato, and wandering farther into the Casinca, I still could not cease thinking on Murat. And I could not help connecting him with the romantic Baron Theodore von Neuhoff, who, seventy-nine years earlier, landed on this same coast, strangely and fantastically costumed, as it had also been Murat's custom to appear. Theodore von Neuhoff was the forerunner in Corsica of those men who conquered for themselves the fairest crowns in the world. Napoleon obtained the imperial crown, Joseph the crown of Spain, Louis the crown of Holland, Jerome the crown of Westphalia—the land of which Theodore King of Corsica was a native,—the adventurer Murat secured the Norman crown of the Two Sicilies, and Bernadotte the crown of the chivalrous Scandinavians, the oldest knights of Europe. A hundred years *before* Theodore, Cervantes had satirized, in his Sancho Panza, the romancing practice of conferring island kingdoms in reward for conquering prowess, and now, a hundred years *after* him, the romance of *Arthur and the Round Table* repeats itself here on the boundaries of Spain, in the island of Corsica, and continues to be realized in the broad daylight of the nineteenth century, and our own present time.

I often thought of Don Quixote and the Spanish romances in Corsica. It seems to me as if the old knight of La Mancha were once more riding through the world's history; in fact, are not antique Spanish names again becoming historical, which were previously for the world at large involved in as much romantic obscurity as the Athenian Duke Theseus of the *Midsummer Night's Dream?*

CHAPTER V
VENZOLASCA—CASABIANCA—
THE OLD CLOISTER

"Que todo se passa en flores

Mis amores,

Que todo se passa en flores." —*Spanish Song.*

Near Vescovato lies the little hamlet of Venzolasca. It is a walk as if through paradise, over the hills to it through the chestnut-groves. On my way I passed the forsaken Capuchin convent of Vescovato. Lying on a beautifully-wooded height, built of brown granite, and roofed with black slate, it looked as grave and austere as Corsican history itself, and had a singularly quaint and picturesque effect amid the green of the trees.

In travelling through this little "Land of Chestnuts," one forgets all fatigues. The luxuriance of the vegetation, and the smiling hills, the view of the plain of the Golo, and the sea, make the heart glad; the vicinity of numerous villages gives variety and human interest, furnishing many a group that would delight the eye of the *genre* painter. I saw a great many walled fountains, at which women and girls were filling their round pitchers; some of them had their spindles with them, and reminded me of what Peter of Corsica has said.

Outside Venzolasca stands a beautifully situated tomb belonging to the Casabianca family. This is another of the noble and influential families which Vescovato can boast. The immediate ancestors of the present French senator Casabianca made their name famous by their deeds of arms. Raffaello Casabianca, commandant of Corsica in 1793, Senator, Count, and Peer of France, died in Bastia at an advanced age in 1826. Luzio Casabianca, Corsican deputy to the Convention, was captain of the admiral's ship, *L'Orient*, in the battle of Aboukir. After Admiral Brueys had been torn in pieces by a shot, Casabianca took the command of the vessel, which was on fire, the flames spreading rapidly. As far as was possible, he took measures for saving the crew, and refused to leave the ship. His young son Giocante, a boy of thirteen, could not be prevailed on to leave his father's side. The vessel was every moment expected to blow up. Clasped in each other's arms, father and son perished in the explosion. You can wander nowhere in Corsica without breathing an atmosphere of heroism.

Venzolasca has a handsome church, at least interiorly. I found people engaged in painting the choir, and they complained to me that the person who had been engaged to gild the wood-carving, had shamefully cheated the village, as he had been provided with ducat-gold for the purpose, and had run off with it. The only luxury the Corsicans allow themselves is in the matter of church-decoration, and there is hardly a paese in the island, however poor, which does not take a pride in decking its little church with gay colours and golden ornaments.

From the plateau on which the church of Venzolasca stands, there is a magnificent view seawards, and, in the opposite direction, you have the indescribably beautiful basin of the Castagniccia. Few regions of Corsica have given me so much pleasure as the hills which enclose this basin in their connexion with the sea. The Castagniccia is an imposing amphitheatre, mountains clothed in the richest green, and of the finest forms, composing the sides. The chestnut-woods cover them almost to their summit; at their foot olive-groves, with their silver gray, contrast picturesquely with the deep green of the chestnut foliage. Half-appearing through the trees are seen scattered hamlets, Sorbo, Penta, Castellare, and far up among the clouds Oreto, dark, with tall black church-towers.

The sun was westering as I ascended these hills, and the hours of that afternoon were memorably beautiful. Again I passed a forsaken cloister— this time, of the Franciscans. It lay quite buried among vines, and foliage of every kind, dense, yet not dense enough to conceal the abounding fruit. As I passed into the court, and was entering the church of the convent, my eye lighted on a melancholy picture of decay, which Nature, with her luxuriance of vegetation, seemed laughingly to veil. The graves were standing open, as if those once buried there had rent the overlying stones, that they might fly to heaven; skulls lay among the long green grass and trailing plants, and the cross—the symbol of all sorrow—had sunk amid a sea of flowers.

CHAPTER VI
HOSPITALITY AND FAMILY LIFE IN
ORETO—THE CORSICAN ANTIGONE

"To Jove belong the stranger and the hungry,
And though the gift be small, it cheers the heart."—
Odyssey.

An up-hill walk of two hours between fruit-gardens, the walls of which the beautiful wreaths of the clematis garlanded all the way along, and then through groves of chestnuts, brought me to Oreto.

The name is derived from the Greek oros, which means *mountain*; the place lies high and picturesque, on the summit of a green hill. A huge block of granite rears its gray head from the very centre of the village, a pedestal for the colossal statue of a Hercules. Before reaching the paese, I had to climb a laborious and narrow path, which at many parts formed the channel of a brook.

At length gaining the summit, I found myself in the piazza, or public square of the village, the largest I have seen in any paese. It is the plateau of the mountain, overhung by other mountains, and encircled by houses, which look like peace itself. The village priest was walking about with his beadle, and the *paesani* stood leaning in the Sabbath-stillness on their garden walls. I stepped up to a group and asked if there was a locanda in the place; "No," said one, "we have no locanda, but I offer you my house—you shall have what we can give." I gladly accepted the offer, and followed my host. Marcantonio, before I entered his house, wished that I should take a look of the village fountain, the pride of Oreto, and taste the water, the best in the whole land of Casinca. Despite my weariness, I followed the Corsican. The fountain was delicious, and the little structure could even make pretensions to architectural elegance. The ice-cold water streamed copiously through five pipes from a stone temple.

Arrived in Marcantonio's house, I was welcomed by his wife without ceremony. She bade me a good evening, and immediately went into the kitchen to prepare the meal. My entertainer had conducted me into his best room, and I was astonished to find there a little store of books; they were of a religious character, and the legacy of a relative. "I am unfortunate," said Marcantonio, "for I have learnt nothing, and I am very poor; hence I must stay here upon the mountain, instead of going to the Continent, and filling some post." I looked more narrowly at this man in the brown blouse and Phrygian cap. The face was reserved, furrowed with passion, and of an iron austerity, and what he said was brief, decided, and in a bitter tone. All the time I was in his company, I never once saw this man smile; and found here, among the solitary hills, an ambitious soul tormented with its thwarted aspirations. Such minds are not uncommon in Corsica; the frequent success of men who have emigrated from these poor villages is a powerful temptation to others; often in the dingiest cabin you see the family likenesses of senators, generals, and prefects. Corsica is the land of upstarts and of natural equality.

Marcantonio's daughter, a pretty young girl, blooming, tall, and well-made, entered the room. Without taking any other notice of the presence of a guest, she asked aloud, and with complete *naïveté*: "Father, who is the stranger, is he a Frenchman; what does he want in Oreto?" I told her I was a German, which she did not understand. Giulia went to help her mother with the meal.

This now made its appearance—the most sumptuous a poor man could give—a soup of vegetables, and in honour of the guest a piece of meat, bread, and peaches. The daughter set the viands on the table, but, according to the Corsican custom, neither she nor the mother took a share in the meal; the man alone helped me, and ate beside me.

He took me afterwards into the little church of Oreto, and to the edge of the rock, to show me the incomparably beautiful view. The young curato, and no small retinue of *paesani*, accompanied us. It was a sunny, golden, delightfully cool evening. I stood wonderstruck at such undreamt-of magnificence in scenery as the landscape presented—for at my feet I saw the hills, with all their burden of chestnut woods, sink towards the plain; the plain, like a boundless garden, stretch onwards to the strand; the streams of the Golo and Fiumalto wind through it to the glittering sea; and far on the horizon, the islands of Capraja, Elba, and Monte Chiato. The eye takes in the whole coast-line to Bastia, and southwards to San Nicolao; turning inland, mountain upon mountain, crowned with villages.

A little group had gathered round us as we stood here; and I now began to panegyrize the island, rendered, as I said, so remarkable by its scenery and by the history of its heroic people. The young curate spoke in the same strain with great fire, the peasants gesticulated their assent, and each had something to say in praise of his country. I observed that these people were much at home in the history of their island. The curate excited my admiration; he had intellect, and talked shrewdly. Speaking of Paoli, he said: "His time was a time of action; the men of Orezza spoke little, but they did much. Had our era produced a single individual of Paoli's large and self-sacrificing spirit, it would be otherwise in the world than it is. But ours is an age of chimeras and Icarus-wings, and yet man was not made to fly." I gladly accepted the curate's invitation to go home with him; his house was poor-looking, built of black stone. But his little study was neat and cheerful; and there might be between two and three hundred volumes on the book-shelves. I spent a pleasant hour in conversation with this cultivated, liberal, and enlightened man, over a bottle of exquisite wine, Marcantonio sitting silent and reserved. We happened to speak of Aleria, and I put a question about Roman antiquities in Corsica. Marcantonio suddenly put in his word, and said very gravely and curtly—"We have no need of the fame of Roman antiquities—that of our own forefathers is sufficient."

Returning to Marcantonio's house, I found in the room both mother and daughter, and we drew in round the table in sociable family circle. The women were mending clothes, were talkative, unconstrained, and *naïve*, like all Corsicans. The unresting activity of the Corsican women is well known. Subordinating themselves to the men, and uncomplainingly accepting a menial position, the whole burden of whatever work is necessary rests upon them. They share this lot with the women of all warlike nations; as, for example, of the Servians and Albanians.

I described to them the great cities of the Continent, their usages and festivals, more particularly some customs of my native country. They never expressed astonishment, although what they heard was utterly strange to them, and Giulia had never yet seen a city, not even Bastia. I asked the girl how old she was. "I am twenty years old," she said.

"That is impossible. You are scarce seventeen."

"She is sixteen years old," said the mother.

"What! do you not know your own birthday, Giulia?"

"No, but it stands in the register, and the Maire will know it."

The Maire, therefore—happy man!—is the only person who can celebrate the birthday of the pretty Giulia—that is, if he chooses to put his great old horn-spectacles on his nose, and turn over the register for it.

"Giulia, how do you amuse yourself? young people must be merry."

"I have always enough to do; my brothers want something every minute; on Sunday I go to mass."

"What fine clothes will you wear to-morrow?"

"I shall put on the faldetta."

She brought the faldetta from a press, and put it on; the girl looked very beautiful in it. The faldetta is a long garment, generally black, the end of which is thrown up behind over the head, so that it has some resemblance to the hooded cloak of a nun. To elderly women, the faldetta imparts dignity; when it wraps the form of a young girl, its ample folds add the charm of mystery.

The women asked me what I was. That was difficult to answer. I took out my very unartistic sketch-book; and as I turned over its leaves, I told them I was a painter.

"Have you come into the village," asked Giulia, "to colour the walls?"

I laughed loudly and heartily; the question was an apt criticism of my Corsican sketches. Marcantonio said very seriously—"Don't; she does not understand such things."

These Corsican women have as yet no notion of the arts and sciences; they read no romances, they play the cithern in the twilight, and sing a melancholy vocero—a beautiful dirge, which, perhaps, they themselves improvise. But in the little circle of their ideas and feelings, their nature remains vigorous and healthy as the nature that environs them—chaste, and pious, and self-balanced, capable of all noble sacrifice, and such heroic resolves, as the poetry of civilisation preserves to all time as the highest examples of human magnanimity.

Antigone and Iphigenia can be matched in Corsica. There is not a single high-souled act of which the record has descended to us from antiquity but this uncultured people can place a deed of equal heroism by its side.

In honour of our young Corsican Giulia, I shall relate the following story. It is historical fact, like every other Corsican tale that I shall tell.

THE CORSICAN ANTIGONE

It was about the end of the year 1768. The French had occupied Oletta, a considerable village in the district of Nebbio. As from the nature of its situation it was a post of the highest importance, Paoli put himself in secret communication with the inhabitants, and formed a plan for surprising the French garrison and making them prisoners. They were fifteen hundred in number, and commanded by the Marquis of Arcambal. But the French were upon their guard; they proclaimed martial law in Oletta, and maintained a strict and watchful rule, so that the men of the village did not venture to attempt anything.

Oletta was now still as the grave.

One day a young man named Giulio Saliceti left his village to go into the Campagna, without the permission of the French guard. On his return he was seized and thrown into prison; after a short time, however, he was set at liberty.

The youth left his prison and took his way homewards, full of resentment at the insult put upon him by the enemy. He was noticed to mutter something to himself, probably curses directed against the hated French. A sergeant heard him, and gave him a blow in the face. This occurred in front of the youth's house, at a window of which one of his relatives happened to be standing—the Abbot Saliceti namely, whom the people called Peverino, or Spanish Pepper, from his hot and headlong temper. When Peverino saw the stroke fall upon his kinsman's face, his blood boiled in his veins.

Giulio rushed into the house quite out of himself with shame and anger, and was immediately taken by Peverino into his chamber. After some time the two men were seen to come out, calm, but ominously serious.

At night, other men secretly entered the house of the Saliceti, sat together and deliberated. And what they deliberated on was this: they proposed to blow up the church of Oletta, which the French had turned into their barracks. They were determined to have revenge and their liberty.

They dug a mine from Saliceti's house, terminating beneath the church, and filled it with all the powder they had.

The date fixed for firing the mine was the 13th of February 1769, towards night.

Giulio had nursed his wrath till there was as little pity in his heart as in a musket-bullet. "To-morrow!" he said trembling, "to-morrow! Let me apply the match; they struck me in the face; I will give them a stroke that shall strike them as high as the clouds. I will blast them out of Oletta, as if the bolts of heaven had got among them!

"But the women and children, and those who do not know of it? The explosion will carry away every house in the neighbourhood."

"They must be warned. They must be directed under this or the other pretext to go to the other end of the village at the hour fixed, and that in all quietness."

The conspirators gave orders to this effect.

Next evening, when the dreadful hour arrived, old men and young, women, children, were seen betaking themselves in silence and undefined alarm, with secrecy and speed, to the other end of the village, and there assembling.

The suspicions of the French began to be aroused, and a messenger from General Grand-Maison came galloping in, and communicated in breathless haste the information which his commander had received. Some one had betrayed the plot. That instant the French threw themselves on Saliceti's house and the powder-mine, and crushed the hellish undertaking.

Saliceti and a few of the conspirators cut their way through the enemy with desperate courage, and escaped in safety from Oletta. Others, however, were seized and put in chains. A court-martial condemned fourteen of these to death by the wheel, and seven unfortunates were actually broken, in terms of the sentence.

Seven corpses were exposed to public view, in the square before the Convent of Oletta. No burial was to be allowed them. The French commandant had issued an order that no one should dare to remove any of the bodies from the scaffold for interment, under pain of death.

Blank dismay fell upon the village of Oletta. Every heart was chilled with horror. Not a human being stirred abroad; the fires upon the hearths were extinguished—no voice was heard but the voice of weeping. The people remained in their houses, but their thoughts turned continually to the square before the convent, where the seven corpses lay upon the scaffold.

The first night came. Maria Gentili Montalti was sitting on her bed in her chamber. She was not weeping; she sat with her head hanging on her breast, her hands in her lap, her eyes closed. Sometimes a profound sob shook her frame. It seemed to her as if a voice called, through the stillness of the night, O Marì!

The dead, many a time in the stillness of the night, call the name of those whom they have loved. Whoever answers, must die.

O Bernardo! cried Maria—for she wished to die.

Bernardo lay before the convent on the scaffold; he was the seventh and youngest of the dead. He was Maria's lover, and their marriage was fixed for the following month. Now he lay dead upon the scaffold.

Maria Gentili stood silent in the dark chamber, she listened towards the side where the convent lay, and her soul held converse with a spirit. Bernardo seemed to implore of her a Christian burial.

But whoever removed a corpse from the scaffold and buried it, was to be punished by death. Maria was resolved to bury her beloved and then die.

She softly opened the door of her chamber in order to leave the house. She passed through the room in which her aged parents slept. She went to their bedside and listened to their breathing. Then her heart began to quail, for she was the only child of her parents, and their sole support, and when she thought how her death by the hand of the public executioner would bow her father and mother down into the grave, her soul shrank back in great pain, and she turned, and made a step towards her chamber.

At that moment she again heard the voice of her dead lover wail: O Marì! O Marì! I loved thee so well, and now thou forsakest me. In my mangled body lies the heart that died still loving thee—bury me in the Church of St. Francis, in the grave of my fathers, O Marì!

Maria opened the door of the house and passed out into the night. With uncertain footsteps she gained the square of the convent. The night was gloomy. Sometimes the storm came and swept the clouds away, so that the moon shone down. When its beams fell upon the convent, it was as if the light of heaven refused to look upon what it there saw, and the moon wrapped itself again in the black veil of clouds. For before the convent a row of seven corpses lay on the red scaffold, and the seventh was the corpse of a youth.

The owl and the raven screamed upon the tower; they sang the vocero— the dirge for the dead. A grenadier was walking up and down, with his musket on his shoulder, not far off. No wonder that he shuddered to his inmost marrow, and buried his face in his mantle, as he moved slowly up and down.

Maria had wrapped herself in the black faldetta, that her form might be the less distinct in the darkness of the night. She breathed a prayer to the Holy Virgin, the Mother of Sorrows, that she would help her, and then she walked swiftly to the scaffold. It was the seventh body—she loosed Bernardo; her heart, and a faint gleam from his dead face, told her that it was he, even in the dark night. Maria took the dead man in her arms, upon her shoulder. She had become strong, as if with the strength of a man. She bore the corpse into the Church of St. Francis.

There she sat down exhausted, on the steps of an altar, over which the lamp of the Mother of God was burning. The dead Bernardo lay upon her knees, as the dead Christ once lay upon the knees of Mary. In the south they call this group Pietà.

Not a sound in the church. The lamp glimmers above the altar. Outside, a gust of wind that whistles by.

Maria rose. She let the dead Bernardo gently down upon the steps of the altar. She went to the spot where the grave of Bernardo's parents lay. She opened the grave. Then she took up the dead body. She kissed him, and lowered him into the grave, and again shut it. Maria knelt long before the Mother of God, and prayed that Bernardo's soul might have peace in heaven; and then she went silently away to her house, and to her chamber.

When morning broke, Bernardo's corpse was missing from among the dead bodies before the convent. The news flew through the village, and the soldiers drummed alarm. It was not doubted that the Leccia family had removed their kinsman during the night from the scaffold; and instantly their house was forced, its inmates taken prisoners, and thrown chained into a jail. Guilty of capital crime, according to the law that had been proclaimed, they were to suffer the penalty, although they denied the deed.

Maria Gentili heard in her chamber what had happened. Without saying a word, she hastened to the house of the Count de Vaux, who had come to Oletta. She threw herself at his feet, and begged the liberation of the prisoners. She confessed that it was she who had done that of which they were supposed to be guilty. "I have buried my betrothed," said she; "death is my due, here is my head; but restore their freedom to those that suffer innocently."

The Count at first refused to believe what he heard; for he held it impossible both that a weak girl should be capable of such heroism, and that she should have sufficient strength to accomplish what Maria had accomplished. When he had convinced himself of the truth of her assertions, a thrill of astonishment passed through him, and he was moved to tears. "Go," said he, "generous-hearted girl, yourself release the relations of your lover; and may God reward your heroism!"

On the same day the other six corpses were taken from the scaffold, and received a Christian burial.

CHAPTER VII
A RIDE THROUGH THE DISTRICT
OF OREZZA TO MOROSAGLIA

I wished to go from Oreto to Morosaglia, Paoli's native place, through Orezza. Marcantonio had promised to accompany me, and to provide good horses. He accordingly awoke me early in the morning, and made ready to go. He had put on his best clothes, wore a velvet jacket, and had shaved himself very smoothly. The women fortified us for the journey with a good breakfast, and we mounted our little Corsican horses, and rode proudly forth.

It makes my heart glad yet to think of that Sunday morning, and the ride through this romantic and beautiful land of Orezza—over the green hills, through cool dells, over gushing brooks, through the green oak-woods. Far as the eye can reach on every side, those shady, fragrant chestnut-groves; those giants of trees, in size such as I had never seen before. Nature has here done everything, man so little. His chestnuts are often a Corsican's entire estate; and in many instances he has only six goats and six chestnut-trees, which yield him his polleta. Government has already entertained the idea of cutting down the forests of chestnuts, in order to compel the Corsican to till the ground; but this would amount to starving him. Many of these trees have trunks twelve feet in thickness. With their full, fragrant foliage, long, broad, dark leaves, and fibred, light-green fruit-husks, they are a sight most grateful to the eye.

Beyond the paese of Casalta, we entered a singularly romantic dell, through which the Fiumalto rushes. You find everywhere here serpentine, and the exquisite marble called Verde Antico. The engineers called the little district of Orezza the elysium of geology; the waters of the stream roll the beautiful stones along with them. Through endless balsamic groves, up hill and down hill, we rode onwards to Piedicroce, the principal town of Orezza, celebrated for its medicinal springs; for Orezza, rich in minerals, is also rich in mineral waters.

Francesco Marmocchi says, in his geography of the island: "Mineral springs are the invariable characteristic of countries which have been upheaved by the interior forces. Corsica, which within a limited space presents the astonishing and varied spectacle of the thousandfold workings of this ancient struggle between the heated interior of the earth and its cooled crust, was not likely to form an exception to this general rule."

Corsica has, accordingly, its cold and its warm mineral springs; and although these, so far as they have been counted, are numerous, there can be no doubt that others still remain undiscovered.

The natural phenomena of this beautiful island, and particularly its mineralogy, have by no means as yet had sufficient attention directed to them.

Up to the present time, fourteen mineral springs, warm and cold, are accurately and fully known. The distribution of these salubrious waters over the surface of the island, more especially in respect to their temperature, is extremely unequal. The region of the primary granite possesses eight, all warm, and containing more or less sulphur, except one; while the primary ophiolitic and calcareous regions possess only six, one alone of which is warm.

The springs of Orezza, bursting forth at many spots, lie on the right bank of the Fiumalto. The main spring is the only one that is used; it is cold, acid, and contains iron. It gushes out of a hill below Piedicroce in great abundance, from a stone basin. No measures have been taken for the convenience of strangers visiting the wells; these walk or ride under their broad parasols down the hills into the green forest, where they have planted their tents. After a ride of several hours under the burning sun, and not under a parasol, I found this vehemently effervescing water most delicious.

Piedicroce lies high. Its slender church-tower looks airily down from the green hill. The Corsican churches among the mountains frequently occupy enchantingly beautiful and bold sites. Properly speaking, they stand already in the heavens; and when the door opens, the clouds and the angels might walk in along with the congregation.

A majestic thunderstorm was flaming round Piedicroce, and echoed powerfully from hill to hill. We rode into the paese to escape the torrents of rain. A young man, fashionably dressed, sprang out of a house, and invited us to enter his locanda. I found other two gentlemen within, with daintily-trimmed beard and moustache, and of very active but polished manners. They immediately wished to know my commands; and nimble they were in executing them—one whipped eggs, another brought wood and fire, the third minced meat. The eldest of them had a nobly chiselled but excessively pale face, with a long Slavonic moustache. So many cooks to a simple meal, and such extremely genteel ones, I was now for the first time honoured with. I was utterly amazed till they told me who they were. They were two fugitive Modenese, and a Hungarian. The Magyar told me, as he stewed the meat, that he had been seven years lieutenant-general. "Now I stand here and cook," he added; "but such is the way of the world, when one has come to be a poor devil in a foreign country, he must not stand on ceremony. We have set up a locanda here for the season at the wells, and have made very little by it."

As I looked at his pale face—he had caught fever at Aleria—I felt touched.

We sat down together, Magyar, Lombard, Corsican, and German, and talked of old times, and named many names of modern celebrity or notoriety. How silent many of these become before the one great name, Paoli! I dare not mention them beside him; the noble citizen, the man of intellect and action, will not endure their company.

The storm was nearly over, but the mountains still stood plunged in mist. We mounted our horses in order to cross the hills of San Pietro and reach Ampugnani. Thunder growled and rolled among the misty summits, and clouds hung on every side. A wild and dreary sadness lay heavily on the hills; now and then still a flash of lightning; mountains as if sunk in a sea of cloud, others stretching themselves upwards like giants; wherever the veil rends, a rich landscape, green groves, black villages—all this, as it seemed, flying past the rider; valley and summit, cloister and tower, hill after hill, like dream-pictures hanging among clouds. The wild elemental powers, that sleep fettered in the soul of man, are ready at such moments to burst their bonds, and rush madly forth. Who has not experienced this mood on a wild sea, or when wandering through the storm? and what we are then conscious of is the same elemental power of nature that men call passion, when it takes a determinate form. Forward, Antonio! Gallop the little red horses along this misty hill, fast! faster! till clouds, hills, cloisters, towers, fly with horse and rider. Hark! yonder hangs a black church-tower, high up among the mists, and the bells peal and peal Ave Maria—signal for the soul to calm itself.

The villages are here small, picturesquely scattered everywhere among the hills, lying high or in beautiful green valleys. I counted from one point so many as seventeen, with as many slender black church-towers. We passed numbers of people on the road; men of the old historic land of Orezza and Rostino, noble and powerful forms; their fathers once formed the guard of Paoli.

At Polveroso, we had a magnificent glimpse of a deep valley, in the middle of which lies Porta, the principal town of the little district of

Ampugnani, embosomed in chestnuts, now dripping with the thunder-shower. Here stood formerly the ancient Accia, a bishopric, not a trace of which remains. Porta is an unusually handsome place, and many of its little houses resemble elegant villas. The small yellow church has a pretty façade, and a surprisingly graceful tower stands, in Tuscan fashion, as isolated campanile or belfry by its side. From the hill of San Pietro, you look down into the rows of houses, and the narrow streets that group themselves about the church, as into a trim little theatre. Porta is the birthplace of Sebastiani.

The mountains now become balder, and more severe in form, losing the chestnuts that previously adorned them. I found huge thistles growing by the roadside, large almost as trees, with magnificent, broad, finely-cut leaves, and hard woody stem. Marcantonio had sunk into complete silence. The Corsicans speak little, like the Spartans; my host of Oreto was dumb as Harpocrates. I had ridden with him a whole day through the mountains, and, from morning till evening had never been able to draw him into conversation. Only now and then he threw out some *naïve* question: "Have you cannons? Have you hells in your country? Do fruits grow with you? Are you wealthy?"

After Ave Maria, we at length reached the canton of Rostino or Morosaglia, the country of Paoli, the most illustrious of all the localities celebrated in Corsican history, and the central point of the old democratic Terra del Commune. We were still upon the Campagna, when Marcantonio took leave of me; he was going to pass the night in a house at some distance, and return home with the horses on the morrow. He gave me a brotherly kiss, and turned away grave and silent; and I, happy to find myself in this land of heroes and free men, wandered on alone towards the convent of Morosaglia. I have still an hour on the solitary plain, and, before entering Paoli's house, I shall continue the history of his people and himself at the point where I left off.

CHAPTER VIII
PASQUALE PAOLI

"Il cittadin non la città son io." — Alfieri's *Timoleon*.

After Pasquale Paoli and his brother Clemens, with their companions, had left Corsica, the French easily made themselves masters of the whole island. Only a few straggling guerilla bands protracted the struggle a while longer among the mountains. Among these, one noble patriot especially deserves the love and admiration of future times — the poor parish priest of Guagno — Domenico Leca, of the old family of Giampolo. He had sworn upon the Gospels to abide true to freedom, and to die sooner than give up the struggle. When the whole country had submitted, and the enemy summoned him to lay down his arms, he declared that he could not violate his oath. He dismissed those of his people that did not wish any longer to follow him, and threw himself, with a faithful few, into the hills. For months he continued the struggle, fighting, however, only when he was attacked, and tending wounded foes with Christian compassion when they fell into his hands. He inflicted injury on none except in honourable conflict. In vain the French called on him to come down, and live unmolested in his village. The priest of Guagno wandered among the mountains, for he was resolved to be free; and when all had forsaken him, the goat-herds gave him shelter and sustenance. But one day he was found dead in a cave, whence he had gone home to his Master, weary and careworn, and a free man. A relative of Paoli and friend of Alfieri — Giuseppe Ottaviano Savelli — has celebrated the memory of the priest of Guagno in a Latin poem, with the title of *Vir Nemoris* — The Man of the Forest.

Other Corsicans, too, who had gone into exile to Italy, landed here and there, and attempted, like their forefathers, Vincentello, Renuccio, Giampolo, and Sampiero, to free the island. None of these attempts met with any success. Many Corsicans were barbarously dragged off to prison — many sent to the galleys at Toulon, as if they had been helots who had revolted against their masters. Abattucci, who had been one of the last to lay down arms, falsely accused of high treason and convicted, was condemned in Bastia to branding and the galleys. When Abattucci was sitting upon the scaffold ready to endure the execution of the sentence, the executioner shrank from applying the red-hot iron. "Do your duty," cried a French judge; the man turned round to the latter, and stretched the iron towards him, as if about to brand the judge. Some time after, Abattucci was pardoned.

Meanwhile, Count Marbœuf had succeeded the Count de Vaux in the command of Corsica. His government was on the whole mild and beneficial; the ancient civic regulations of the Corsicans, and their statutes, remained in force; the Council of Twelve was restored, and the administration of justice rendered more efficient. Efforts were also made to animate agriculture, and the general industry of the now utterly impoverished country. Marbœuf died in Bastia in 1786, after governing Corsica for sixteen years.

When the French Revolution broke out, that mighty movement absorbed all private interests of the Corsicans, and these ardent lovers of liberty threw themselves with enthusiasm into the current of the new time. The Corsican deputy, Saliceti, proposed that the island should be incorporated with France, in order that it might share in her constitution. This took place, in terms of a decree of the Legislative Assembly, on the 30th of November 1789, and excited universal exultation throughout Corsica. Most singular and contradictory was the turn affairs had taken. The same France, that twenty years before had sent out her armies to annihilate the liberties and the constitution of Corsica, now raised that constitution upon her throne!

The Revolution recalled Paoli from his exile. He had gone first to Tuscany, and thereafter to London, where the court and ministers had given him an honourable reception. He lived very retired in London, and little was heard of his life or his employment. Paoli made no stir when he came to England; the great man who had led the van for Europe on her new career, withdrew into silence and obscurity in his little house in Oxford Street. He made no magniloquent speeches. All he could do was to act like a man, and, when that was no longer permitted him, be proudly silent. The scholar of Corte had said in his presence, in the oration from which I have quoted: "If freedom were to be gained by mere talking, then were the whole world free." Something might be learned from the wisdom of this young student. When Napoleon, like a genuine Corsican, taking refuge as a last resource in an appeal to hospitality, claimed that of England from on board the Bellerophon, he compared himself to Themistocles when in the position of a suppliant for protection. He was not entitled to compare himself with the great citizen of Greece; Pasquale Paoli alone was that exiled Themistocles!

Here are one or two letters of this period:—

PAOLI TO HIS BROTHER CLEMENS,

(Who had remained in Tuscany.)

"London, *Oct. 3, 1769.*—I have received no letters from you. I fear they have been intercepted, for our enemies are very adroit at such things.... I was well received by the king and queen. The ministers have called upon me. This reception has displeased certain foreign ministers: I hear they have lodged protests. I have promised to go on Sunday into the country to visit the Duke of Gloucester, who is our warm friend. I hope to obtain something here for the support of our exiled fellow-countrymen, if Vienna does nothing. The eyes of people here are beginning to be opened; they acknowledge the importance of Corsica. The king has spoken to me very earnestly of the affair; his kindness to me personally made me feel embarrassed. My reception at court has almost drawn upon me the displeasure of the opposition; so that some of them have begun to lampoon me. Our enemies sought to encourage them, letting it be understood with a mysterious air, that I had sold our country; that I had bought an estate in Switzerland with French gold, that our property had not been touched by the French; and that they had an understanding with these ministers, as they too are sold to France. But I believe that all are now better informed; and every one approved of my resolution not to mix myself up with the designs of parties; but to further by all means that for which it is my duty to labour, and for the advancement of which all can unite, without compromising their individual relations.

"Send me an accurate list of all our friends who have gone into banishment—we must not be afraid of expense; and send me news of Corsica. The letters must come under the addresses of private friends, otherwise they do not reach me. I enjoy perfect health. This climate appears to me as yet very mild.

"The Campagna is always quite green. He who has not seen it can have no conception of the loveliness of spring. The soil of England is crisped like the waves of the sea when the wind moves them lightly. Men here, though excited by political faction, live, as far as regards overt acts of violence, as if they were the most intimate friends: they are benevolent, sensible, generous in all things; and they are happy under a constitution than which there can be no better. This city is a world; and it is without doubt a finer town than all the rest put together. Fleets seem to enter its river every moment; I believe that Rome was neither greater nor richer. What we in Corsica reckon in paoli, people here reckon in guineas, that is, in louis-d'ors. I have written for a bill of exchange; I have refused to hear of contributions intended for me personally, till I know what conclusion they have come to in regard to the others; but I know that their intentions are good. In case they are obliged to temporize, finding their hands tied at present, they will be ready the first war that breaks out. I greet all; live happy, and do not think on me."

CATHERINE OF RUSSIA TO PASQUALE PAOLI

"St. Petersburg, *April 27, 1770.*

"Monsieur General de Paoli!—I have received your letter from London, of the 15th February. All that Count Alexis Orloff has let you know of my good intentions towards you, Monsieur, is a result of the feelings with which your magnanimity, and the high-spirited and noble manner in which you have defended your country, have inspired me. I am acquainted with the details of your residence in Pisa, and with this among the rest, that you gained the esteem of all those who had opportunities of intercourse with you. That is the reward of virtue, in whatever situation it may find itself; be assured that I shall always entertain the liveliest sympathy for yours.

"The motive of your journey to England, was a natural consequence of your sentiments with regard to your country. Nothing is wanting to your good cause but favourable circumstances. The natural interests of our empire, connected as they are with those of Great Britain; the mutual friendship between the two nations which results from this; the reception which my fleets have met with on the same account, and which my ships in the Mediterranean, and the commerce of Russia, would have to expect from a free people in friendly relations with my own, supply motives which cannot but be favourable to you. You may, therefore, be assured, Monsieur, that I shall not let slip the opportunities which will probably occur, of rendering you all the good services that political conjunctures may allow.

"The Turks have declared against me the most unjust war that perhaps ever *has* been declared. At the present moment I am only able to defend myself. The blessing of Heaven, which has hitherto accompanied my cause, and which I pray God to continue to me, shows sufficiently that justice cannot be long suppressed, and that patience, hope, and courage, though the world is full of the most difficult situations, nevertheless attain their aim. I receive with pleasure, Monsieur, the assurances of regard which you are pleased to express, and I beg you will be convinced of the esteem with which I am,

"Catherine."

Paoli had lived twenty long years an exile in London, when he was summoned back to his native country. The Corsicans sent him a deputation, and the French National Assembly, in a pompous address, invited him to return.

On the 3d of April 1790, Paoli came for the first time to Paris. He was fêted here as the Washington of Europe, and Lafayette was constantly at his side. The National Assembly received him with stormy acclamations, and elaborate oratory. His reply was as follows:—

"Messieurs, this is the fairest and happiest day of my life. I have spent my years in striving after liberty, and I find here its noblest spectacle. I left my country in slavery, I find it now in freedom. What more remains for me to desire? After an absence of twenty years, I know not what alterations tyranny may have produced among my countrymen; ah! it cannot have been otherwise than fatal, for oppression demoralizes. But in removing, as you have done, the chains from the Corsicans, you have restored to them their ancient virtue. Now that I am returning to my native country, you need entertain no doubts as to the nature of my sentiments. You have been magnanimous towards me, and I was never a slave. My past conduct, which you have honoured with your approval, is the pledge of my future course of action: my whole life, I may say, has been an unbroken oath to liberty; it seems, therefore, as if I had already sworn allegiance to the constitution which you have established; but it still remains for me to give my oath to the nation which adopts me, and to the monarch whom I now acknowledge. This is the favour which I desire of the august Assembly."

In the club of the Friends of the Constitution, Robespierre thus addressed Paoli: "Ah! there was a time when we sought to crush freedom in its last retreats. Yet no! that was the crime of despotism—the French people have wiped away the stain. What ample atonement to conquered Corsica, and injured mankind! Noble citizens, you defended liberty at a time when I did not so much as venture to hope for it. You have suffered for liberty; you now triumph with it, and your triumph is ours. Let us unite to preserve it for ever, and may its base opponents turn pale with fear at the sight of our sacred league."

Paoli had no foreboding of the position into which the course of events was yet to bring him, in relation to this same France, or that he was once more to stand opposed to her as a foe. He left for Corsica. In Marseilles he was again received by a Corsican deputation, with the members of which came the two young club-leaders of Ajaccio—Joseph and Napoleon Bonaparte. Paoli wept as he landed on Cape Corso and kissed the soil of his native country; he was conducted in triumph from canton to canton; and the Te Deum was sung throughout the island.

Paoli, as President of the Assembly, and Lieutenant-general of the Corsican National Guard, now devoted himself entirely to the affairs of his country; in the year 1791 he also undertook the command of the Division, and of the island. Although the French Revolution had silenced the special interests of the Corsicans, they began again to demand attention, and this was particularly felt by Paoli, among whose virtues patriotism was always uppermost. Paoli could never transform himself into a Frenchman, or forget that his people had possessed independence, and its own constitution. A coolness sprang up between him and certain parties in the island; the aristocratic French party, namely, on the one hand, composed of such men as Gaffori, Rossi, Peretti, and Buttafuoco; and the extreme democrats on the other, who saw the welfare of the world nowhere but in the whirl of the French Revolution, such as the Bonapartes, Saliceti, and Arenas.

The execution of the king, and the wild and extravagant procedure of the popular leaders in Paris, shocked the philanthropic Paoli. He gradually broke with France, and the rupture became manifest after the unsuccessful French expedition from Corsica against Sardinia, the failure of which was attributed to Paoli. His opponents had lodged a formal accusation against him and Pozzo di Borgo, the Procurator-general, libelling them as Particularists, who wished to separate the island from France.

The Convention summoned him to appear before its bar and answer the accusations, and sent Saliceti, Lacombe, and Delcher, as commissaries to the island. Paoli, however, refused to obey the decree, and sent a dignified and firm address to the Convention, in which he repelled the imputations made upon him, and complained of their forcing a judicial investigation upon an aged man, and a martyr for freedom. Was a Paoli to stand in a court composed of windy declaimers and play-actors, and then lay his head, grown gray in heroism, beneath the knife of the guillotine? Was this to be the end of a life that had produced such noble fruits?

The result of this refusal to obey the orders of the Convention, was the complete revolt of Paoli and the Paolists from France. The patriots prepared for a struggle, and published such enactments as plainly intimated that they wished Corsica to be considered as separated from France. The commissaries hastened home to Paris; and after receiving their report, the Convention declared Paoli guilty of high treason, and placed him beyond the protection of the law. The island was split into two hostile camps, the patriots and the republicans, and already fighting had commenced.

Meanwhile Paoli had formed the plan of placing the island under the protection of the English Government. No course lay nearer or was more natural than this. He had already entered into communication with Admiral Hood, who commanded the English fleet before Toulon, and now with his ships appeared on the Corsican coast. He landed near Fiorenzo on the 2d of February. This fortress fell after a severe bombardment; and the commandant of Bastia, General Antonio Gentili, capitulated. Calvi alone, which had withstood in previous centuries so many assaults, still held out, though the English bombs made frightful havoc in the little town, and all but reduced it to a heap of ruins. At length, on the 20th of July 1794, the fortress surrendered; the commandant, Casabianca, capitulated, and embarked with his troops for France. As Bonifazio and Ajaccio were already in the hands of the Paolists, the Republicans could no longer maintain a footing on the island. They emigrated, and Paoli and the English remained undisputed masters of Corsica.

A general assembly now declared the island completely severed from France, and placed it under the protection of England. England, however, did not content herself with a mere right of protection—she claimed the sovereignty of Corsica; and this became the occasion of a rupture between Paoli and Pozzo di Borgo, whom Sir Gilbert Elliot had won for the English side. On the 10th of June 1794, the Corsicans declared that they would unite their country to Great Britain; that it was, however, to remain independent, and be governed by a viceroy according to its own constitution.

Paoli had counted on the English king's naming him viceroy; but he was deceived, for Gilbert Elliot was sent to Corsica in this capacity—a serious blunder, since Elliot was totally unacquainted with the condition of the island, and his appointment could not but deeply wound Paoli.

The gray-haired man immediately withdrew into private life; and as Elliot saw that his relation to the English, already unpleasant, must soon become dangerous, he wrote to George III. that the removal of Pasquale was desirable. This was accomplished. The King of England, in a friendly letter, invited Paoli to come to London, and spend his remaining days in honour at the court. Paoli was in his own house at Morosaglia when he received the letter. Sadly he now proceeded to San Fiorenzo, where he embarked, and left his country for the third and last time, in October 1795. The great man shared the same fate as most of the legislators and popular leaders of antiquity; he died rewarded with ingratitude, unhappy, and in exile. The two greatest men of Corsica, Pasquale and Napoleon, foes to each other, were both to end their days and be buried on British territory.

The English government of Corsica—from ignorance of the country very badly conducted—lasted only a short time. As soon as Napoleon found himself victorious in Italy, he despatched Generals Gentili and Casalta with troops to the island; and scarcely had they made their appearance, when the Corsicans, imbittered by the banishment of Paoli and their other grievances, rose against the English. In almost inexplicable haste they relinquished the island, from whose people they were separated by wide and ineradicable differences in national character; and by November 1796, not a single Englishman remained in Corsica. The island was now again under the supremacy of France.

Pasquale Paoli lived to see Napoleon Emperor. Fate granted him at least the satisfaction of seeing a countryman of his own the most prominent and the most powerful actor in European history. After passing twelve years more of exile in London, he died peacefully on the 5th of February 1807, at the age of eighty-two, his mind to the last occupied with thoughts of the people whom he had so warmly loved. He was the patriarch and oldest legislator of European liberty. In his last letter to his friend Padovani, the noble old man, reviewing his life, says humbly:—

"I have lived long enough; and if it were granted me to begin my life anew, I should reject the gift, unless it were accompanied with the intelligent cognisance of my past life, that I might repair the errors and follies by which it has been marked."

One of the Corsican exiles announced his death to his countrymen in the following letter:—

GIACOMORSI TO SIGNOR PADOVANI.

"London, July 2, 1807.

"It is, alas! true that the newspapers were correctly informed when they published the death of the poor General. He fell ill on Monday the 2d of February, about half-past eight in the evening, and at half-past eleven on the night of Thursday he died in my arms. He leaves to the University at Corte salaries of fifty pounds a year each, for four professors; and another mastership for the School of Rostino, which is to be founded in Morosaglia.

"On the 13th of February, he was buried in St. Pancras, where almost all Catholics are interred. His funeral will have cost nearly five hundred pounds. About the middle of last April, I and Dr. Barnabi went to Westminster Abbey to find a spot where we shall erect a monument to him with his bust.

"Paoli said when dying:—My nephews have little to hope for; but I shall bequeath to them, for their consolation, and as something to remember me by, this saying from the Bible—'I have been young, and now am old, yet have I not seen the righteous forsaken, nor his seed begging bread.'"

CHAPTER IX
PAOLI'S BIRTHPLACE

It was late when I reached Rostino, or Morosaglia. Under this name is understood, not a single paese, but a number of villages scattered among the rude, stern hills. I found my way with difficulty through these little neighbour hamlets to the convent of Morosaglia, climbing rough paths over rocks, and again descending under gigantic chestnuts. A locanda stands opposite the convent, a rare phenomenon in the country districts of Corsica. I found there a lively and intelligent young man, who informed me he was director of the Paoli School, and promised me his assistance for the following day.

In the morning, I went to the little village of Stretta, where the three Paolis were born. One must see this Casa Paoli in order rightly to comprehend the history of the Corsicans, and award a just admiration to these singular men. The house is a very wretched, black, village-cabin, standing on a granite rock; a brooklet runs immediately past the door; it is a rude structure of stone, with narrow apertures in the walls, such as are seen in towers; the windows few, unsymmetrically disposed, unglazed, with wooden shutters, as in the time of Pasquale. When the Corsicans had elected him their general, and he was expected home from Naples, Clemens had glass put in the windows of the sitting-room, in order to make the parental abode somewhat more comfortable for his brother. But Paoli had no sooner entered and remarked the luxurious alteration, than he broke every pane with his stick, saying that he did not mean to live in his father's house like a Duke, but like a born Corsican. The windows still remain without glass; the eye overlooks from them the magnificent panorama of the mountains of Niolo, as far as the towering Monte Rotondo.

A relative of Paoli's—a simple country girl of the Tommasi family—took me into the house. Everything in it wears the stamp of humble peasant life. You mount a steep wooden stair to the mean rooms, in which Paoli's wooden table and wooden seat still stand. With joy, I saw myself in the little chamber in which Pasquale was born; my emotions on this spot were more lively and more agreeable than in the birth-chamber of Napoleon.

Once more that fine face, with its classic, grave, and dignified features, rose before me, and along with it the forms of a noble father and a heroic brother. In this little room Pasquale came to the world in April of the year 1724. His mother was Dionisia Valentina, an excellent woman from a village near Ponte Nuovo—the spot so fatal to her son. His father, Hyacinth, we know already. He had been a physician, and became general of the Corsicans along with Ceccaldi and Giafferi. He was distinguished by exalted virtues, and was worthy of the renown that attaches to his name as the father of two such sons. Hyacinth had great oratorical powers, and some reputation as a poet. Amid the din of arms those powerful spirits had still time and genial force enough to rise free above the actual circumstances of their condition, and sing war-hymns, like Tyrtæus.

Here is a sonnet addressed by Hyacinth to the brave Giafferi, after the battle of Borgo:—

"To crown unconquer'd Cyrnus' hero-son,
See death descend, and destiny bend low;
Vanquish'd Ligurians, by their sighs of wo,
Swelling fame's trumpet with a louder tone.
Scarce was the passage of the Golo won,
Than in their fort of strength he storm'd the foe.
Perils, superior numbers scorning so,
Vict'ry still follow'd where his arms had shone.
Chosen by Cyrnus, fate the choice approved,
Trusting the mighty conflict to his sword,
Which Europe rose to watch, and watching stands.
By that sword's flash, e'en fate itself is moved;
Thankless Liguria has its stroke deplored,
While Cyrnus takes her sceptre from his hands."

Such men are as if moulded of Greek bronze. They are the men of Plutarch, and resemble Aristides, Epaminondas, and Timoleon. They could resign themselves to privation, and sacrifice their interests and their lives; they were simple, sincere, stout-hearted citizens of their country. They had become great by facts, not by theories, and the high nobility of their principles had a basis, positive and real, in their actions and experiences. If we are to express the entire nature of these men in one word, that word is Virtue, and they were worthy of virtue's fairest reward—Freedom.

My glance falls upon the portrait of Pasquale. I could not wish to imagine him otherwise. His head is large and regular; his brow arched and high, the hair long and flowing; his eyebrows bushy, falling a little down into the eyes, as if swift to contract and frown; but the blue eyes are luminous, large, and free—full of clear, perceptive intellect; and an air of gentleness, dignity, and benevolence, pervades the beardless, open countenance.

One of my greatest pleasures is to look at portraits and busts of great men. Four periods of these attract and reward our examination most—the heads of Greece; the Roman heads; the heads of the great fifteenth and sixteenth centuries; and the heads of the eighteenth century. It would be an almost endless labour to arrange by themselves the busts of the great men of the eighteenth century; but such a Museum would richly reward the trouble. When I see a certain group of these together, it seems to me as if I recognised a family resemblance prevailing in it—a resemblance arising from the presence in each, of one and the same spiritual principle— Pasquale, Washington, Franklin, Vico, Genovesi, Filangieri, Herder, Pestalozzi, Lessing.

Pasquale's head is strikingly like that of Alfieri. Although the latter, like Byron, aristocratic, proud, and unbendingly egotistic, widely differs in many respects from his contemporary, Pasquale—the peaceful, philanthrophic citizen; he had nevertheless a soul full of a marvellous energy, and burning with the hatred of tyranny. He could understand such a nature as Paoli's better than Frederick the Great. Frederick once sent to this house a present for Paoli—a sword bearing the inscription, *Libertas, Patria*. Away in distant Prussia, the great king took Pasquale for an unusually able soldier. He was no soldier; his brother Clemens was his sword; he was the thinking head—a citizen and a strong and high-hearted man. Alfieri comprehended him better, he dedicated his *Timoleon* to him, and sent him the poem with this letter:—

TO SIGNOR PASQUALE PAOLI, THE
NOBLE DEFENDER OF CORSICA.

"To write tragedies on the subject of liberty, in the language of a country which does not possess liberty, will perhaps, with justice, appear mere folly to those who look no further than the present. But he who draws conclusions for the future from the constant vicissitudes of the past, cannot pronounce such a rash judgment. I therefore dedicate this my tragedy to you, as one of the enlightened few—one who, because he can form the most correct idea of other times, other nations, and high principles—is also worthy to have been born and to have been active in a less effeminate century than ours. Although it has not been permitted you to give your country its freedom, I do not, as the mob is wont to do, judge of men according to their success, but according to their actions, and hold you entirely worthy to listen to the sentiments of *Timoleon*, as sentiments which you are thoroughly able to understand, and with which you can sympathize.

Vittoria Alfieri."

Alfieri inscribed on the copy of his tragedy which he sent to Pasquale, the following verses:—

"To Paoli, the noble Corsican

Who made himself the teacher and the friend

Of the young France.

Thou with the sword hast tried, I with the pen,

In vain to rouse our Italy from slumber.

Now read; perchance my hand interprets rightly

The meaning of thy heart."

Alfieri exhibited much delicacy of perception in dedicating the *Timoleon* to Paoli—the tragedy of a republican, who had once, in the neighbouring Sicily, given wise democratic laws to a liberated people, and then died as a private citizen. Plutarch was a favourite author with Paoli, as with most of the great men of the eighteenth century, and Epaminondas was his favourite hero; the two were kindred natures—both despised pomp and expensive living, and did not imagine that their patriotic services and endeavours were incompatible with the outward style of citizens and commoners. Pasquale was fond of reading: he had a choice library, and his memory was retentive. An old man told me that once, when as a boy he was walking along the road with a school-fellow, and reciting a passage from Virgil, Paoli accidentally came up behind him, slapped him on the shoulder, and proceeded himself with the passage.

Many particulars of Paoli's habits are still remembered by the people here. The old men have seen him walking about under these chestnuts, in a long green, gold-laced coat,[N] and a vest of brown Corsican cloth. When he showed himself, he was always surrounded by his peasantry, whom he treated as equals. He was accessible to all, and he maintained a lively recollection of an occasion when he had deeply to repent his having shut himself up for an hour. It was one day during the last struggle for independence; he was in Sollacaro, embarrassed with an accumulation of business, and had ordered the sentry to allow no one admission. After some time a woman appeared, accompanied by an armed youth. The woman was in mourning, wrapped in the faldetta, and wore round her neck a black ribbon, to which a Moor's head, in silver—the Corsican arms—was attached. She attempted to enter—the sentry repelled her. Paoli, hearing a noise, opened the door, and demanded hastily and imperiously what she wanted. The woman said with mournful calmness: "Signor, be so good as listen to me. I was the mother of two sons; the one fell at the Tower of Girolata; the other stands here. I come to give him to his country, that he may supply the place of his dead brother." She turned to the youth, and said to him: "My son, do not forget that you are more your country's child than mine." The woman went away. Paoli stood a moment as if thunderstruck; then he sprang after her, embraced with emotion mother and son, and introduced them to his officers. Paoli said afterwards that he never felt so embarrassed as before that noble-hearted woman.

He never married; his people were his family. His only niece, the daughter of his brother Clemens, was married to a Corsican called Barbaggi. But Paoli himself, capable of all the virtues of friendship, was not without a noble female friend, a woman of talent and glowing patriotism, to whom the greatest men of the country confided their political ideas and plans. This Corsican Roland, however, kept no *salon*; she was a nun, of the noble house of Rivarola. A single circumstance evinces the ardent sympathy of this nun for the patriotic struggles of her countrymen; after Achille Murati's bold conquest of Capraja, she herself, in her exultation at the success of the enterprise, went over to the island, as if to take possession of it in the name of Paoli. Many of Pasquale's letters are addressed to the Signora Monaca, and are altogether occupied with politics, as if they had been written to a man.

The incredible activity of Paoli appears from his collected letters. The talented Italian Tommaseo (at present living in exile in Corfu) has published a large volume containing the most important of these. They are highly interesting, and exhibit a manly, vigorous, and clear intellect. Paoli disliked writing—he dictated, like Napoleon; he could not sit long, his continually active mind allowed him no rest. It is said of him that he never knew the date; that he could read the future, and that he frequently had visions.

Paoli's memory is very sacred with his people. Napoleon elates the soul of the Corsican with pride, because he was his brother; but when you name the name of Paoli, his eye brightens like that of a son, at the mention of a noble departed father. It is impossible for a man to be more loved and honoured by a whole nation after his death than Pasquale Paoli; and if posthumous fame is a second life, then Corsica's and Italy's greatest man of the eighteenth century lives a thousandfold—yes, lives in every Corsican heart, from the tottering graybeard who knew him in his youth, to the child on whose soul his high example is impressed. No greater name can be given to a man than "Father of his country." Flattery has often abused it and made it ridiculous; among the Corsicans I saw that it could also be applied with truth and justice.

Paoli contrasts with Napoleon, as philanthropy with self-love. No curses of the dead rise to execrate his name. At the nod of Napoleon, millions of human beings were murdered for the sake of fame and power. The blood that Paoli shed, flowed for freedom, and his country gave it freely as that mother-bird that wounds her breast to give her fainting brood to drink.

No battle-field makes Paoli's name illustrious; but his memory is here honoured by the foundation-school of Morosaglia, and this fame seems to me more human and more beautiful than the fame of Marengo or the Pyramids.

I visited this school, the bequest of the noble patriot. The old convent supplies an edifice. It consists of two classes; the lower containing one hundred and fifty scholars, the upper about forty. But two teachers are insufficient for the large number of pupils. The rector of the lower class was so friendly as to hold a little examination in my presence. I here again remarked the *naïveté* of the Corsican character, as displayed by the boys. There were upwards of a hundred, between the ages of six and fourteen, separated into divisions, wild, brown little fellows, tattered and torn, unwashed, all with their caps on their heads. Some wore crosses of honour suspended on red ribbons; and these looked comical enough on the breasts of the little brown rascals—sitting, perhaps, with their heads supported between their two fists, and staring, frank and free, with their black eyes at all within range—proud, probably, of being Paoli scholars. These honours are distributed every Saturday, and worn by the pupil for a week; a silly, and at the same time, hurtful French practice, which tends to encourage bad passions, and to drive the Corsican—in whom nature has already implanted an unusual thirst for distinction—even in his boyhood, to a false ambition. These young Spartans were reading Telemachus. On my requesting the rector to allow them to translate the French into Italian, that I might see how they were at home in their mother-tongue, he excused himself with the express prohibition of the Government, which "does not permit Italian in the schools." The branches taught were writing, reading, arithmetic, and the elements of geography and biblical history.

The schoolroom of the lower class is the chapter-hall of the old convent in which Clemens Paoli dreamed away the closing days of his life. Such a spacious, airy Aula as that in which these Corsican youngsters pursue their studies, with the view from its windows of the mighty hills of Niolo, and the battle-fields of their sires, would be an improvement in many a German university. The heroic grandeur of external nature in Corsica seems to me to form, along with the recollections of their past history, the great source of cultivation for the Corsican people; and there is no little importance in the glance which that Corsican boy is now fixing on the portrait yonder on the wall—for it is the portrait of Pasquale Paoli.

CHAPTER X
CLEMENS PAOLI

"Blessed be the Lord my strength, who teacheth my hands to war, and my fingers to fight." —Psalm cxliv.

The convent of Morosaglia is perhaps the most venerable monument of Corsican history. The hoary structure as it stands there, brown and gloomy, with the tall, frowning pile of its campanile by its side, seems itself a tradition in stone. It was formerly a Franciscan cloister. Here, frequently, the Corsican parliaments were held. Here Pasquale had his rooms, his bureaus, and often, during the summer, he was to be seen among the monks—who, when the time came, did not shrink from carrying the crucifix into the fight, at the head of their countrymen. The same convent was also a favourite residence of his brave brother Clemens, and he died here, in one of the cells, in the year 1793.

Clemens Paoli is a highly remarkable character. He resembles one of the Maccabees, or a crusader glowing with religious fervour. He was the eldest son of Hyacinth. He had served with distinction as a soldier in Naples; then he was made one of the generals of the Corsicans. But state affairs did not accord with his enthusiastic turn of mind. When his brother was placed at the head of the Government he withdrew into private life, assumed the garb of the Tertiaries, and buried himself in religious contemplation. Like Joshua, he lay entranced in prayer before the Lord, and rose from prayer to rush into battle, for the Lord had given his foes into his hand. He was the mightiest in fight, and the humblest before God. His gloomy nature has something in it prophetic, flaming, self-abasing, like that of Ali.

Wherever the danger was greatest, he appeared like an avenging angel. He rescued his brother at the convent of Bozio, when he was besieged there by Marius Matra; he expelled the Genoese from the district of Orezza, after a frightful conflict. He took San Pellegrino and San Fiorenzo; in innumerable fights he came off victorious. When the Genoese assaulted the fortified camp at Furiani with their entire force, Clemens remained for fifty-six days firm and unsubdued among the ruins, though the whole village was a heap of ashes. A thousand bombs fell around him, but he prayed to the God of hosts, and did not flinch, and victory was on his side.

Corsica owed her freedom to Pasquale, as the man who organized her resources; but to Clemens alone as the soldier who won it with his sword. He signalized himself also subsequently in the campaign of 1769, by the most splendid deeds of arms. He gained the glorious victory of Borgo; he fought desperately at Ponte Nuovo, and when all was lost, he hastened to rescue his brother. He threw himself with a handful of brave followers in the direction of Niolo, to intercept General Narbonne, and protect his brother's flight. As soon as he had succeeded in this, he hastened to Pasquale at Bastelica, and sorrowfully embarked with him for Tuscany.

He did not go to England. He remained in Tuscany; for the strange language of a foreign country would have deepened his affliction. Among the monks in the beautiful, solitary cloister of Vallombrosa, he sank again into fervent prayer and severe penance; and no one who saw this monk lying in prayer upon his knees, could have recognised in him the hero of patriot struggles, and the soldier terrible in fight.

After twenty years of cloister-life in Tuscany, Clemens returned shortly before his brother to Corsica. Once more his heart glowed with the hope of freedom for his country; but events soon taught the grayhaired hero that Corsica was lost for ever. In sorrow and penance he died in December of the same year in which his brother was summoned before the Convention, to answer the charge of high treason.

In Clemens, patriotism had become a cultus and a religion. A great and holy passion, stirred to an intense glow, is in itself religious; when it takes possession of a people, more especially when it does so in periods of calamity and severe pressure, it expresses itself as religious worship. The priests in those days preached battle from every pulpit, the monks marched with the ranks into the fight, and the crucifixes served instead of standards. The parliaments were generally held in convents, as if God himself were to preside over them, and once, as we saw in their history, the Corsicans by a decree of their Assembly placed the country under the protection of the Holy Virgin.

Pasquale, too, was religious. I saw in his house the little dark room which he had made into a chapel; it had been allowed to remain unchanged. He there prayed daily to God. But Clemens lay for six or seven hours each day in prayer. He prayed even in the thick of battle—a figure terrible to look on, with his beads in one hand and his musket in the other, clad like the meanest Corsican, and not to be recognised save by his great fiery eyes and bushy eyebrows. It is said of him that he could load his piece with furious rapidity, and that, always sure of his aim, he first prayed for mercy to the soul of the man he was about to shoot, then crying: "Poor mother!" he sacrificed his foe to the God of freedom. When the battle was over, he was gentle and mild, but always grave and profoundly melancholy. A frequent saying of his was: "My blood and my life are my country's; my soul and my thoughts are my God's."

Men of Pasquale's type are to be sought among the Greeks; but the types of Clemens among the Maccabees. He was not one of Plutarch's heroes; he was a hero of the Old Testament.

CHAPTER XI
THE OLD HERMIT

I had heard in Stretta that a countryman of mine was living there, a Prussian—a strange old man, lame, and obliged to use crutches. The townspeople had also informed him of my arrival. Just as I was leaving the chamber in which Clemens Paoli had died, lost in meditation on the character of this God-fearing old hero, my lame countryman came hopping up to me, and shook hands with me in the honest and hearty German style. I had breakfast set for us; we sat down, and I listened for several hours to the curious stories of old Augustine of Nordhausen.

"My father," he said, "was a Protestant clergyman, and wished to educate me in the Lutheran faith; but from my childhood I was dissatisfied with Protestantism, and saw well that the Lutheran persuasion was a vile corruption of the only true church—the church in spirit and in truth. I took it into my head to become a missionary. I went to the Latin School in Nordhausen, and remained there until I entered the classes of logic and rhetoric. And after learning rhetoric, I left my native country to go to the beautiful land of Italy, to a Trappist convent at Casamari, where I held my peace for eleven years."

"But, friend Augustine, how were you able to endure that?"

"Well, it needs a merry heart to bear it: a melancholy man becomes mad among the Trappists. I understood the carpenter-trade, and worked at it all day, beguiling my weariness by singing songs to myself in my heart."

"What had you to eat in the convent?"

"Two platefuls of broth, as much bread as we liked, and half a bottle of wine. I ate little, but I never left a drop of wine in my flask. God be praised for the excellent wine! The brother on my right was always hungry, and ate his two platefuls of broth and five rolls to the bargain."

"Have you ever seen Pope Pio Nono?"

"Yes, and spoken with him too, just like a friend. He was then bishop in Rieti; and, one Good-Friday, I went thither in my capote—I was in a different convent then—to fetch the holy oil. I was at that time very ill. The

Pope kissed my capote, when I went to him in the evening to take my leave. 'Fra Agostino,' said he, 'you are sick, you must have something to eat.' 'My lord bishop,' said I, 'I never saw a brother eat on Good-Friday.' 'No matter, I give you a dispensation; I see you are sick.' And he sent to the best inn in the town, and they brought me half a fowl, some soup, wine, and confectionary; and the bishop made me sit down to table with him."

"What! did the holy Father eat on Good-Friday?"

"Only three nuts and three figs. After this I grew worse, and removed to Toscana. But one day I ceased to find pleasure in the ways of men; their deeds were hateful to me. I resolved to become a hermit. So I took my tools, purchased a few necessaries, and sailed to the little island of Monte Cristo. The island is nine miles[O] round; not a living thing dwells on it but wild goats, serpents, and rats. In ancient times the Emperor Diocletian banished Saint Mamilian there—the Archbishop of Palermo. The good saint built a church upon the island; a convent also was afterwards erected. Fifty monks once lived there—first Benedictines, then Cistercians, and afterwards Carthusians of the Order of St. Bruno. The monks of Monte Cristo built many hospitals, and did much good in Toscana; the hospital of Maria Novella in Florence, too, was founded by them. Then, you see, came the Saracens, and carried off the monks of Monte Cristo with their oxen and their servants; the goats they could not catch—they escaped to the mountains, and have ever since lived wild among rocks."

"Did you stay in the old convent?"

"No, it is in ruins. I lived in a cave, which I fitted up with the help of my tools. I built a wall, too, before the mouth of it."

"How did you spend the long days? You prayed a great deal, I suppose?"

"Ah, no! I am no Pharisee. One can't pray much. Whatever God wills must happen. I had my flute; and I amused myself with shooting the wild goats; or explored the island for stones and plants; or watched the sea as it rose and fell upon the rocks. I had books to read, too."

"Such as?" —

"The works of the Jesuit Paul Pater Segneri."

"What grows upon the island?"

"Nothing but heath and bilberries. There are one or two pretty little green valleys, and all the rest is gray rock. A Sardinian once visited the island, and gave me some seeds; so I grew a few vegetables and planted some trees."

"Are there any fine kinds of stone to be found there?"

"Well, there is beautiful granite, and black tourmaline, which is found in a white stone; and I also discovered three different kinds of garnets. At last I fell sick in Monte Cristo—sick to death, when there happily arrived a number of Tuscans, who carried me to the mainland. I have now been eleven years in this cursed island, living among scoundrels—thorough scoundrels. The doctors sent me here; but I hope to see Italy again before a year is over. There is no country in the world like Italy to live in, and they are a fine people the Italians. I am growing old, I have to go upon crutches; and I one day said to myself, 'What am I to do? I must soon give up my joiner's work, but I cannot beg;' so I went and roamed about the mountains, and by good fortune discovered Negroponte."

"Negroponte? what is that?"

"The clay with which they make pipes in the island of Negroponte; we call it *meerschaum* at home, you know. Ah, it is a beautiful earth—the very flower of minerals. The Negroponte here is as good as that in Turkey, and when I have my pipes finished, I shall be able to say that I am the first Christian that has ever worked in it."

Old Augustine would not let me off till I had paid a visit to his laboratory. He had established himself in one of the rooms formerly occupied by poor Clemens Paoli, and pointed out to me with pride his Negroponte and the pipes he had been engaged in making, and which he had laid in the sun to dry.

I believe that, once in his life, there comes to every man a time when he would fain leave the society of men, and go into the green woods and be a hermit, and an hour when his soul would gladly find rest even in the religious silence of the Trappist.

I have here told my reader the brief story of old Augustine's life, because it attracted me so strongly at the time, and seemed to me a true specimen of German character.

CHAPTER XII
THE BATTLE-FIELD OF PONTE NUOVO

"Gallia vicisti! profuso turpiter auro

Armis pauca, dolo plurima, jure nihil!" — *The Corsicans.*

I left Morosaglia before Ave Maria, to descend the hills to Ponte Nuovo. Near the battle-field is the post-house of Ponte alla Leccia, where the Diligence from Bastia arrives after midnight, and with it I intended to return to Bastia.

The evening was beautiful and clear—the stillness of the mountain solitude stimulated thought. The twilight is here very short. Hardly is Ave Maria over when the night comes.

I seldom hear the bells pealing Ave Maria without remembering those verses of Dante, in which he refers to the softened mood that descends with the fall of evening on the traveller by sea or land:—

"It was the hour that wakes regret anew

In men at sea, and melts the heart to tears,

The day whereon they bade sweet friends adieu,

And thrills the youthful pilgrim on his way

With thoughts of love, if from afar he hears

The vesper bell, that mourns the dying day."

A single cypress stands yonder on the hill, kindled by the red glow of evening, like an altar taper. It is a tree that suits the hour and the mood—an Ave Maria tree, monumental as an obelisk, dark and mournful. Those avenues of cypresses leading to the cloisters and burying-grounds in Italy are very beautiful. We have the weeping-willow. Both are genuine churchyard trees, yet each in a way of its own. The willow with its drooping branches points downwards to the tomb, the cypress rises straight upwards, and points from the grave to heaven. The one expresses inconsolable grief, the other believing hope. The symbolism of trees is a significant indication of the unity of man and nature, which he constantly draws into the sphere of his emotions, to share in them, or to interpret them. The fir, the laurel, the oak, the olive, the palm, have all their higher meaning, and are poetical language.

I saw few cypresses in Corsica, and these of no great size; and yet such a tree would be in its place in this Island of Death. But the tree of peace grows here on every hand; the war-goddess Minerva, to whom the olive is sacred, is also the goddess of peace.

I had fifteen miles to walk from Morosaglia, all the way through wild, silent hills, the towering summits of Niolo constantly in view, the snow-capped Cinto, Artiga, and Monte Rotondo, the last named nine thousand feet in height, and the highest hill in Corsica. It stood bathed in a glowing violet, and its snow-fields gleamed rosy red. I had already been on its summit, and recognised distinctly, to my great delight, the extreme pinnacle of rock on which I had stood with a goatherd. When the moon rose above the mountains, the picture was touched with a beauty as of enchantment.

Onwards through the moonlight and the breathless silence of the mountain wilds; not a sound to be heard, except sometimes the tinkling of a brook; the rocks glittering where they catch the moonlight like wrought silver; nowhere a village, nor a human soul. I went at hap-hazard in the direction where I saw far below in the valley the mists rising from the Golo. Yet it appeared to me that I had taken a wrong road, and I was on the point of crossing through a ravine to the other side, when I met some muleteers, who told me that I had taken not only the right but very shortest road to my destination.

At length I reached the Golo. The river flows through a wide valley; the air is full of fever, and is shunned. It is the atmosphere of a battle-field — of the battle-field of Ponte Nuovo. I was warned in Morosaglia against passing through the night-mists of the Golo, or staying long in Ponte alla Leccia. Those who wander much there are apt to hear the ghosts beating the death-drum, or calling their names; they are sure at least to catch fever, and see visions. I believe I had a slight touch of the last affection, for I saw the whole battle of the Golo before me, the frightful monk, Clemens Paoli in the thickest of it, with his great fiery eyes and bushy eyebrows, his rosary in the one hand, and his firelock in the other, crying mercy on the soul of him he was about to shoot. Wild flight — wounded — dying!

"The Corsicans," says Peter Cyrnæus, "are men who are ready to die." The following is a characteristic trait: — A Frenchman came upon a Corsican who had received his death-wound, and lay waiting for death without complaint. "What do you do," he asked, "when you are wounded, without physicians, without hospitals?" "We die!" said the Corsican, with the laconism of a Spartan. A people of such manly breadth and force of character as the Corsicans, is really scarcely honoured by comparison with the ancient heroic nations. Yet Lacedæmon is constantly present to me here. If it is allowable to say that the spirit of the Hellenes lives again in the wonderfully-gifted people of Italy, this is mainly true, in my opinion, as applied to the two countries—and they are neighbours of each other—of Tuscany and Corsica. The former exhibits all the ideal opulence of the Ionic genius; and while her poets, from Dante and Petrarch to the time of Ariosto, sang in her melodious language, and her artists, in painting, sculpture, and architecture, renewed the days of Pericles; while her great historians rivalled the fame of Thucydides, and the philosophers of her Academy filled the world with Platonic ideas, here in Corsica the rugged Doric spirit again revived, and battles of Spartan heroism were fought.

The young Napoleon visited the battle-field of the Golo in the year 1790. He was then twenty-one years old; but he had probably seen it before when a boy. There is something fearfully suggestive in this: Napoleon on the first battle-field that his eyes ever lighted on—a stripling, without career, and without stain of guilt, he who was yet to crimson a hemisphere—from the ocean to the Volga, and from the Alps to the wastes of Lybia—with the blood of his battle-fields.

It was a night such as this when the young Napoleon roamed here on the field of Golo. He sat down by the river, which on that day of battle, as the people tell, rolled down corpses, and ran red for four-and-twenty miles to the sea. The feverous mist made his head heavy, and filled it with dreams. A spirit stood behind him—a red sword in its hand. The spirit touched him, and sped away, and the soul of the young Napoleon followed the spirit through the air. They hovered over a field—a bloody battle was being fought there—a young general is seen galloping over the corpses of the slain. "Montenotte!" cried the demon; "and it is thou that fightest this battle!" They flew on. They hover over a field—a bloody battle is fighting there—a young general rushes through clouds of smoke, a flag in his hand, over a bridge. "Lodi!" cried the demon; "and it is thou that fightest this battle!" On and on, from battle-field to battle-field. They halt above a stream; ships are burning on it; its waves roll blood and corpses. "The Pyramids!" cries the demon; "this battle too thou shalt fight!" And so they continue their flight from one battle-field to another; and, one after the other, the spirit utters the dread names—"Marengo! Austerlitz! Eylau! Friedland! Wagram! Smolensk! Borodino! Beresina! Leipzig!" till he is hovering over the last battle-field, and cries, with a voice of thunder, "Waterloo! Emperor, thy last battle!—and here thou shalt fall!"

The young Napoleon sprang to his feet, there on the banks of the Golo, and he shuddered; he had dreamt a mad and a fearful dream.

Now that whole bloody phantasmagoria was a consequence of the same vile exhalations of the Golo that were beginning to take effect on myself. In this wan moonlight, and on this steaming Corsican battle-field, if anywhere, it must be pardonable to have visions. Above yon black, primeval, granite hills hangs the red moon—no! it is the moon no longer, it is a great, pale, bloody, horrid head that hovers over the island of Corsica, and dumbly gazes down on it—a Medusa-head, a Vendetta-head, snaky-haired, horrible. He who dares to look on this head becomes—not stone, but an Orestes seized by madness and the Furies, so that he shall murder in headlong passion, and then wander from mountain to mountain, and from cavern to cavern, behind him the avengers of blood and the sleuthhounds of the law that give him no moment's peace.

What fantasies! and they will not leave me! But, Heaven be praised! there is the post-house of Ponte alla Leccia, and I hear the dogs bark. In the large desolate room sit some men at a table round a steaming oil-lamp; they hang their heads on their breasts, and are heavy with sleep. A priest, in a long black coat, and black hat, is walking to and fro; I will begin a conversation with the holy man, that he may drive the vile rout of ghosts and demons out of my head.

But although this priest was a man of unshaken orthodoxy, he could not exorcise the wicked Golo-spirit, and I arrived in Bastia with the most violent of headaches. I complained to my hostess of what the sun and the fog had done to me, and began to believe I should die unlamented on a foreign shore. The hostess said there was no help unless a wise woman came and made the *orazion* over me. However, I declined the *orazion*, and expressed a wish to sleep. I slept the deepest sleep for one whole day and a night. When I awoke, the blessed sun stood high and glorious in the heavens.

FOOTNOTES

[A] Thus referred to by Boswell in his *Account of Corsica*: — "The Corsicans have no drums, trumpets, fifes, or any instrument of warlike music, except a large Triton shell, pierced in the end, with which they make a sound loud enough to be heard at a great distance.... Its sound is not shrill, but rather flat, like that of a large horn." — *Tr.*

[B] There is a discrepancy which requires explanation between the sum of these and the population given for 1851. Their total is 50,000 below the other figure. — *Tr.*

[C] A hectar equals 2 acres, 1 rood, 35 perches English.

[D] Of raw tobacco grown in the island, since manufactured tobacco was mentioned among the exports. — *Tr.*

[E] German, *Eiferartig*. The word referred to is probably θυμοειδής, usually translated *high-spirited, hot-tempered*. See Book II. of the *Republic*. — *Tr.*

[F] The hero of Schiller's tragedy of *The Robbers*. — *Tr.*

[G] A kilometre is 1093·633 yards.

[H] Usually given along with Seneca's Tragedies; but believed to be of later origin — *Tr.*

[I] The olive.

[J] It may be worth while to notice a contradiction between this epigram and the preceding, in order that no more insults to Corsica may be fathered on Seneca than he is probably the author of. It is not quite easy to imagine that the writer who, in one epigram, had characterized Corsica as "traversed by fish-abounding streams" — *piscosis pervia fluminibus* — would in another deny that it afforded a draught of water — *non haustus aquæ*. Such an expression as *piscosis pervia fluminibus* guarantees to a considerable extent both quantity and quality of water. — *Tr.*

[K] "Die Sonne sie bleibet am Himmel nicht stehen,

Es treibt sie durch Meere und Länder zu gehen."

[L] For this unblushing assertion, Livius Geminus had actually received from Caligula a reward of 250,000 denarii.

[M] *Sic* in the German, but it seems a pseudonym, or a mistake. — *Tr.*

[N] Green and gold are the Corsican colours.

[O] *Miglien*—here, as in the other passages where he uses the measurement by miles, the author probably means the old Roman mile of 1000 paces.